Health and Holism

A journey from Birth to Death

Angela Bea

Disclaimer; All the material in this book is presented as non-medical self-help care and advice, and as such each person can decide for themselves what feels appropriate to use or not.

Contents

		Page
Chapter 1	Understanding the problem	7
Chapter 2	What is Holism?	11
Chapter 3	Cell health and why we create illness	17

Childhood

Chapter 4	Childbirth	27
Chapter 5	The decision to conceive	31
Chapter 6	Pregnancy and preparation	39
Chapter 7	The first stage of labour	49
Chapter 8	Transition, second stage and the birth	55
Chapter 9	Complications of labour	59
Chapter 10	Care of the new-born	61
Chapter 11	The older baby and feeding	69
Chapter 12	Life with a toddler	77
Chapter 13	Living with problems	83
Chapter 14	Working and having a family	85
Chapter 15	Siblings and bigger families	89
Chapter 16	Growing into school	95
Chapter 17	Ideas for new eating habits	99
Chapter 18	Qualities of parenting	107
Chapter 19	Caring for sick children	109
Chapter 20	The Immune System	113
Chapter 21	Acidity and Alkalinity	117
Chapter 22	Nature or nurture	119
Chapter 23	Caring for a sick child at home	131

Teenagers

Chapter 24	Teenagers	153
Chapter 25	Growing up	157
Chapter 26	Who am I?	161
Chapter 27	Physical care of teenagers	167
Chapter 28	Nutrition of teenagers	173
Chapter 29	Exercise in the teens	177
Chapter 30	Emotional care of the teenager	179
Chapter 31	Education for life	185
Chapter 32	Going out into the world	189
Chapter 33	Parent care	191
Chapter 34	Finding the link from teens into adulthood	195

Health and Dis-ease in adults

Chapter 35	Working with the planet Gaia	201
Chapter 36	On Nutrition	207
Chapter 37	Diabetes, arthritis, cancer, hypertension and heart disease	219
Chapter 38	Fibromyalgia, chronic fatigue, candida and ME	223

The Age of Wisdom

Chapter 39	Elders	227
Chapter 40	Aging bodies	233
Chapter 41	The problem	237
Chapter 42	Right living for elders; nutrition	241
Chapter 43	Right living; exercise of body and mind	247
Chapter 44	St John Communities	251
Chapter 45	Personal power and creativity	255

Chapter 46	Dementia, Alzheimer's and Parkinson's	257
Chapter 47	On being a grandparent	261
Chapter 48	Living with terminal illness and dying	263
Chapter 49	Preparing for death	269
Chapter 50	Afterwards	273
Chapter 51	In conclusion	277
Appendix notes		279
Appendix 1	The pH of some foods	281
Appendix 2	The water Ioniser	285
Useful resources		287

Chapter 1

Understanding the problem

The majority of people in the western world think of their bodies as machines, which have within them various 'systems'. We are taught at school that we have a nervous system, including the brain, which gives us all our intelligence and a feeling of who we are; the digestive system which breaks down the food we eat and transports it to cells for energy; the hormones, or endocrine system, which are chemical messengers and control the functioning of everything, and the blood and circulation which act as transport. The heart is a pump, and when it stops we die.

When our 'machine' goes wrong we have to go to a mechanic (the Doctor), like our car does, and get it fixed. This may involve taking tablets, having surgery, x-rays and other tests done by specialists in one or other system. We have an expectation that we will then get better and can go on as before, until something else goes wrong. Just as an aging car can be expected to perform less well and begin to show problems, so we too as we age can expect to get some problems. How often does the Doctor gently remind us of our age!

If we want to 'do our own thing' with our health we are made to feel slightly guilty that we are not accepting the free help which is offered on the NHS, and we then invariably have to pay quite large sums to go and see a Holistic Practitioner, who is quite often regarded as a quack by the establishment. 20% of the British population use some form of Complementary therapies. These various practitioners have trained in widely differing types of treatments, and it can be very confusing going from one to another trying to fix the problem, and find some respite from unpleasant symptoms. Even with these 'alternative' or 'complementary' therapies there is still an attitude that if we pay enough our body, the machine, will get fixed, and we can carry on with our lives as before.

In other parts of the world health is regarded very differently. In Ayurvedic Medicine (the way the Indians have regarded health for thousands of years) they speak of Doshas which can become imbalanced. Everyone has a predominant Dosha, which needs particular food and treatments to stay in balance. Massage of various kinds, and other specific treatments, yoga and meditation, as well as diet are used to come back into a 'state of balance'.

In Chinese Medicine they speak of the 5 elements, (Water, Metal, Wood, Fire and Air) and again the aim is to be in balance in order to obtain a state of 'ease'. They use acupuncture and herbs to help to rebalance the patient's dis-ease.

African witch doctors prescribe herbs, read runes and perform rituals to help to heal someone. This is also the case in other tribes and early civilisations, and can still be found amongst some Aborigines and North American Indians, as well as other groups living away from the influences of modern civilization.

The Ancient Greeks, with Hippocrates, Aristotle and others, developed healing and medicine to quite a sophisticated level, with exercise, diet, herbs and astrology also being used.

Man has always apparently had some form of sickness which is addressed by healers or medicine men, using plants or natural substances to redress imbalances.

After the time of Alexander the Great healing temples were established throughout the Middle East and beyond, which were truly Holistic.

Back in the middle ages great store was put on Healers in this country and other northern European areas. There were alchemists who explored the elements. There were 'good witches' who gave advice with astrology readings and natural herbal mixtures. They become confused with witches who performed 'black magic' and many of them were burned at the stake or hounded out of their practices.

Gradually things become more 'scientific', with doctors performing such things as blood-letting, purges, poultices, baths and mixing up potions.

My father was a pharmacist who trained in the 1930's. The University degree and training was highly regarded in those days. At that time local pharmacists would spend most of their time making up ointments, lotions and potions using basic chemical elements and herbal remedies. Even tablets were made by hand. By the 1960's, when I observed my father working in a pharmacy, he was making up the GPs prescriptions, counting pills out of big bottles supplied by the pharmaceutical industry, and many of his specific skills were no longer needed.

The development of pharmaceuticals in the last years has changed everything. Now chemical elements are isolated from either mineral or plant substances and they are carefully controlled to create complex chemicals which change the very nature of our bodies. Unfortunately these drugs are not without their side effects.

Most pharmacists these days spend the majority of their time checking the doctor's prescriptions and ensuring that there are no errors or incompatibilities between different drugs. Drugs are mainly pre-packaged, but errors are still quite common. Repeat prescriptions are often doled out unnecessarily. Pharmacists will also try to keep patients on track to take their medicines, checking doses and the side effects from time to time.

The drug companies now have enormous financial and political power, as prescribing has become such a huge part of the NHS budget, which is regulated by the Government. Drug companies are some of the most powerful economic influences in the world. Drug 'reps' are employed to visit GP's and sell them their new products, giving incentives (such as free gifts and holidays) if they use them.

New drugs are constantly being developed for different illnesses, and prescription numbers have gone through the roof! If you do not go home from a visit to your GP with a prescription now, you feel as if the doctor is not doing his work properly.

There are also some unfortunate people who feel they are being deprived of care as the expensive drugs, which are said to cure them, cost too much to be prescribed on the NHS.

Many painkillers, antibiotics, steroids, statins, antidepressants and tranquilisers as well as contraceptive pills are prescribed, as well as costly new treatments for cancer and inflammatory diseases.

There are now more drug related deaths in this country than ever before. Concoctions of drugs are taken and build up as toxins in the body, especially the liver and kidneys. People may react differently to various compounds and often adverse effects are felt. Some other side-effects are less obvious but just as dangerous.

More people are taking medication than ever before and there are also more and more tablets being thrown away into the mains water supply, which we then drink and reabsorb back into our bodies as toxic substances.

As well as this, many antibiotics are becoming less efficacious from overprescribing in the last years, as 'superbugs' develop resistant strains.

The older members of our society can be overheard frequently talking about their health, saying "I went to the GP and he gave me some tablets". There is an assumption, especially amongst the older population, that this is the way to get better and that the doctor knows best. Doctors have become demigods in our society!

Doctors are highly trained in physical symptoms and disease pictures. They look at the physical outcome of a body which has long been abused, and make a diagnosis by taking tests, but they have little time to go into the whole story or give any advice on changes which may be necessary to stay healthy. In the short time which is allocated to each patient there is barely the chance to reach a diagnosis and prescribe a drug which might help the patient.

Everything then has to be logged into the computer and, as many patients experience, the doctor may spend more time looking at the computer screen than actually relating to the human being in front of them. It can be very frustrating, not only for the patients but also for the doctors.

Practice Nurses, and also now recently installed machines, will check your blood pressure, urine, weight and even cholesterol as a measure of the 'health of the nation'. I worked as a Practice Nurse for some time in the '90's and much of my time was spent then doing 'well man' and 'well women' clinics, for which the Doctors were paid a sum per capita by the government.

All successes in the practice were measured by HOW MANY patients were being treated for a particular condition, such as diabetes, or how many were willing to be inoculated.

Statistics of these measurements are then gathered by civil servants who give a definitive prognosis of the 'Health of the Nation' and how much of our national expenditure needs to go to keeping us healthy. One statistic which has appeared is that we are all going to live longer. Perhaps this is good news, until it affects the funding of pensions and facilities for older people!

Most citizens in this country take all this fairly much for granted, and would feel very let down by the government if all this disappeared overnight!

For a moment I would ask you to ignore all this habitual behaviour and knowledge and try to think from a totally different perspective.

If there were no tablets and no doctors, what would we do to keep ourselves happy and healthy? My aim here is NOT to undermine our worthy overworked doctors and nurses! It is to ask the basic question "WHAT IS HEALTH and how do we maintain it?"

The majority of people do not think twice about health. It is a natural state of being, and until something starts to go wrong it is taken for granted. We assume that the body will adjust to anything that we throw at it; be that stress, a diet consisting of coffee and sugar, nicotine or junk food, and a lifestyle where we sit at desks all day, commute in trains or cars to work in a polluted environment, and relax at the weekend by slumping on the sofa watching the TV or drinking alcohol.

This may sound extreme but it is what the majority of the British population are doing without stopping for a moment to consider the implications of such action.

The mere fact that you are reading this book is an indication that you have started to think about what you are doing, and might like to change a few things.

In the following chapter I will explain the term Holism which is how we look at life and health from the broadest perspective.

Chapter 2

What is Holism?

Holism, the subject of this book, is about the WHOLE PERSON, which includes not only their body and mind, but also their emotions, social environment and their path through life which we can term 'destiny.' It is the higher energies, (by which I mean vibrational energy which is all around us and can be photographed in Kirlian photography) explained in various terms by religious and spiritual practices, which concern us also. Who we truly are and what affects our health in the very broadest sense is Holism.

Holism means understanding the whole picture. It observes people not from the point of view of a symptom, but as a person who has a life story and has developed their dis-ease very gradually over many years, quite possibly by abusing themselves by their lifestyle and diet.

It is the basic recognition that the human being has not only a physical body but also higher more refined energies which interweave with the physical, and are sometimes referred to as the soul or spirit, as well as the emotions. Everything is interdependent.

Holism goes further than that even. It recognises existence even before birth, assuming a life before birth and after death. It also asks questions about the inherited genetic traits going back over several generations. What illnesses have appeared in parents and grandparents on both sides?

Holism might also look at the astrological birth chart of an individual, and what was happening at the time of their birth. How did the energy of the Universe at the moment of birth affect the child at its first breath of life?

One might also ask what was happening emotionally with the mother and father during conception and pregnancy. How did their energy affect the growing child?

It asks questions about siblings, upbringing, and education; diet in childhood, childhood illnesses and fevers; or any accidents which may have happened.

It looks at social status, income, employment factors.

It looks at what is going on with the person right NOW and what their emotional and spiritual wellbeing is. Are they happily employed and active? How do they spend their leisure time? What is their exercise level now and in the past? How are their relationships and their love life? Do they take in toxins regularly in the form of nicotine, soft drugs, alcohol or a poor diet? How has their medical history and any medication prescribed affected their health up to this point?

Some of these questions are sometimes posed by a practice nurse filling in a form, or one may be asked to fill in a questionnaire whilst waiting to see a new doctor. But the observation of any doctor nowadays is severely curtailed by the fact that they are mainly looking at a computer screen, reading what is written there and filling in new symptoms and treatments prescribed, while you are sitting there hoping to have an intelligent conversation about your worries.

They have only approximately 10 minutes per person to review treatments, listen to the patient's symptoms and perhaps do a brief examination of the physical body. However committed they are, and interested in their patients, how CAN they do a proper job in these circumstances?

In the 'Good Old days' GPs used to help deliver babies at home, visit the mothers afterwards, perhaps several times, get to know the whole family and their environment, and so when one of the family came to the surgery later they would already have a picture of the living conditions and social setting of their patients. They could envisage the daily stresses, financial, social and environmental, that they might be experiencing and give some social care and advice. They might get to know the grandparents too, before they perhaps needed to move in with an adult daughter, and be able to support early dementia and other problems of aging.

Now, with busy surgeries of usually well over 2000 patients per GP, and group practices of up to 20, where GPs share lists and rotas, there is often little continuity of care and everything becomes less personalised. Added to this is the pressure of financial responsibility, of 'buying in' care as needed, and allocating money for specific areas of treatment, which the doctors now have to do. Practices have become more like businesses, with targets, budgets and savings having to be made. There are choices about priorities of treatments and care, which lead to endless meetings. Time is wasted on administration and pointless communication, especially form filling and work on computers.

When I was a Practice Nurse, just before the big changes which brought many rural practices 'up to date' with modern thinking, computers were being introduced into practice rooms and surgeries for the first time. More and more time was needed to fulfil the demands of government bureaucracy and less and less attention was given to the patients. 20 years on we are giving no better care and people are no fitter or healthier than they were then!

Now the NHS cutbacks have put even more stress on GPs and surgery staff and people seem to be losing touch with WHAT HEALTH REALLY IS!

All this may seem like a very negative view of a huge problem. Only when things develop into a real crisis can we start to learn to look again at the true human being and how they can learn to live in a healthier holistic way.

As you have found this book and others like it, I trust you may become part of the new wave of consciousness in the 21st century which will help to turn the tide so that mankind can survive this major crisis, which is affecting not only our own health and wellbeing but also that of the animals, plants and very fabric of the planet on which we live.

Simplicity is the key word in all this. If we could only simplify our lives, back to a point where we have TIME to relax, enjoy and contemplate life we would be a much healthier nation. We could take our lives back into our own responsibility.

Whose responsibility is it anyway? Why do we rely on professionals constantly to advise us about something which in essence is a very personal question? Nowadays the shelves of bookshops are full of self-help volumes on how to live a better more relaxed life. If you weren't interested in self-help, I doubt you would have this book in your hands right now. However I trust that while I am writing this I can always bear in mind the fact that there is no 'single path to righteousness' and that there are 'very many ways up the mountain', in fact as many ways as there are people on this planet!

My aim therefore is not to give recipes of 'How to', but to raise questions so that you, the individual searching for a better healthier lifestyle, can ponder for a while and perhaps consciously decide to make some positive changes which will enable you to live a longer, more fulfilling and healthier life.

I hope very much that some of the ideas which I suggest here you may feel able to try, not just for a week or two, but as a lifestyle change. All changes are gradual, and taking the first step is the biggest one along the way. Realising there is a problem is the very first thing, finding some alternatives and trying them comes next, and discovering that they work for you and you can sustain them as a new habit is the final step towards realising inner and outer changes.

Why might you want to change the status quo anyway? Most people who go to their doctor and are given a diagnosis of disease get a big shock. They may fear pain, or not really want to go through the suggested treatments, or they may be afraid of death. It is usually a wake-up call that for some time you have been abusing your body and treating it in a way that will create illness.

It may be something relatively minor like excessive weight gain, or rising blood pressure, or it may show something more serious; sugar in your urine, chest pain and an abnormal ECG, or a positive test for cancer. Some illnesses are symptom free whilst others start to make you feel decidedly unwell and lacking in energy or you may start to experience pain.

In the following chapters I will look at what health is, from the moment of conception to death, and what we mean by dis-ease. The hyphen in this word is intentional and gives the emphasis on the 'ease', which we all understand as being an easy happy state, and 'dis' is when it all goes wrong!

Whilst looking in detail at nutrition in several sections, I am not a qualified nutritionist, but have cured myself of Fibromyalgia through learning to live in a healthier way and eat food which is full of Energy. My life has been 'given back to me' in full and yours can be too, if you are suffering from any chronic condition, you are full of pain and your life activities are curtailed.

Many thousands of adults nowadays are constantly suffering from some form of ill health. We are not generally a very healthy society! If you are active and young and abusing your body on a daily basis, you will have no idea how the clock is ticking towards a time when you will experience pain, lack of energy or other symptoms which will lead you to the surgery for some tablets. Or maybe you will start to self-medicate on things such as Paracetamol, Nurofen or antacids which will hide the symptoms for a while until one day they become acute and you need urgent admission to a hospital.

Or you may wander into a health food shop and start to take some herbal or homeopathic remedies which may or may not work, because they may not be the right ones for you, or your illness needs a more rounded approach to change. You are still just pill popping!

Whilst taking this rather for granted, as being what happens as we age, it is by no means necessary to age in an unhealthy way. In fact our health can even improve as we get older, so that our natural aging is delayed and people comment on how well we look!

There ARE alternatives to being chronically below par. If you have positive thoughts, living each day to the full and enjoying everything you do with plenty of energy, then you can be said to be healthy.

Being in a healthy state is not just physical; it is also emotional, mental and spiritual, as you may be aware. I will expand on this during this book.

As the World Health Organisation defines it:

"Health is a state of complete physical, mental and social well-being, not merely the absence of disease or infirmity."

Having worked not only as a nurse, working with the elderly in many different settings but also a midwife, maternity nurse and nanny I feel a deep interest in the different phases of life and the challenges that each stage brings from the point of view of healthy living.

I perceive that many of the difficulties of young people stem from our illusion that health can be 'fixed' by taking a pill from the doctor. Therefore the following chapters are there to help give an alternative version of the norm of childbearing and care, the care of young people and also the responsibility we have towards those who are becoming frail, and needing our help in the last part of their lives.

As adults we can help both the young and the old to live healthier lives. What we can do ourselves is also covered in the chapter on specific conditions, such as diabetes, fibromyalgia, hypertension and arthritis, all common conditions which are becoming ever more frequently diagnosed.

Chapter 3

Cell health and why we create illness

How illnesses develop and what we can do to heal ourselves is a fascinating subject. In order to understand the essence of life I need to start at the beginning! What is the Life Energy which we find within each single cell?

Each day we wake up and see the sun rise, either bright and clear or behind the clouds. We take it for granted! The sun, the centre of our Solar system, is our all-pervading source of Life Energy, or LIGHT. We are part of a group of planets which make up our small solar group; our Earth being the only place where there is obvious life within this galaxy. If we look out at night without the street lamps we see the vast Heavens spread out above our heads and we start to marvel at the enormity of it all.

We, our whole solar system, our world, are only as small as one of those tiny blinking stars out there! We cannot comprehend 'light years' to another star, 'black holes' where nothing exists, or the other things we hear about our Universe. Where is Infinity and what happens when you reach it and mathematically can turn around and come back?

A sense of wonder starts to develop as we contemplate these things. We may start to feel a sense of awe and devotion as we look at all the tiny perfect creatures scampering along in our garden, busy with what they have to do. We may go into a daytime reverie and our brain thoughts slow down a little as we start to use the right side or intuitive part of our brain, which is where we can start to access the secrets of the Universe.

This is not 'fairy tale land' or 'namby pamby rubbish' cooked up to be 'Spiritual' but it is a real scientific phenomenon; that when we slow our left-brained intellects right down and consciously focus on inner worlds through Meditation, and go into an Alpha, Beta and Theta or even Delta brain state, we start to experience more and more of other dimensions, of unknown truths and things which otherwise we only read about.

At this level our differences all fade and we may glimpse Eternal Truth, and feel true Bliss. Colour, sound and light, the basic ingredients of our whole world measured as vibrational Energy are all here, beautiful and peaceful. People may access this world artificially by the use of drugs, and do so, as it is a happy and calm space to be in. However, when they return it is to a greyer and more depressing earth, and they would like to escape again.

If one is awake and able to slow down the day-to-day busyness of our intellect, one can become aware of this 'other world' out in nature also; the specks of light moving around plants and trees, rainbows and forms in water, the 'lasting quality' of even crystal and rock face.

Where is 'God' in all this? We learn in Christian schools that God created the world in 7 days.

Start studying embryology in detail and you will be amazed to find the 7 Days of Creation as told in the Bible playing out there in front of you! We can find the separation of the light and dark, the creation of water and then the creatures. Have you ever thought that an embryo looks like a little fish? It is a little known phenomenon that the heart is created by the circulation of the first primitive blood. The movement of fluids and the pulse <u>actually forms</u> the heart organ. There is movement at the very beginning of all new life. No-one has yet discovered where this movement originates, unless from 'God'?

Stand and watch carefully as a double rainbow stretches across the sky. See the purity of the colours and know that this also is God. Be aware in each moment and you will catch the magic of a loving glance, a synchronicity, music on the wind, the growth of new buds in spring. God is here and everywhere we wish to perceive Him/Her. Every day miracles happen right under our noses.

Quantum Physics as a new science is breaking through the boundaries of matter, speed, light, making a link between science and religion ever more possible. In Switzerland there is now a huge tunnel built under the mountains to measure scientifically some of these phenomena. Recently scientists have been able to break down the atom yet further.

In a vacuum we can observe photons (sub-atomic particles) taking on the shapes of DNA samples put into the vacuum, acting in a totally 'sacrificial way' to all that is around them. Experiments on water in different surroundings and influenced by different feelings, create either harmonious beautiful crystals, or malformed ugly ones. What IS this phenomenon?

We are beginning to be able to measure **Life Energy** which is everywhere in the Universe. We can begin to understand how it works and appreciate that Healers and Reiki masters, Chi gung practitioners, Homeopaths and Biofeedback techniques and many others, may be working with a reality which we are just coming to recognise and understand. Is this what we refer to as 'God'?

Everyone on this planet is capable of becoming a Healer. It is the ability to work consciously with Life Energy, with the <u>intent</u> of enabling another person, animal or plant to heal. One has to learn first to still the busy mind and open the heart in Love.

The seven Chakras, referred to in many Eastern philosophies, are nothing more or less than nerve centres which act on the endocrine system of the physical body, but also reflect the Energies around, going out and out in many layers, becoming ever more rarefied.

Our emotions directly affect our breathing, heart rate and blood pressure, as our thoughts also affect our bodies. The mind/body connection is becoming more and more recognised in Western medicine.

Auras, referred to in Spiritual teachings, are layers of coloured energy, pulsating ever faster, and more purely, which surround our bodies, going out in great circles. They are visible to some who have developed the 'Third Eye', or psychic ability to see things not normally perceived by everyman. Edgar Cayce was one such person, who established the ideas of Holistic health. Rudolf Steiner was another.

By the very way we live day-to-day we can begin to become aware of the Positive and Negative within us. We can work consciously to overcome our Negativity and by meditating and practising love, humility and consciousness towards our neighbours and all people on the planet we become self-aware and able to start to radiate Peace and Light which affects those around us, and ultimately the whole Universe.

The two sides of our brains work very differently. In our society we are predominantly using our Left Brains to make decisions and act in the modern world. This is a world of logic, business, accruing power, and masculine energy.

Our Right Brains are used in intuition, meditation, creativity, and lateral thinking and these are known more as feminine qualities.

These differing qualities can be found in both men and women, and ideally should be well balanced.

Cell health at the microscopic level is perhaps the most important aspect that we can start to understand and work with. Without healthy cellular structure we are unable to sustain life, grow and develop to our full potential.

All our cells are made up of millions of different chemical activities which are constantly changing, dependent on the time of day, nutrition, and hydration. This latter aspect is of vital importance and one of the main reasons for ill health.

The electric impulses which are present in the workings of each individual cell cannot work effectively without fluid, light and correct nutrition. Our DNA controls and masterminds all these activities.

Cellular health and the amount of light (Life Energy) carried within each cell is therefore also intimately linked with our genetic inheritance of illness. If a child is born with a weakness towards eczema, for example, (often inherited if one or more grandparent has had active TB) and this is suppressed with steroid creams from an early age, then the illness will 'push deeper' into the body and develop into asthma. If this is treated inappropriately with Steroid inhalers, it may be forced yet deeper to show up as depression and lack of direction in the teenage years, or may develop into mental illness or addictions. This phenomenon has been well researched and written about by Barbara Wren. All illnesses can be traced back in this way, and if we do not understand this then we can make our health worse by suppressing symptoms.

Sometimes illnesses which affect the immune system, such as ME, AIDS or Chronic fatigue and Candida and which are becoming quite common nowadays and are complex and virtually untreatable by medical practitioners, can be traced back to a sequence of events, or too many immunisations being given early on to a child. The body goes into a crisis state **when it becomes dehydrated at cell level**. Only by gentle and very deep detoxification and rehydration can healing be achieved.

Homeopathy works in this way, giving subtle messages at a cellular Energetic level. Science cannot yet fully comprehend these changes which are possible, although animals can be well treated by homeopathy, proving there is no 'placebo effect'.

What is happening to our bodies and Life Energy that we become SICK? We are whole beings, not just the physical manifestation, and our physical structures reflect what is happening to us energetically.

EVERY CELL IN OUR BODY HAS ITS OWN INTELLIGENCE. Every cell is teaming with life and messages from the whole Universe at a sub-atomic level. We are reflections of the greater whole; as without, so also within.

We are also constantly recreating ourselves. Every 7 years we have completely changed every cell in our body and grown anew. We are no longer the same body as 7 years previously! Every cell has changed! But we still look the same, we still have the same scars on us from traumas of various kinds, we still think the same way very often!

We are made up of between 70% and 90% water. As we know, water is unstructured; it flows, and carries substances around. It is very 'selfless.' Why do we not float around as formless blobs; what gives us our structure? What recreates the unique cells in each moment and maintains them in hot and cold situations? We are not amoebic creatures, but highly complex, evolved, thinking, sensitive and conscious beings with Free Will. It is not just about our DNA. Scientists are close to making a breakthrough on this subject.

Increasingly nowadays, through much research and experimentation with placebos, scientists are beginning to acknowledge that the mind affects the body in many ways. Our thinking patterns send messages to each cell and we react accordingly.

We are not only mind and body though. There is the so-called soul or spirit which is unique to every individual. It is the pattern of built up life experiences, the shimmering 'aura' of energy patterns, and our very own blueprint that makes us who we are. It is what gazes out of the eyes of a new born baby, or what comes to us from the eyes of our beloved.

Many world religions believe that the spirit continues from one life to the next, on a journey of learning. If we do reincarnate then why do we not remember? It is increasingly recognised that maybe some people can and do remember other life experiences. Many books are written on this interesting phenomenon. Often a small child will refer to some past life experience and the parent is baffled or thinks they are talking nonsense.

Stress

Stress is a much discussed subject nowadays. It is the body's and mind's inability to cope with prolonged changes and demands which are not innately natural to us. Our minds no longer feel in charge. We are no longer on our correct 'soul journey'; we are going against our 'life purpose' in some way.

We have developed a long way since the days when we hunted the large woolly mammals and lived in caves. Then we developed part of our brains which we now call instincts, or the hind brain. We learned to run away in fear, and we created a mechanism whereby our bodies protected us, by producing more adrenalin so we could run or fight back. This still functions today.

But if there is a gap between our physical reality and what we would LIKE to see happen; that is, what our fore brains or thinking intelligence would have us believe and do and our hind brains, then we experience stress. This gap grows ever wider for some people nowadays.

We live in a society of high expectations, of media advertising, of broken relationships, of living in the fast lane! We sit stuck in queues of traffic whilst trying to meet deadlines; we have umpteen phone calls and emails to attend to; we miss mealtimes and watch fast moving flashing images on TV while we eat; we have constant financial pressure to get rich fast and spend fast! What has happened to our balance and sanity?

It is not just about going backwards to the 'good old days' when life was slower. We have intelligence to develop onwards and upwards. We are inventing cars for the future when fossil fuels run low; we are developing new means of harnessing energy from the sun, waves and wind; we are able to sustain life (albeit artificially), fly to the moon and beyond; we can communicate across the world in seconds with computers which get ever more complex yet smaller. We can now predict and warn about strange new weather patterns which are threatening our humanity.

But all this development has its cost. We have lost touch with 'Healthy Living' and living in harmony with nature, the cycle of the seasons, growing our own food, celebrating the rituals of Harvest, Fertility, Birth and Death in our local community.

We live stressed lives, with deadlines and pressure to the extent that we have to take tablets, go to the gym, consult psychologists and therapists, have broken relationships and get more and more obese and sick.

Conversely, in developing countries, there is much starvation and unrest, massive suffering, with ill health, poverty and AIDS. There comes from the west a huge supply of ammunitions available for the young men to use in 'tribal' warfare.

A lack of clean water, lack of education, and an aspiration for 'everything that glitters' which comes from the West, creates a great loss of family bonds, cultural values and creative outlets. These people are immensely creative and also fun-loving and have such a lot to contribute to the whole of society.

We have been responsible for creating this situation by going out there to 'teach' them how to be 'Westernised,' expecting monetary reward, dispersing the nuclear families and village communities, with promises of work in cities, mines and factories, which will give a 'better' lifestyle. We have been responsible for the 'development' of much of the world, through colonialization, and the Commonwealth. Our Victorian ancestors believed that education of the 'heathens' was a good thing. We are also responsible for the massive changes occurring through pollution and rape of the earth.

We are creating droughts and floods by unbalancing the planet's weather patterns because we are living in a way to cause extreme global imbalance. AIDS is just a symptom of the stress we have helped to create. Stress immediately affects the immune system.

Dis-ease (or lack of ease) is caused primarily by stress, whatever the cause. Our bodies are trying hard to adapt, and do a very good job most of the time, but when our spirits, minds and bodies are at odds with each other and what we are doing day by day, and more importantly we have not found our true 'Life Purpose', then sickness follows.

What do I mean by 'Life Purpose?' Each one of us is an Individual Intelligence in the greatest picture of things. Before we are born we have the impulse to work in a certain way on earth. There are many different ways of approaching life or colour 'rays' and we all belong to one of these unique 'rays.' If we can consciously find the 'Leitmotif' or thread which drives us, we can understand more clearly if we are following our intended path. Sometimes a crisis situation will wake us up to this truth.

Many people go through life as though asleep and often it is only in the final painful illness before death, or through a life threatening illness or accident that realisation starts to dawn. Material needs, atheistic outlooks and selfishness are ever more common in our society in Britain, and only if we start to talk to people in depth do we find a great longing for Truth, and a searching mind and soul.

There is a lot of anger amongst young people, more than ever before, and it reflects a deep yearning for our communities to recognise that change is desperately needed in the way we live our lives. The violence and unrest we see currently in many countries is a 'dis-ease' of our young people who yearn to be heard. Fundamentalism in any form is a symptom of unmet Spiritual questioning.

Young people are grieving the loss of our beautiful planet and the many creatures which are becoming extinct.

Again, we are responsible for all this! How often do you have the opportunity to talk in depth to an angry/grieving young person? Are we not afraid of them? Do we not criticize them inwardly, if not overtly? They may be rude to us or threaten us with violence. They smash the environment and drop litter, using foul language.

True health can only be found and maintained when we are feeling at one with our lives, in terms of our work, community and relationships. If we once become physically sick it is much harder for the body to find its healthy balance again, as sickness may have been going on in the body/mind connection for many years already in an un-manifested way.

Our lifestyles may be 'sickness inducing' also. We smoke, drink large quantities of alcohol, take little healthy exercise in the fresh air and sunshine (Life Energy giving!) and live in pollution of mind and body, to the point where we are truly toxic.

One of the greatest causes of ill health is dehydration. Lack of pure water within the cells themselves causes the cells to start reacting abnormally and the balance of substances goes awry. Cells become over-acidic and surround themselves with a sticky membrane which is for self-preservation. This reads as raised cholesterol in a blood test.

So many people nowadays are not aware that their illness will only be healed by their own change and effort with diet, exercise and new thinking. It is NOT an answer to take a magic pill, which only further poisons our systems

Once we are toxic there is only one way out; to detoxify!

The following chapters will look at the various stages of life from birth to death and some basic changes that could be made to reach a state of health, including an Alkaline system, Light filled cells and good hydration, as well as a sense of Purpose and Peace.

Childhood

Chapter 4

Childbirth

Having a child for the first time is seen as a blessing and can be an extremely joyful experience. From a personal perspective I believe it is the single most important and creative thing I have ever achieved in my life. Most parents however would admit that in hindsight they had absolutely no idea what it would be like becoming a parent and that many of the changes involved in becoming a fulltime carer to an infant were hard to cope with.

Looking back, many of the things I saw and did as a young trainee midwife in the '70's (and again in the late '80's when I returned to Midwifery), and also when I was a young inexperienced mother, are rather abhorrent to me now, as wisdom and life experience gives broader views of what is and should be a very natural and basic process.

When I was having my own 3 children I gave up midwifery for ten years and trained, and then worked, as a teacher for the National Childbirth Trust for several years, giving classes to mothers and couples in my own home. I sometimes felt that new mothers came to me for a course in 'GCSE Childbirth'! They wanted to learn 'the Breathing' so that they could perform well during labour. It was very difficult to speak to them about 'Afterwards'. NCT classes can still be found in most towns in Britain, and teachers try to give a picture of what may happen in labour in a hospital environment to empower parents to get the choices they want. When things 'go wrong' and they end up with a Caesarean or forceps delivery it is often seen as a failure.

Going beyond just the practical implications of birth and parenting will enable you to feel what is actually happening on a deeper level, so that you can start to change your inner BEINGNESS and become a mother (or father) with a new consciousness. It is about becoming a selfless vessel for another human being to come into this world. After conception it is no longer "I want and need", but "What is right for US?" Becoming a worthy parent is about *giving* in the very broadest sense. It is a path of learning which will enable one to learn to *love* with a much greater selflessness.

Energy, as described before, is the Movement which creates the flow of liquid in the embryo, the pulsing of which then *forms* the heart organ *from* that Movement. It is the Energy which is so vibrant in a young child but naturally diminishes as we get older. As we walk through woods or by the sea we can feel this Energy in nature also and it refreshes us. We can observe a dog charging along a beach; that is Energy!

It is the single most important aspect of welcoming new life into the world and as mothers going through the process of conception, pregnancy, and birth and nurturing their children in the early years; it is most helpful to <u>always</u> keep it in mind!

There are hundreds of books written about childbirth. The consciousness of each potential parent becomes 'knowingness' of what is essentially a totally natural process. Through modern living and cerebral thinking this knowingness has been largely lost. It is perhaps better described as INSTINCT.

If we watch animals or mothers of less developed cultures giving birth and becoming parents we can begin to have an inkling of this natural process. We, as 'intelligent' humans, have lost many of these instincts. We have become too cerebral or fore-brained about the whole process. Perhaps our subconscious minds, where these instincts are seated, in the hind brain, have become so full of FEAR that we can only react out of fear? Fear directly affects the body's ability to labour and give birth naturally, as I will explain in the chapter about birth.

Observing many mothers in labour, as I did as a practicing midwife, I noticed that the mothers who delivered most easily were those who were unafraid, relaxed and instinctual; young teenage girls, poor working class women, or those who had prepared themselves on a deeper spiritual level tended to have quicker less painful labours with fewer complications. They entered into a deep almost meditative space during labour so that they <u>let go</u> and were completely taken over by the Energy of labour.

By reading this as a preparation for childbirth and parenting my greatest hope is that you too may become more 'instinctual' and allow your body to work in its <u>natural</u> way as it 'knows' how to. **Trust** it to work for you, in what is a totally natural process!

Some of the ideas which I present may seem rather old fashioned! I do not apologise for this! Nowadays we have lost much of the inherent wisdom of our own grandmothers and great grandmothers. It was not just the 'bad old days' but also the 'good old days' and we can learn much from returning to this wisdom in a new way.

Keeping in mind that science and medicine have now got to the point where we can both create and take life, we have a Godlike power which also needs a morality to keep it sane. Our population in Britain now has a huge diversity of worldwide cultures, and as such has become much enriched. It does have a danger however of being apologetic for anything which stands for the old fashioned 'Victorian British Christian Values'. How can we find a new morality to guide us through these stormy waters? How do we hold fast to the right way of doing things when we no longer have those boundaries in our society?

Becoming parents today holds the responsibility for the next generation. It is the future of humanity. If we can give our children a good start both physically and emotionally we are ensuring the survival of the human race. It is a grave responsibility indeed and worth musing upon.

Chapter 5

The decision to conceive

When we are young children we often have inklings as to whether we are destined to become parents ourselves. Listen to children playing together in Kindergarten or playgroup and they often act out being mothers and fathers! They may recently also have had a new baby brother or sister and this comes into their games. Dolls or teddies are stuffed up inside their jumpers and then hauled out again and often the baby then cries. They know what happens!

These lessons are soon forgotten as children grow up into the exciting world around and 'more important things' occupy their minds. It is only in the teenage years when our natural hormones kick in and boys and girls become interested in each other and start to have their first experiments in sex that the question of becoming a parent seems again to be a dim reality.

But very many young working people nowadays are waiting right into their 30s or even early 40's before considering having a family. By this stage it becomes much more of a conscious decision, based often on economic and social pressures. How easy is it to afford the big mortgage and for both parents to keep working? How much of their social and leisure life will be impacted by the arrival of a child, who cannot be taken on adventure holidays or to parties? We become increasingly selfish and materialistic by earning good wages and living comfortably in the style we have become accustomed to. Children will change all that!

Sex, the coming together of male and female for the purpose of reproducing, is seen by some as 'dirty' and by others as 'blissful'. In humans it is usually more than just for procreation. It is a form of communication and *sharing and creation* of natural Energy between loved ones. There is much cultural taboo around it and it is normally a very private thing between couples which is not discussed, except perhaps with close friends. Each relationship is different and sex often reflects the nature of the emotional human relationship, or how the couple bond energetically. It can reflect a give/give relationship or be more one sided, where one or other partner needs to *take* the Energy from the other.

As soon as a woman and man come together in the sexual act <u>there is a third person present</u> and that is the *potential* of a new human life! This is very important to recognise. The very act of coming together creates a huge amount of Energy, as seen in the orgasmic bliss, and the sperm swim strongly and joyfully up into the darkness, searching for the ovum in the fallopian tubes and the strongest fastest one penetrates the egg and division of the cells starts almost immediately.

When the woman is at the right moment of her cycle then fertilisation usually occurs. This is exactly 14 days before the *next* period is due. As many women do not have a very regular cycle this is not a moment usually recognised or calculated, but some women who are very in tune with their bodies can know when they ovulate, or release the egg from the ovary (alternate ovaries each month) and fertilisation can happen for several hours after this occurs. There may also be 'Mittelschmerz' which can be felt as an ache similar to period pain, which occurs on ovulation.

Although much sex is enjoyed in both married and unmarried relationships these days, with the only intention being to have fun, enjoy the sensation, and be close to another human being in the physical sensation that our society calls 'love', nature originally intended the act to be a reproductive one on an instinctive level. Only as human beings have developed freedom and intelligence has this changed into a much broader physical/emotional enjoyment and pastime!

As modern human beings many things need to be considered when having regular sexual intercourse with a loving partner, and this includes the decision to start a family. It is fairly easy now to 'plan' exactly when children should appear. Contraception is now well developed and applied by most couples.

The 'pill' changes the woman's hormones so that the release of ova cannot occur naturally and it cannot imbed in the uterine wall. This is very convenient nowadays, providing that one remembers to take the pill at the prescribed time, it is of the correct hormonal strength, and no sickness or diarrhoea occurs.

There are always disadvantages though with all contraceptive methods, the biggest one with the pill being the change in the woman's hormone levels. It is not natural to tamper with the body's own hormone levels. Some women put on weight, especially around their breasts; there is a higher incidence of blood clotting, and other circulatory disturbances and the woman may feel unwell on the pill. There may also be a higher incidence of cancer. The natural cleansing of the uterus each month does not work so thoroughly either, so that conception and implantation when it *is* planned may not be so immediate. Women with low levels of hormones may become so out of balance that when a family *is* planned they cannot conceive at all. Secondary infertility due to prolonged use of the pill is not uncommon.

Taking the pill is also an environmental hazard, as hormones are excreted into the sewerage system and thus to the water table via urine and are imbibed by anyone drinking tap water, which may affect their health adversely.

What other methods are there to prevent an unwanted pregnancy? The barrier methods (the sheath, cap and creams) are literally what they claim to be; a way of stopping the sperm from swimming up into the uterus. Some are more efficient than others. With all of them there is the risk that they may break or leak. Most methods need a certain amount of sensitivity between partners to cope with the practicalities. There may be a certain amount of anxiety about their safety when used long-term. These methods have evolved over the ages, from simple sponges and even camel dung!

The coil is a form of contraception which prevents a fertilised egg from implanting in the womb. It is therefore almost like a form of early abortion, as is also the 'morning after' pill.

Abortion is a very loaded subject. Many people believe it is fine to do away with an unborn baby and as such it can almost be classed as a form of contraception. There are all sorts of social reasons why it might be better to terminate a pregnancy rather than having an unwanted or deformed baby. It is relatively easy to obtain an abortion anywhere these days, and this is much more preferable to the old back-street abortions which were life threatening to the mother.

However if one truly thinks about the potential of new life from an Energetic perspective and honours the creation and sustaining of all life, then abortion can be seen as an act of murder! As a young student nurse I worked on a gynaecological ward and had to help mothers with their abortions, done via a hormonal drip. One day a mother delivered into a bedpan and I had to carry a live perfect tiny baby, which was still moving, out to the sluice area and leave it there for Sister to check. Such experiences enable one to realise the reality of such an act! There is no moral judgement of abortion here, but I wish to point out that taking life before birth is just as meaningful as taking it after birth, as the foetus is already created as a human form and is alive and growing.

Often after an abortion the mother is aware of the spiritual 'essence' or Energy of the unborn child which lingers close to her for many years until she becomes pregnant again. This can cause her much distress and even deep depression, as a longing for the unborn child is always there.

This is not intended to be a 'guilt trip' for any mothers who have already had abortions, but may help them to understand these feelings of ill ease which may be around after such an event. Millions of abortions have been performed and all that potential Energy has been blocked at source. Incarnating souls may need to look elsewhere for less than perfect parents, or they may not be able to come to earth at all.

Are there any natural ways of avoiding a baby? Saying "No!" is the simplest! Avoiding sex altogether unless a baby is truly wished for ensures that unwanted pregnancy does not occur, but it also denies the couple their closeness and pleasure. Therefore understanding, affectionate cuddles and conversations about this are vitally important. 'Coitus interupticus,' or withdrawing the penis before ejaculation is one way of doing things naturally, but needs consciousness and control by the man and may not be 100% safe. Giving each other pleasure without actual penetration is always a possibility.

Abstaining from intercourse just at the most fertile times of the month is the most natural way of avoiding pregnancy but needs a very good solid relationship between the man and woman who can work together with real consciousness. The woman takes her temperature every day at the same time. This rises slightly at ovulation. Then the couple must not have intercourse for 3-4 days afterwards. The mucous in the woman's vagina also changes and can be observed as more slimy and clinging. This entices and helps the sperm up when fertilisation is optimal.

If this method is going to be used it is worth getting a good book and studying it in detail beforehand. It is also important to consider whether a baby would be welcome if this method does fail. Don't be casual about contraception if you cannot cope with a child! It is the responsibility of both partners, not just the potential mother.

Natural cycle observation can be useful also if the couple are not very fertile, in helping to find the best times to have intercourse to ensure conception. It is a tried and tested method often used between children, when the timing of another baby is not crucial.

Some women are so finely tuned to the moon phases that their periods also follow the ebb and flow of the moon and the tides and they know exactly when they are fertile. The sex of the baby can also be 'controlled' if the mother knows her exact time of ovulation, as male and female sperm swim up and fertilise at different rates.

Working in this natural way, the woman may also become more in tune and intuitive to the incoming *soul* of the child. This statement assumes that there is a consciousness before conception and that a unique individual choses its parents in order to provide it with the body and inherited traits which will help it to live out its life to the full as intended by the 'destiny impulse' of that approaching soul.

This thought is based on my personal belief that there is a meaning and purpose to our lives which is predestined. We do not have a choice in our destiny, but we do have total *free will* as to how we fulfil or work through our destiny. This belief is held by many people in the world today.

Women may have a strong urge to become pregnant at a particular time. They talk of being 'broody'! They may even have a dream or a 'vision' of the child and 'know' that the child is waiting to come. This is a not uncommon experience of mothers, and sometimes also fathers.

The child's name may also be heard at any time during the early weeks of pregnancy or may come through strongly to either parent at the time of the birth.

If a child is waiting to incarnate they may become disappointed if they have to wait too long and go elsewhere to find a parent. Then the broodiness feelings diminish again as the soul moves away.

It is also possible with humans and animals to have a phantom pregnancy. This is a strange phenomenon where the hormones start to change giving the appearance of pregnancy and the mother may be positive that she is carrying the child without physical fertilisation having ever happened.

There is currently an increase in the number of children being born in Britain.70, 000 babies are due to be born this year. Statistics show rises and falls of the population which often mirror economic growth or confidence in the state of the country. At present this seems to be the opposite in Britain! One can wonder why? Many children seem to want to be born at these exciting times. We are living in a time of huge transitions, where we are becoming ever more conscious of the potential to destroy ourselves, through wars, natural disasters and famine. Many animals are already becoming extinct, through pollution and manmade disasters. We are becoming greedier and raping the earth of her natural resources.

But at the same time we are now ever more aware of our Spiritual dimension which calls on our conscience to do the RIGHT thing. There is a big shift of our human social potential going on at present and it seems that more incarnating souls wish to be part of this Shift of Consciousness.

Preconception care

There are a number of practical things both mother and father can do to help ensure that their bodies are in tip top condition before they start trying to get pregnant, to give the baby and themselves the best chance of remaining healthy throughout pregnancy, birth and afterwards.

Diet is of the utmost importance. Nowadays people who eat a so-called 'healthy diet' are often severely lacking in minerals and vitamins as the soil in which most food is grown is heavily toxic with pesticides and fertilizers; so Organic vegetables and grains in large quantities are a first step to becoming healthy. Eating lots of variety of vegetables and fruit, raw foods whenever possible, and regular meals is all important.

A good quality multivitamin/mineral supplement, particularly containing zinc, folic acid, iron, Vitamins A B's C D E and K, copper, selenium, magnesium and calcium should be taken every day to boost the normal levels. Most people are mineral deficient nowadays. Patrick Holford has developed some very good quality daily supplements for different times in life.

Meat eating is generally accepted as being important, because of the need for extra iron, but only organic meat should be eaten, as the growth hormones and antibiotics given to animals are toxic to oneself and the baby. This is especially important when eating liver, which is often advised to pregnant women. Many perfectly healthy mothers eat only vegetarian food, fish or poultry whilst being pregnant with no ill effects. Whole-grains and green vegetables can provide much essential iron and folic acid, as well as beans and pulses.

Cutting out tea, coffee, alcohol, coke, artificial sweeteners, MSG, and large amounts of sugar will also help the liver and gut to detoxify and be healthier to receive the child. Many additives in foods can be harmful to the growing child, so ALWAYS READ THE LABELS, and try if possible to prepare simple food from basic ingredients rather than resorting to quick ready meals which go into the microwave.

Remember that food contains Energy just as we do and it is the Energy which nourishes you and the child. To eat food which has been picked for a long time and flown in from abroad after being irradiated, which has been processed, canned, frozen, or flavours, colours and preservatives added, or has lain in the fridge for several days, will not give you much vital Energy. It is far better to eat locally produced and freshly picked vegetables, which will also support the local economy and help the earth too.

Drugs, whether over the counter, prescribed or illegal should be completely avoided. If you are taking any regular medication from the doctor for health issues you should discuss pregnancy and see if you can come off it. Many problems both to the pregnancy and the baby can be avoided or reduced by keeping to this cleansing regime.

Nicotine is now known to be deadly to the foetus and mother. If you have been a smoker go and get help to stop smoking *before* you even think about becoming pregnant! Also encourage your partner to do the same. Babies born to smokers are smaller and less intelligent. 'Side smoking' in the house or car with young children has been proved to increase asthma, bronchitis and allergies. Is it worth damaging the child that you love?

Environmental toxins need to be considered too. How many hours do you sit at a computer? How much time do you spend on a mobile phone? Do you sleep on an electric blanket or waterbed with heated filaments? Do you drive long distances? Do you live on a polluted street in a city? Do you have to operate machinery or have to work in a highly stressed environment?

It is not always possible to avoid these toxins nowadays but being conscious of them is the first step. If you can try to offset their effects by having a good long walk in the fresh country air regularly, keeping relaxed and happy, and plan your work and family balance beforehand, so you will have fewer problems with yourself and the baby during pregnancy, birth and afterwards.

All these things one can start to think about when planning a family. You are preparing the space both mentally, emotionally and physically for welcoming a new human being. Pre-conceptual care is becoming more widely recognised. Being in best condition at the outset will help to avoid unnecessary delays in becoming pregnant or losing a child in the early weeks of pregnancy due to miscarriage.

Fear is one of the greatest toxins in our society. It is most often held at a subconscious level and may reflect experiences from your parents or even grandparents. Ask your mother how your own birth experience was if you can? Was it easy? Did it have complications or trauma? Was your own mother very frightened? Becoming aware of these traumas is the first step to clearing them from the subconscious level, where they sit and may have bad effects on your own labour and birth. A re-birthing experience done under hypnosis may be helpful if you are worried about anything. Practising meditation and relaxation before you even become pregnant is also helpful as it will be essential during labour.

Nest building is a basic instinct practised by most animals in one way or another. In humans it often shows itself as a wish to move house and create a nice family environment. Be warned that this can be remarkably stressful and takes a large amount of Energy to achieve! Paint chemicals are toxic and heavy lifting of boxes or furniture in the early weeks of pregnancy can cause a miscarriage. So try to pre plan your move *before* you fall pregnant so you have the bulk of the work done and there is no dust, smell or stressful chaos when you are most vulnerable! Sewing curtains, choosing the nursery décor or knitting are more suitable 'nesting' activities for pregnancy!

Paid employment or a career is now fairly normal before starting a family. Many couples are reluctant to give up a second income so the mother can stay at home to care for the children. This causes untold stress in our modern society, where women have been educated and trained to become earners alongside their husbands. There are often expectations that a mother should do both and endless juggling will need to be done to ensure the needs of young children are met adequately.

Financial implications of 'Maternity Leave' will need to be worked out, so as to optimise the time that the woman can take off from work. Women also do not want to become 'just a mother and housewife' nowadays, as this is considered menial and boring mindless work, which society does not value highly. It is often cheaper to get in a nanny on a lower wage to bring up the children and continue with one's own career and our current government is encouraging this.

Having worked for many years as a nanny, mother's help and maternity nurse I can say that I have seen much emotional deprivation amongst top earning middle and upper class families who chose to go straight back to work. The child often has to contend with foreign speaking au-pairs or nannies with a different cultural background. The child becomes confused about the role of the real mother who appears just at bedtime or at the weekends. She may be tired and stressed after work and feeling guilty that her child is upset at seeing her again. The child is often 'spoilt' as the parent tries to compensate for lack of care during the day.

Quite often there are conflicting sets of rules being imposed by the parents and the nannies. If the child is taken to a nursery from a young age, this can be an even worse scenario as the child then has to contend with much *different* Energy. The child absorbs and grows from the mother's and father's Energy which it has chosen, rather as a plant grows from light and water. A peaceful loving environment is what is needed. If they are away from the natural parents for long periods in the early years before that natural separation is due, there may be subconscious stresses which play into the child and only show much later on in life as health issues.

If you want to do the BEST for your baby, then try to organise your life so that one or other parent or a grandparent can be with the child most of the time. I said that some of my ideas may seem old fashioned, but seen in the light of Energy they are true!

I will speak more of this in later chapters on young children. Suffice to say that the decision to have a family at all is not one to be taken lightly and needs the agreement and consideration of both parents to make it work. A child is not just a baby to be dressed up and cuddled, a status symbol! Becoming a parent is a total change of lifestyle and the oportunity to 'grow up' in wisdom and love over many years.

Chapter 6

Pregnancy and preparation

So now conception has been successful! The sperm has penetrated the ovum and the first division of the cells has started. The cells multiply rapidly into a tiny ball which travels down the Fallopian tube and imbeds into the wall of the ready prepared Uterus or womb. It nestles in and puts out tiny roots rather like a plant would.

This eventually becomes the placenta, an amazing new organ neither part of the baby nor the mother but acting as an intermediary for both, rich in hormones and blood supply. The placenta sustains the pregnancy and comes away after the child is born as the 'afterbirth'. It only causes any concern if it implants low down in the uterus, blocking or partially blocking the outlet of the uterus, or if the hormone levels drop too much too early and the placenta starts to die off prematurely. It is primarily the hormones in the placenta which control the onset of labour too.

The tiny bunch of cells, the potential embryo, starts to divide in a more specialised way and there is a division of cells between the baby embryo and the yolk sac. The membranes which enclose the foetus, (as the unborn fully formed baby is called,) in a watery world during pregnancy start to form and the first division of cells into the spinal cord and brain occur. The pulsating Energy which is creating all these changes continues to work strongly and some tiny beating blood cells gather together to form the first primitive heart. Before many days have passed little buds appear which form into tiny hands and feet. The embryo looks a bit like a tiny fish, but the process continues as if by some miracle until about 2 months has gone by and the tiny baby or foetus is clearly recognisable. Hair and nails, eyes, ears, limbs and organs have all been formed as though by a magician!

Many women are able to see their babies now at this stage if they go for an Ultrasound scan at about 10-12 weeks. It seems strange that for many mothers this is the first time they really believe they are pregnant! 'Seeing believes', whereas all the amazing creative work has already taken place, often unrecognised and unknown by the parents. Nowadays the sex of the baby can also be seen from the scan, but many parents still choose not to be told so that it remains a surprise at birth.

While these changes are taking place in the uterus, unseen, other big changes are occurring in the mother's body too. She does not look pregnant yet but her body is starting to soften and increase in weight. The hormones work from the pituitary, or master gland, and the ovaries, increasing the blood supply by several pints, softening the ligaments and muscles, changing the elasticity of the skin, the texture of the hair, the nipples and breasts. These may leak a little milky substance in the latter stages of pregnancy.

Many women experience huge tiredness during the first weeks of pregnancy. This may mean that they fall asleep in the armchair when they get home from work or need to get really early nights. They may become moody, depressed or weepy for no reason. They may have skin rashes or other skin changes. Their breasts may become sore or tingly and start to increase in size.

Apart from the tell-tale sign of a missed period, nausea is a thing which many women look for when becoming pregnant. Not all women experience nausea or morning sickness. It does not always appear first thing in the morning but can also be later in the day if one is tired or hungry. I used to vomit regularly between 4-6 p.m. in the first 12 weeks when preparing the evening meal for my husband and children! It is mainly associated with a low blood sugar, as the changes of pregnancy may affect the insulin levels. Having a dry sweetish biscuit first thing before getting out of bed may help, and eating small regular meals every 3-4 hours including some carbohydrate will help to sustain the blood sugar levels.

Some women experience extreme vomiting to the extent of needing hospitalization. This is known as 'Hyperemesis gravidarum'. This is an interesting condition if one remembers what was said about the incarnating soul of the child. A strong soul, or even two souls as in the case of twins, may so displace the soul of the mother that she feels rather 'spaced out', and no longer sufficiently in her body to cope with digestion. The mother's instinctive body then tries to reject the incarnating child and literally vomit it out! It becomes a battle of wills between the baby and the mother on a subconscious level. Meditation on the incarnating soul and allowing the child more 'space' inwardly will help the situation. The mother needs to peacefully accept the pregnancy without FEAR. All sorts of anxieties may be present mainly deeply seated in the unconscious, possibly inherited from the ancestral line.

Nausea usually wears off by the third or fourth month and the woman may start to feel very well. This is known as the 'bloom of pregnancy'. There may be brown marks on her cheekbones which make the woman looked tanned, she will have thick lustrous hair, her eyes may shine more and she is filled with a blessed Energy of creativity.

It is at about 10-12 weeks, when the uterus with the foetus growing inside it comes up out of the bony pelvis, that the first tiny movements may be felt (later with the first child; about 18-20 weeks) and the waistline starts to expand so that looser clothes are needed. Often the woman has had her first antenatal appointment with the doctor and midwife by then and she has been given her expected delivery dates (EDD)

The length of pregnancy is 10 lunar months (a lunar month being approximately 27.5 days) *from the time of conception*. As the date of conception is often not known, dates are generally worked out from the date of the last period, assuming that menstruation was regular. This gives quite a lot of leeway for error, and so nowadays it is common practice to do Ultrasonic scans at various points during pregnancy to check on the size of the baby's head circumference. By plotting the measurements at various stages, an accurate growth chart can be worked out, giving the average time to birth.

Our cerebral minds can become very focused on this due date! Life needs to be planned around the birth! Many modern women even book in for a particular date to have a Caesarean which means they know exactly when their husbands or the maternity nurse have to be available!

Babies do not work in this way! Just as feeds cannot be regimented afterwards, so the birth cannot be planned! Each pregnancy is different in its quality and length, each incarnating soul chooses its own particular moment of birth and as the first breath is taken so the imprint of the Energy of the entire Universe colours how we live out our lives. This ancient knowledge is known as Astrology and a reading of the planets and the zodiac signs at birth give an accurate picture of the forces at work at this important moment in our lives. It is obviously open to different interpretations, but in essence the child *chooses* its moment of birth.

Seen in this light we can ask ourselves what the effect might be on the destiny and connection with its true life purpose for a child who is induced in labour early or has a planned Caesarean birth? Are we meddling with deeper things than we realise?

Patience and careful observation by the midwife is needed to ensure that everything is safe and well managed throughout pregnancy, to check that the baby is growing and moving well, in a good position for delivery and there are no abnormalities.

For this reason the mother is visited at home or asked to attend antenatal clinic at very regular intervals throughout the pregnancy. Initially this will be every month or so, then every 2 weeks and finally every week up to the birth. Once the EDD has been reached and passed the doctor likes to keep a good eye on their progress.

At this check-up the mother, if she is going to a small local maternity unit, can start to get to know the midwives and doctor who will be assisting at the delivery. She can visit the hospital too where she is booked in, so she feels more confident about going in when the time comes, although she is unlikely to have met her midwife before. If she is booking for a home birth and everything appears normal she will see the local team of midwives for most of her care.

At each subsequent visit to the clinic she will be given a blood pressure check, her urine is tested for sugar and protein and she is weighed. This is to check whether her body is 'rejecting' the baby and creating a condition known as **pre-eclampsia**. If this starts to happen it could lead on to full blown eclampsia which is a very serious condition for both the mother and baby and may even cause the death of either or both. The kidneys start to fail and the blood pressure rises to extremes.

The only cure for eclampsia is to deliver the baby immediately. Fortunately this is now a rare occurrence since regular antenatal checks pick up the slightest signs of this condition, such as puffy ankles and fingers, protein in the urine, or rising blood pressure. If it is beginning, the mother is advised to rest at home or in more extreme cases may need to rest in the hospital.

The size of the baby is assessed at each visit and the mother is palpated, meaning that the midwife feels where and how the baby is lying and then she listens to the baby's heartbeat. This is done with a special machine which picks up the sounds or by an ear trumpet which the midwife listens through. The latter is rarely used now! The normal heartbeat is usually between 120-140 beats per minute, much faster than an adult's.

It is reassuring for the mother to be told that all is well. And antenatal care provides a good oportunity for the mother to ask questions too and find out about minor problems in pregnancy, such as pain on walking, due to the baby's head pressing down and the pelvic joints relaxing, bladder pressure, heartburn, sleeping problems, and Braxton Hicks contractions (practice ones, which don't last long and just tone up the uterus). The midwife always asks about the baby's movements too, as these help to indicate the health of the growing foetus.

In the last three months of pregnancy (the last Trimester) the baby becomes much larger and heavier and the mother slows up considerably. Now the waiting game begins! Once the head moves down into the pelvis and becomes deeply 'engaged', as usually happens after about 36 weeks with the first child, then labour can start any time after this.

Most mothers enjoy being pregnant despite the times when it becomes a bit uncomfortable. There is a pride and joy about carrying new life and most mothers actually feel very fulfilled and well. People tend to treat them as a bit special, getting up to let them have a seat on the train, treating them with respect, or just joking about their changing figure! This extra attention is very good for both the mother and baby. It is a way of giving love and Energy when it is most needed. Most people love the prospect of a new baby, but it may be an oportunity to give unwelcome advice and hear all the gory stories too!

All this time the baby is being nourished by the foods and oxygen from the mother's blood, which filter across to the placenta, and is growing steadily stronger and larger in utero while the mother is supplying the vital Energy for its growth. She must therefore really look after herself and ensure that the child gets plenty of Energy, as otherwise the baby will take it from *her directly* and she may become weakened, perhaps anaemic or extremely tired.

Energy, as we have learned, is obtained from the Universe in the form of fresh healthy food, sunlight and fresh air and love and hugs from others. The mother can also access Universal Energy through meditation and relaxation, and also through some forms of creativity. Being aware of this phenomenon she can plan times alone with her child, to focus in and send love to the baby, and also ensure that she has enough relaxation time out in nature which will refresh her. Eating healthy alive food is also her main responsibility, as is ensuring that the pollutants that are so prevalent in our society do not come near the child. She is the child's protector and nourisher in the widest sense.

Emotions can also affect the pregnancy and it is important that she remains calm and fearless, so that the unborn child does not pick up these emotions from her. If she becomes stressed then the child may respond to that extreme fear by becoming restless or worse still failing to thrive in utero. The process of being a good mother starts from before conception, not just at the birth! Talking to other new mothers, or one's own mother or sisters at this stage is often helpful.

Being careful of the incarnating child is often negated nowadays, with mothers getting involved in many unsuitable activities; not only working full time in a stressful environment, but also going on journeys, flying long distances or even taking part in some extreme sports. She may also watch fearful aggressive films on television which upset her.

Often the mother is more sensitive to such things, if her instincts are working well, and she has a natural inclination to protect the unborn child from danger. It must be said though that pregnancy is a perfectly natural condition and the mother should remain active and not treat herself like an invalid during this special time.

Early nights, or a short rest during the day, will give her time to be quietly at one with the baby. It is often the case that when she lies down the baby starts kicking and moving around, as it now gets more oxygen and she is more relaxed. Instead of being disturbed by this she can link even more strongly with the little being growing inside her.

During this daily rest time it is also a very good idea to practise complete relaxation and simple deep breathing, nothing forced or extreme, which when practised can become familiar as a means of focusing the mind when labour starts. With each breath it is important to concentrate on blowing OUT, rather like trying to blow out a candle gently with pursed lips, rather than deep breathing IN which might lead to Hyperventilation. This can disturb the balance of CO_2 and O_2 in the body and create too much acid in the blood which will adversely affect the baby, especially when it may become tired during labour; so learning specific breathing patterns which become exaggerated during labour is NOT a good idea. If you over-breath you may become slightly dizzy, but breathing in and out of a paper bag can help equalise the gases and stop this happening.

Lying flat on your back during pregnancy is also not a good idea, especially late on, as the weight of the baby presses against the mother's large blood vessels and may create low blood pressure which is not good for either mother or baby.

It is very comforting to have a couple of extra pillows in the bed as time gets close to delivery. Try putting one between your legs and another in the small of your back or just under your 'bump' if you get backache or pain in your groin when you lie on your side.

Mothers may become quite forgetful or irrational during pregnancy! This is normal and due to the hormonal changes going on, but is also recognised as the beginnings of 'maternal absorption' which is a very natural phenomenon and helps to ensure the child is properly cared for. Fathers beware of this!

Sleep may become quite disturbed in the last weeks too, as the baby's head pushes against the bladder, so the mother needs to get up several times at night. This is good training ground for the demands of the baby in the first months after the birth!

As the baby grows, so the mother finds it harder to eat big meals. Small high energy meals taken more frequently are best, with not too many spices or rich foods. This is also a suitable diet for early labour, as it is important not to go long periods without food then.

Drinking Raspberry Leaf tea can be helpful in toning up the muscles of the uterus. Drink 2-3 cups a day in the last weeks of pregnancy. A little honey and lemon added can help overcome the rather bland taste.

As 'D DAY' approaches is a good idea to have everything prepared in the 'nursery' or wherever the baby is going to sleep, (which could also be your own bedroom.) A simple layette can be pre-prepared consisting of 6 nightgowns or baby-grows (size 1), vests and a couple of soft hats, nappies, rubbish bags and bin for disposing of nappies, 2-3 soft large wraps for swaddling and 6 muslin wipes, a changing place which is warm and flat with a good defuse light, soft towels, cotton wool and 2 dishes for water, a baby bath, and an instantly controllable heater. Initially one doesn't need much more!

There will always be plenty of presents arriving afterwards with modern outfits for winter walks and umpteen bootees and mits from aunties! Keep things simple to begin with and tidy, with perhaps a portable changing mat/bag for trips out too.

Babies grow incredibly fast, and often first size outfits are hardly worn. Once you are established properly you can chose some more clothes to suit your child, preferably made from natural fabrics such as cotton, and prewashed using mild soap powder and ironed to reduce the factory dressing. Baby's skin is incredibly sensitive and cannot cope with biological washing powders or bleaches.

The bed for the baby is important to think about. Many parents like to prepare a traditional crib for the first few weeks as this is cosier than a big cot or a carry cot. Preparing a new lining for a second hand crib which may have been used by several families enables Mum to have a nice 'nesting' feeling. Rockers attached underneath are very worthwhile for sending the child into a sweet sleep! A head covering made of light soft material and draped over like a hood shelters the child in a gentle way after it has come out from the very dark warm place of the womb. The fewer shocks the child has in the early weeks the more it can conserve its Energy for all the new experiences such as seeing, breathing and digesting. A peaceful soft environment is therefore helpful. Mobiles and squeaky garish plastic or fluffy toys are unnecessary in the first few weeks.

Grandparents often like to be involved in giving some equipment for a first grandchild, a pram or buggy/car-transporter. It is considered unlucky to buy these in advance, but they can be ordered, or better still second hand ones can be recycled via second hand sales, charity shops, the local newspaper, or borrowed from friends. Cutting costs at this stage will enable you to spend a bit more later on when the child will benefit more. It is also much more ecological to do this.

Becoming a father for the first time can be quite a scary business, especially if you have never had any contact with children or pregnant mothers before, which is often the case nowadays. Talking to colleagues and work mates may be a good idea, as well as coming along to some of the antenatal classes, which are held at the clinic or hospital by the midwives, or by the National Childbirth Trust, often in the evenings. Sharing your anxieties and hearing about the process of labour and afterwards, many future fathers enjoy giving some special care to their wives and following the growth and development of the baby at the various stages, through feeling it's kicking, or even listening to its heartbeat through a cardboard toilet role, placed gently on the mother's abdomen! Another interesting thing for fathers can be attending the clinic appointment when a scan is done, so they get to see the baby moving around inside.

Fathers can also learn to massage their wives, which can be extremely helpful in the latter stages of pregnancy and as labour commences, and they are often the ones who take charge when the mother needs to transfer to the hospital, and assess how far the labour is progressing.

Mothers can get busy in the kitchen in the last weeks and prepare a few meals to put into the freezer to save time and energy in the first days after coming home when everything seems chaotic. Good choices for these ready meals are soups, lasagne, shepherd's pie or fish pie, cooked without too many spices or onions, as eating these whilst breast feeding can upset the baby's delicate stomach and cause wind.

Baking some high energy granola bars using dates, oats, coconut or chocolate can be useful for early labour, or to keep Dad happy in the early hours! Savoury flapjacks made with cheese and grated carrots are also useful for hungry moments! Try, as D day approaches, to keep your cupboards and fridge topped up with healthy food so that there is not a panic when labour does start. The odd takeaway can be useful too, providing it is not full of additives and heavily spiced.

Also try and keep the washing and ironing baskets empty as far as possible beforehand, as there will be extra work once you are home again with the new baby, and husbands can create lots of washing suddenly while you are away! Fathers are usually good at lending a hand with such chores.

Why am I writing about such mundane stuff? Anything you can do in advance to prepare 'the nest' so that it is clean, tidy and calm to welcome the child when you come home as a new family will help both you and the baby in the early days.

The last few weeks of pregnancy can be a bit daunting. You may have given up work and be missing the normal routine and company of colleagues. Your body feels heavy and cumbersome and you are not sleeping well. Your mind is turning more and more to the task ahead and you may be getting nervous about how you will 'perform' in labour! The baby is making itself ever more known to you with its movements, hiccups and sudden kicks which may be just on your bladder!

Apart from gentle 'nesting', try to spend a bit of extra time each day with the unborn child, listening inwardly to the approaching Energy of the child. If the weather allows have a rest in the garden on a recliner chair, or take a gentle walk out in nature. It can be a very content time as one waits patiently, providing you get into the right frame of mind. **Fear must be overcome to prepare for mothering.**

Avoid going to busy high streets or polluted noisy places if you can, cut right down on longer car journeys, don't plan any major events and even consider not driving at all. The brain is affected by your hormones in late pregnancy and your concentration can be affected!

Keep an open diary and know where your husband is going to be. Enjoy the company of other new mothers and practice holding their babies if possible. The NCT groups are useful for this with first time mothers. Becoming 'just a housewife' for the first time may feel strange and a bit lonely or boring. In the previous generations mothers and sisters were often around to support you in this transition to a new status. Nowadays, unless you already have friends with babies, you may feel a bit isolated and wonder how to fill the long days. Husbands may not feel entirely comfortable about the new dependence and vulnerability you are showing now. Just bear in mind that this is entirely natural and ensures that as mothers we are in a state of mind to nurture the next generation, to give our entire attention and Energy to the incoming soul, which is necessary for it to thrive and grow. If you accept this task **selflessly** and adapt your life to slow down and be just a Mum you will enjoy this creative role all the more. It is about 'losing you' for the sake of another and it can be a blessed time. You WILL be able to do things for yourself again once the children are older. You have not lost your independence and brain for ever. Don't fight it, just go with it and it will be less daunting and confusing!

The relationship between a mother and her child is a unique one and starts during pregnancy. It is about give and take, as in any relationship. Babies are naturally demanding of us, otherwise they would not survive, but as time goes on and the baby is more independent parents can also demand personal space, routine and obedience. It is not about being a control freak or having 'perfect' children, but more about listening to and respecting the personality of the unique child but still giving parameters within which the child feels secure. Allowing the child to demand constantly and rule your lives totally will not make for happy parents or a happy childhood.

These things can be pondered as the child starts naturally to demand of you during pregnancy. Do you ignore its basic needs of food and oxygen which are diminished if you 'carry on as usual', or do you pamper to the foetus' needs to the extent that you give up your normal life entirely? Only you, in discussion with your partner, can find these answers. Everyone is different.

Travel is a good example of what I have just been writing about. Is it right to travel by plane during pregnancy? Certainly it IS possible, but what effect will it have on the foetus? Being in this environment is bound to have some effect. Balancing your needs with those of the baby will help you decide. Is it ok to drink alcohol or smoke? The medical profession are now advising on this, but are you giving up with resentment, or joy that you are caring for your child in the best way? Other things to consider in this light might be a stressful job in a polluted environment. How important is the income, versus the stress on the foetus?

You are already beginning to think not only of yourself (and also your partner), but also for the needs of your child. This shift in priorities goes on for years and years; in fact it probably never stops, as once you are a parent you are irrevocably linked to the needs of another human being in a loving way for ever. Even if you cannot keep your child and have it adopted, you will never be quite the same again! Even after your children have grown up and flown the nest, you still think about them constantly and wish them well in their decisions about life. You do not *own* them, they are not your possessions but because you have nurtured them and given them the possibility of LIFE they are forever connected to you in a special way.

This is sometimes referred to as being 'connected by the umbilical cord.' Our children *are* connected to us by this in utero. At birth the cord is cut, leaving the child to fend for itself in terms of oxygen and foodstuffs. Now it has to breathe and digest for itself. As the child grows up, and becomes more and more independent, the Energy cords which still exist are cut one by one. Some landmarks of this cutting of the cord are having a first night away with a grandparent or family friend, going to school for the first time, and finally leaving home. We may take this for granted, but sometimes it is necessary to do it consciously to enable the child to stand on its own feet in the world in a healthy way. We have completed our task as parents and can feel proud of our part in enabling another human being to come into this world.

Chapter 7
The first stage of labour

The due date is approaching, everything is prepared and the excitement is mounting! At a particular moment the pregnancy is 'ripe' and the child is ready to be born. What ascertains this moment in time? Why will an apple or an acorn fall off the tree when ripe?

The placenta, which has sustained the pregnancy and acted as a huge filter for nutrition and oxygen, passing these substances over to the baby via the umbilical cord, is maintained by hormones. It is these constantly changing levels of hormones which affect the onset of labour. Things which can upset this fine balance of hormones are the MOTHER'S FEAR or stress of any kind and therefore the **production of adrenalin which stops labour**; and imbibing alcohol! If, for some reason, the child wants to come early, premature labour can even be stopped by putting up an infusion of alcohol.

There may be deeper reasons for a child deciding to be born early or late. Most pregnancies last ten lunar months, but some babies are eager to arrive before this. As a midwife I observed more births around new moon and full moon. There seems to be an Energy surge around these times. The Universal Laws are complex and we only tip the iceberg when we study astrology. Suffice to say that Nature knows best and inducing labour unnaturally may have disturbing consequences on the child's future destiny.

But how do you know whether or not you are going into labour? It doesn't 'just happen', but is a gradual 'warming up' process of mounting Energy, rather like a huge machine getting going which once started has its own perpetual motion!

The Braxton Hick's contractions get ever stronger towards the end of pregnancy and may even feel painful, especially if you are lying awake at night waiting for the next one to come.

They are often felt at regular intervals and the midwife may have told you to ring the hospital once the contractions are regular. Actually they are doing very little to progress the birth except toning up the hugely powerful muscles which make up the uterus, lying in three different directions so as to squeeze and propel the baby out and also draw the cervix up out of the way, to enable the baby to pass down into the 'birth canal', which was previously the vagina.

How do you recognise a real contraction as appose to a Braxton Hicks one? Many mothers come into the hospital *too soon* with their first baby and have to wait around feeling anxious and getting hungry. They are often told to lie down flat on the bed, so that the baby's heartbeat can be monitored with a continuous machine onto a paper graph, which will give the doctor in charge an instant reading and means that the woman can be left alone for periods if the labour room is busy and no midwives are available, while the baby's heartbeat is monitored.

This is the worst possible scenario for the onset of labour and often results in tired mothers, tired hungry babies and then forceps or Caesarean deliveries. As the cervix can only be assessed by a qualified doctor or midwife, by doing an internal examination, at this very early stage of labour, little dilatation will be felt. As said before, the body is just warming up to labour. Dilatation is referred to as 1-10 cms. When you are 'fully' (dilated) you are ready to push!

Therefore be very aware of what the contractions are doing and only call the hospital and prepare to go in if:

1. There has been a 'show'; i.e. the plug of mucous which sits in the entrance of the vagina comes away as the cervix starts to dilate, and the contractions ARE LASTING at least 40 seconds from beginning to end. If they are only 30 seconds duration, even if painful, chances are they are not dilating the cervix very effectively. So *timing* the contractions is crucial!
2. The 'waters' break. The strong amniotic sac which protects the baby and holds up to 500ml of clear fluid which the baby has been swimming in for the last few months, breaks and there is a sudden gush of warm fluid. This can be very disconcerting, especially if you have not reached your due date yet, and it is a good idea to wear an absorbent pad in the last couple of weeks, especially when you are out and about. Labour does not necessarily start right away when the waters go, but it is one of the signs of the onset of labour and a midwife should be spoken to.
Very occasionally, if the head is still lying quite high up in the pelvis, the baby's cord can slip down in front of the head if the waters break and as labour goes on the cord is compressed and the baby starved of oxygen. This then becomes an obstetric emergency warranting immediate delivery. So call a midwife or the hospital if your waters do pop and prepare to go in to get checked.
If the waters break, the baby is happy and there is no dark meconium (baby poo) in the liquid draining out, some hospitals will let you wait around till labour starts on its own, (or they may send you home again) but there is sometimes a danger of rising infection into the womb, so observations of pulse and temperature will be done often and the liquor observed. Mothers have to shower rather than bath to cleanse in preparation for the birth, for the same reason.
More often the doctor will deem it wise to start the labour using a hormonal infusion into the bloodstream of the mother, via a drip, increasing the natural hormonal levels to force contractions. Because this is unnatural for the body, labour will be shorter and fiercer than intended and the baby

may become distressed; so monitoring, lying down for most of the duration of labour and a less 'natural' labour becomes inevitable, and the outcome may well be forceps or a Caesarean birth. The mother copes less well with these fiercer contractions induced by medication and may need more pain relief and even an epidural. Doctors, who like to know the labour will only last a certain number of hours, tend to encourage this type of 'managed labour' as they have more input and control of the whole process. They may try to persuade you that it is safer. The ultimate decision is yours but try to avoid the reasons for a managed labour in the first place.

3. The last reason for going into hospital is that the contractions are getting stronger. As previously said, you will have to time these accurately and fathers are very good at this! Try to hang out at home until they are lasting at least 45 seconds and coming REGULARLY at about 5-7 minutes. Depending on where you live and the distance/time to the hospital, this may vary somewhat, but keep in touch with the labour ward and talk it through with them if you are unsure.

So you are in early labour at home and getting nervous and excited. What do you do? If it is night time try to get some more sleep if you can! You have a long hard day in front of you. Tell your partner what is happening and have a warm herbal tea and a light nourishing snack. This could be a banana and some cereal, some honey halva, a boiled egg if you fancy it, some porridge, and dried fruit. Keep it fairly light (not a spicy curry) as your digestion more or less stops as labour intensifies. Ensure that you have some fructose or glucose to give you energy. If everything is going completely normally you can nibble a little as labour goes on, but sometimes if you need an anaesthetic this may become a problem later on in labour and for that reason eating is normally forbidden once you get to hospital.

Relaxation is of the utmost importance. You are now at the moment where SURRENDER is the only way forward. Huge Energy is about to take over your body and mind, and you will feel totally displaced by the force of it. You cannot stay 'in control' during natural labour, you can only psyche yourself up to feeling totally taken over and practice your relaxation beforehand, so that each time a contraction starts you just flop like a rag doll and breath out gently through your parted lips. This way you will not over-breath or become tense and distressed. Everything is going along perfectly naturally and all you have to do is allow it to work!

If it is daytime, take a gentle walk nearby, with a friend or your partner, enjoying the sunshine and nature. Stop when each contraction comes and breathe gently, concentrating on the out breath.

Have a nice long warm bath, again with a friend or your partner around and the door unlocked, just in case things speed up, or you feel dizzy. Water is a lovely medium in which to labour, as the watery element is so natural to labour Energy.

You can add some Lavender oil to it to help you relax, or some Melissa to help the labour. Other oils may be recommended by an aromatherapist if you have visited one in pregnancy. These oils can be very powerful, and can be used in the bath, in oil burners or rubbed on gently with massage, especially on the feet and lower back. Always dilute oils before you apply them to the body in a carrier such as almond oil, as they are very potent. Don't use anything that has not been checked and recommended.

Foot massage can be done by a friend, your partner/husband or the midwife caring for you. There are several 'trigger points' on the feet which help strengthen and maintain labour, so getting to know a good Reflexologist who specialises in childbirth can be most helpful. She may be able to come and give you a treatment in early labour to help things along, or even visit you in the labour ward. (This is my current work.)

Contractions are very like huge waves which gradually increase in strength and crash onto a beach. Just like a surfer does, you can ride on each big wave as it comes, jumping in front of the wave, or you sometimes fall off the surf board and the pain crashes over you leaving you breathless and spluttering! If this does happen on occasion don't panic, just keep focused and remember that the next contraction (wave) will be easier and each one is one less to go through.

Quite often nowadays the waters are broken during an examination, early on when you reach hospital. The advantage for the medics is that a clip can be put on the baby's head (ouch!) to accurately monitor the heartbeat. It also has the effect of speeding up labour, but making contractions fiercer. The midwife can see if the baby is distressed by the colour of the liquor. However if they are left intact they normally rupture of themselves just before the second stage and the cushioning effect for the baby is helpful. Very occasionally babies are born in a caul, meaning that the waters never broke. It is supposed to be special. This is common with mammals, which then bite the caul open after the birth, and lick the baby to stimulate breathing.

Having had 2 of my 3 births at home I can assure you that it is much easier and more relaxing if you don't have the worry and upset of changing your environment during labour and getting in the car to go to the hospital. The midwife comes to you! If you can just quietly settle down to doing something domestic and relax each time a contraction comes, then they become stronger and stronger and you hardly notice the time passing or the pain. There is also a chance to eat and drink fairly normally and remain upright and active throughout.

Most doctors and midwives are unwilling to allow a first child to be born at home; as there is no guarantee that the pelvic outlet is big enough. With good obstetric practice and scans of the baby's growth this should be possible to check. Midwives usually work as a team for home births, so you cannot ensure you have the same midwife, but it is helpful to build up a personal relationship with those most likely to be on duty, and discuss your wishes with them. The decision to have a homebirth will need to be made with your partner first and foremost, as they will support you through it more fully than in the hospital. As pregnancy progresses it will become clearer whether this is a safe option or not.

Active childbirth became a vogue in the 1980's and subsequently, and it is still possible to find antenatal teachers who will give you loads of ideas, using stretching exercises, upright and squatting positions, yoga breathing and all about water births. Some hospitals have 'birthing rooms' where you can opt for an Active Birth and use the pool either for labour or delivery, and cushions on the floor to relax and keep active. It is worth asking about the hospital's policies when you visit.

- Do they expect you to be monitored? And for how long?
- Can you use the pool as much as you want? And for the actual delivery?
- What is their policy about eating during labour?
- What pain relief is normally offered?
- Do they put the baby to the breast as soon as possible after delivery?
- Do they accept and refer to the mother's birth plan?
- Birth plans are a list of your Do they cut the cord straight away?

wishes, after you have read all the books and idealised your perfect delivery! I sound cynical but many parents go into labour with their birth plans, and come out feeling a failure because it hasn't gone according to plan. Is there a reason for this? They have become stressed and their bodies could not work optimally because they were frightened!

So much of easy labouring has to do with the spiritual and emotional preparation which has gone on in the previous weeks and months; learning to relax and surrender, learning to listen to and welcome the baby, learning to become selfless and intuitive. It is not about performing well, doing as one was told by the antenatal teacher or fighting battles to have no intervention at the hospital.

Labour, as all parenting, is about YOU and the BABY and your intimate relationship. It is about *allowing* the child to be born from you, of becoming a selfless vessel through which another human being can incarnate.

Chapter 8

Transition, second stage and the birth

There comes a moment towards the end of labour when everything becomes chaotic, known as 'Transition'.

Up to this point the mother has been labouring steadily for several hours, the contractions have come closer together and are getting stronger, the child will be descending down with its head pressing on the cervix, usually with its back towards the mother's front. Every few hours the midwife looking after the mother and child will examine the cervix to ensure it is dilating evenly and steadily. She will check that the baby's head is in a good position for birth and flexing well to help it through the bony pelvis. She will regularly listen to the baby's heartbeat, especially during a contraction, to make sure that the baby isn't getting tired; she will check the draining fluid, the mother's pulse and blood pressure. She acts as the watchdog for what is going on. A good midwife will know how labour is progressing but *will not interfere*. She will just observe and support the natural process.

But suddenly the contractions are irregular, doubling up, double peaking, or much stronger. The woman may start to have an urge to push, and she may become irrational or quite bolshie, demanding to go home, wanting to lie down or have an epidural, or she just goes very quiet and distant. This is the moment when she is nearly ready to give birth and the rhythm of the Energy is changing. She is often completely 'taken over' at this moment by the strength of it all.

The cervix occasionally has not dilated evenly and there is a rim of cervix inside left on one side, which if pushed against could become swollen and split or delay the head coming down. So it is very important to follow instructions at this time and only push when the midwife allows you to.

The easiest way to prevent oneself pushing against this huge physical urge, if you are told not to, is to 'bounce' the breathing by repeating very rhythmically the words "I must not push, I must not push" making sure that the breath is like panting! While the diaphragm is bouncing it is impossible to breath-hold and push!

Husbands need to be warned about the changes in transition, so they know that the end is close, otherwise they might be frightened that something is wrong. They can help at this moment by reminding her of the panting mantra and doing it with her.

Generally this phase lasts no more than a few contractions. If it is prolonged however it is helpful to get up on hands and knees and work 'against gravity' with your bottom in the air while you do the breathing. Alternatively lying on your side may help.

The Second Stage

The midwife will tell you when it is safe to push and then another change takes place. It is a much more positive and focused time, as now it is YOUR job to be active. No longer are you at sea with mighty waves washing over you, but you can sit up or squat and DO something positive. But again a huge amount of your energy can be lost by doing it the wrong way. It is not about screwing up your face and getting angry and pushing in your throat, but about concentrating on the perineum, the bit of flesh between the anus and the vagina, which is thinning out to allow the head through. It is rather like a flower unfurling and the more relaxed you can be down there the better stretch will occur. Bearing down is a better word than pushing, as it is about assisting the uterus in its mighty piston-like action from above, and 'letting go', or thinking 'out and up' as the best way to achieve this stage of labour.

Position in the second stage is very important. Many babies are born in hospital with the woman lying fairly flat on the bed, and this means that it is going AGAINST gravity, uphill! No wonder that the mother and baby get tired! Try to sit up as much as possible or better still squat up, as they do in developing countries. The pelvis is at its most open in this position and the birth canal is easier to negotiate for the child. With my second child my husband was behind me on the bed, supporting my squat; a very comfortable position! Some women like to stand by the edge of the bed and let the baby hang down between their legs. This is ideal for a long slow delivery but rather hard on the midwife's back. Years ago most mothers were delivered on their sides. Up onto your hands and knees works well too, except at the last moment when the head is born you may want to swivel round. It all depends on the moment and how you feel.

I once watched fascinated as my cat gave birth to kittens. She was moving all the time into different positions and licking her perineum all the time, which stimulated the endorphins, or 'feel good' hormones. It can be quite a sexual experience giving birth and therefore it is best to go with the body's instincts at this time. There is no right way to do it! It is really important to have it quiet and calm in the labour room. Dimmed lights and TV off will help to focus you.

The baby's head descends slowly and surely down the birth canal on the most dangerous journey that we ever make! It is a tight squeeze for the baby but the tissues of their heads are soft and move to fit the pelvic bones. Mother's joints are also softened and give to make way for the child. The head 'crowns', or becomes visible on the outside, and then again one must listen to the instructions of the midwife as she guides the head very gently out over the thin skin, working with the contractions. She must check if the cord is around the baby's neck, which it quite often is, and then she guides the head out, the body rotates and with the next contraction the shoulders are born. The rest of the body follows with a warm rush of amniotic fluid.

Immediately the baby is surrounded by very bright light for the first time, they feel gravity and cold and the touch of human hands; a very different world from the quiet watery dark world they emerge from. Their immediate response is to give a lusty yell and in so doing they take their first gulp of earthly air. This cry is the thing listened for by the parents and a huge smile will come across the mother's face as she looks down to greet her baby. A sensitive midwife will gently wrap the child in a warm towel, without rubbing off the white creamy substance which is often still on the child as protection, and bring it up onto Mum's tummy, so that she can hold it and check it's little fingers and toes are all there. Dad is beside her and they will often decide a name there and then.

Huge changes are taking place in those first few moments as the foetal heart valves close and the circulating blood goes through the lungs for the first time, taking in oxygen from the air. The child may want to suck, so it is important for someone to stay near to help and also observe the child, their colour and movements.

The Third Stage of Labour

At the 'other end', the mother's body is still busy with labour! The contractions continue until the large placenta is sheared off the wall of the uterus and starts to slide down into the birth canal. This is a crucial moment for the midwife to observe and cannot be hurried, as incomplete separation or tearing of the placenta can cause the mother to bleed massively from the uterine 'scar', and if any bits are left behind these may fester and become infected, also causing a secondary bleed.

Nowadays it is normal practice to inject a strong hormone (Syntometrine) into the mother's leg just as the head is born, so assisting the uterus to clamp down soon after the birth and maintain this tension. The effect for the mother is a cramping of the uterus which may be painful like a contraction. The effect on the baby is less good unless the cord is clamped immediately, as a surge of blood is pushed down the cord into the child's circulation. This can cause new-born jaundice as the excess blood cells have to be broken down after birth, and the little liver cannot cope with the by-products of this process.

There are few midwives nowadays though who are willing to risk the danger of post-partum haemorrhage for the mother, and take things slowly as nature intended and work without Syntometrine. It is something worth discussing if you are trying to avoid the injection. Breastfeeding the infant very soon after delivery will release natural hormones into the mothers blood and cause the uterus to contract, but this may take as much as half an hour, before the third stage of labour is complete, and few midwives on a busy maternity unit have the time or patience to wait this long.

In either scenario it is important that the mother and child are both safe and well before leaving them to rest and enjoy their cuddles.

Chapter 9

Complications of labour

I have just described a perfectly normal labour and as such, things go smoothly and are a joy to behold. Nowadays it is fairly unusual to see a perfectly 'normal' delivery in hospital, unless possibly a second or third child coming in at night, as there are so many deviations and complications which arise as a result of induction or speeding up of labour, which seems to be accepted as perfectly normal by the 'status quo'.

When I was working as a hospital midwife in the 1980's I found it hard to attend women and encourage normal labour within the remits of safe practice that we were given. Every mother had to be monitored. All labours had to end within a given number of hours, so labours were artificially speeded up with drugs. Many women opted out of normal labour and had epidurals for their pain and eventually forceps, Ventouse suction or Caesareans.

Pain relief is a gritty subject, which may be needed to some extent for most labours. The pain of labour is strong and intense. However it is a positive pain which comes and goes with each contraction and has a known end. Some women cope better than others with pain. Again *FEAR INCREASES PAIN!* A relaxed mother can get through labour with little or no pain relief. What are your fears?

Nowadays there is plenty of pain relief and women are encouraged to ask for it. However all drugs cross to the baby whether immediately or even through the first milk the mother feeds.

I am not going to elaborate on all the different problems that can arise. These can be learnt about in antenatal classes, textbooks and on films. You may also hear about everyone else's horror stories!

I would however like to mention multiple births. This can be natural twins, where either two eggs are fertilized and the twins are unidentical, or the egg splits in the first hours after conception and then all the genes are shared and the infants will be identical. There is often a fascination with two people looking completely alike, but at the same time it is obvious to the parents that although these two souls decided to incarnate together and are extremely connected, they are in fact two totally different people.

Twins are most commonly passed on through the maternal line and may jump a generation. Triplets are also possible, as are quads and more. The mother in this situation shares her vital Energy between more than one child and therefore everything in the preparation for birth is emphasised and more extreme; more rest, better food, more vitamins, more movements, more discomforts and minor complaints of pregnancy, more sickness. When it comes to labour, few doctors nowadays are content to allow the mother to deliver normally at full term. A Caesarean is usually booked for 38 weeks depending on the condition of the babies. The mother may have to spend the last weeks in hospital if she is very tired or her blood pressure is rising.

When I was a student midwife, before the days of routine scans, I was supervised to deliver what we anticipated would be a normal birth. The child came out without complications. Directly afterwards I felt the mother's tummy and it was larger than it should have been! The midwife in charge confirmed that another child was in there, in breech position (bottom first). I was allowed to deliver the second twin, with guidance from the experienced midwife, with a roomful of medical students, paediatricians and other student nurses looking on. It was an experience I shall never forget, the most vivid impression being the shock on the father's face! I was fortunate to deliver a breech normally, something which rarely happens these days. In rural areas in third world countries it can be routine to deliver these unusual lies and situations, but there are often post-partum haemorrhages or the baby is born very distressed.

Modern obstetrics has come a long way and the child is now observed and protected from harm if things go wrong. The responsibility of good obstetric practice though is not to interfere too hastily and to maintain a calm supportive atmosphere where normal labour can still be the best outcome.

How do you prepare for a normal labour, trusting that your body knows best and that only when you fear, do things start going awry? Meditation, relaxation, trust, relaxation, trust, meditation! There is no greater way of staying at ease with your process. Tune in again and again to your baby; *trust* that your body will work for you, that you have the Energy to do it normally. I am not being a woolly idealist but a mature midwife who has attended many births and knows what does and doesn't work.

It is often the young teenagers who have had no antenatal preparation at all who labour best. They have no expectations and are rather like young animals (excuse the expression) who are labouring intuitively. They do not use their intellects to *think* about labour, to feel their pain, but enter into that intuitive space where they KNOW what to do.

Thus it is during labour and birth that your *own* maternal/paternal instincts can and will be born, if they are not already there. We all have them within us. It is for you to find them! I sincerely wish you strength in your adventure as new parents, as you are 'born' and grow into selfless carers of the new life which has been entrusted to you.

Chapter 10

The care of the new-born

So now you are at home with your new family member! It is probably one of the most exciting and scariest moments of your life when you come home from the hustle and bustle of the hospital for the first time and realise that you actually have a child of your own to care for, night and day with no let-up until they are self-sufficient. You have been on a blissful high since the birth; suddenly all that crumbles into the stark reality of the endless round of feeding and changing.

In the hospital there was always someone to ask help from, if not a midwife then at least another new mother or even the cleaner. You have been shown how to change, top and tail, and bath this wriggling squawking demanding little creature. You may have taken them to the nursery at night so you could have a good sleep; you may have been struggling with breastfeeding, which is supposed to be totally 'natural', but you have persevered because the midwife helped the baby to latch on.

Your own body may feel stiff and sore where you were pushing hard in labour, and you may be bruised down below with even some stitches in your perineum if you were cut or tore a bit as the baby's head came through. Your breasts feel enormous and the nipples may be sore. Will you ever get your gorgeous figure back? At present your stomach looks and feels like a heap of jelly and you even still look pregnant! You can't find anything to wear that fits; you don't want to come home in a maternity dress. Your hair is lank and needs a wash and you have dark rings under your eyes. What a sight!

But your full attention is on the child now. When did he last feed? Will he go on sleeping for a few more minutes while I unpack his things and make a cup of tea? Is he even still breathing? When should I feed him next, should I wake him? What is he now crying for, I've fed him and changed his nappy; does he need changing yet again? Has he got wind? Shall I put him back on the breast for a top-up?

All these things and more go whizzing through your mind when you first get home. Will you cope? Can you be relied upon to fulfil the needs of this small infant who has turned your world totally upside down? You feel anxious and tearful and may find it hard to get back to sleep at night after a feed because you feel so wound up.

The first few hours and days pass like a blur of feeding and nappy changing. There may be visitors, friends and family who come and 'coo' at the baby and even wake him up. Mealtimes sitting down with your husband become a thing of the past. You are lucky if you have a cup of tea by 10 a.m. and are dressed by midday and can have a quick shower before the baby wakes up again. Your husband looks equally dishevelled but then disappears back to work again looking grim, just when you need him most, and starts to sleep in the study as he complains he's shattered!

The washing piles up, you don't have any bread in the house, you have a pile of unanswered cards and letters that need attending to; just as you've got the baby to sleep the midwife or health visitor rings the doorbell and wakes him up again to check everything is ok!

Every day feels like the last one, but gradually the fog starts to clear and you realise what day it is and that you *can* spend a bit of 'me time' between feeds, and that you *are* surviving on less than 5 hours sleep a night!

Do I exaggerate? No, the first few days and weeks *can* feel just like that. That is why I suggested you leave major house renovations to another time, stock up the freezer, and make sure you get some help for afterwards, be it mother, mother-in-law, sister, friend, or an expensive maternity nurse who will need a room for herself, time off in the day and plenty of space to be proficient and professional! She may be a godsend, or may leave you feeling rather inadequate and wanting to care for the baby yourself. And your bank balance will certainly be much dented, by about £180+ per day plus agency fees.

In the old days mothers were expected to 'lie in' for 10 days. The midwife visited every day, and some sort of household help was often provided, as is the case still in Holland. Mothers do need a lot of rest afterwards, especially if they are to get back on their feet after a Caesarean, which after all is a major operation, as well as having a baby.

Nowadays mothers leave hospital after as little as 48 hours and have little help or support. They are expected to be up and around and doing everything as usual. No wonder the rates of post-natal depression are rising. Exhaustion does not allow the mother's hormones to rebalance, and she may get little or no help with breast feeding and resort to bottle feeding as it seems an easier option.

What you need is someone to cook a meal and bring you a glass of water when you settle down to feed the baby, someone to cuddle the baby and settle it down while you go and get dressed or sort out some phone calls; someone to walk the poor deflated dog, or hang out the washing or pop out to the shops for some fresh vegetables; and someone with experience just to chat to. Someone to make you feel you are the best Mum in the world and you are so clever to keep breastfeeding and doing everything well. Criticism is often forthcoming, but how often do you need other's advice when you are instinctively just being a mother?

This may sound like a black picture but it highlights the need for support after birth, so that the baby can be given all the attention it needs and the mother can remain happy and relaxed in her new role. She is the king pin of the entire household. Without her Energy the baby will not thrive and the relationship with her husband may become strained.

Hormones are weird things and after birth there are huge changes enabling the mother to create milk for the child. Prostaglandins are produced and levels of oestrogen and progesterone have to rebalance after the high levels in pregnancy. It is not uncommon to have 'baby blues' on the 4th day as the milk is just gushing in, after the first rich colostrum, so being especially gentle with yourself on that day will help avert you dissolving into tears at the least thing.

Now for the more positive version of your homecoming! You have had an easy birth, it being 'normal', and have started breast feeding. You are a 'natural' as the midwives put it. You are not sore down below because you relaxed enough not to need stitches.

The baby, because you feel relaxed and happy, settles well after each feed and sleeps for 3-4 hours. Each time he wakes up you first change his nappy and give him a little cuddle and then quietly sit down to enjoy the love and sexual enjoyment of giving him the breast. It is an Energy Gift which you are giving him. He latches on well, filling his mouth with the *whole areola,* or dark part, not just the tip of the nipple. He stimulates the sacs behind the nipple which hold the 'foremilk' and then, after about a minute, with a warm 'rush' feeling in your breasts, the milk comes down and is released into the fine tubes, so he gets a rich perfectly balanced meal, thirst quenching at the beginning and more nourishing after the first few sucks. All beautifully controlled by your magic body; right consistency, content, temperature and amount for your baby at each stage. While he feeds you sit comfortably, supported at your back with extra cushions and he is also perhaps supported on a cushion so he doesn't need to stretch up to reach you; or maybe you are lying down sideways in bed, resting, while you enjoy the communication with your new baby. The TV is off, the phone too, and all is quiet and harmonious. Only you and the child fill your whole world. After he has taken one side (about 10 minutes) you sit him up quietly and support his back so he is very upright. Then you wait until a burp comes!

If he is still 'rooting' and the first breast feels soft again, you can put him back to the second side for his pudding! He may not need so long this time as he will be getting satisfied. Always start on alternate sides so that one breast is emptied properly each alternate feed. A good tip to remember which side comes first is to keep a safety pin on your feeding bra on the starting side. The total feeding time should not exceed 20 minutes, after which you can gaze at him in rapt attention, giving him love and communication. He will focus on your face quite soon. If his mouth looks a little blue, or he is 'smiling' (real smiles come a bit later) wind him again very gently. Holding him upright, supported under the arms, with one finger holding his little floppy head, should be sufficient to get another burp. Endless back rubbing with a curled up baby only makes him sick. Another good position is just to lift him up onto your shoulder, and gently rub his back. Put a muslin over your shoulder first, as jumpers get spoilt with small 'posits' that may come up.

Having winded him fully (don't stint on this) lay him down on a soft folded blanket or knitted shawl, triangular in shape, and wrap him up quite tightly like a papoose, tucking in the ends under him. He will feel secure and warm like this and will settle much better. Make sure his arms are comfortably down as well and not waving like flags. Give him another cuddle and kiss and lay him gently down in the bassinette to go back to sleep. Most mothers know instinctively which side their child prefers to lie on. Nowadays it is advised to sleep on their backs, rather than their front. Slightly on their side is fine too.

Hearing your voice singing or talking quietly will give him confidence, as he is used to your being very close. No need for 'womb music' tapes. A good feed won't overstimulate him and allow him to settle quickly. The things which unsettle him are your anxiety, noise which is not natural (radio, TV etc.) and any feeling of stress in the situation. He becomes just like a sponge to how you are feeling. Don't fuss around the baby! Make your movements calm but firm. It will give them confidence too.

Using the rockers on the crib may be helpful if he becomes fretful. It is quite normal for babies to have a crying period at some time in the day. If they are fed, winded, changed and relaxed during a feed and still crying, then try 'the 5 minute method'. They may just be tired. Think what you have put them through in terms of stimulation. A car-ride? A visit to the shops? Too many visitors lifting them around? They are telling you that there has been too much input. Crying is a way of letting go of all this negative energy. Put them as usual in their bed and leave them for 5 minutes to cry themselves to sleep. If they are 'revving up' after this time, carry them around for a little while. It won't spoil them and will make them feel secure. After all they have been carried around for 9 months. Hopefully they will go to sleep with the motion. Many Dads are good at settling babies, because there is no smell of milk.

Some babies always fill their nappy during a feed. If this happens, it is easiest to change them in the middle of the feed, but beware; cold tummies create hiccups and indigestion, so have the room extra warm and try not to expose their abdomens unnecessarily. Work quickly and with confidence. It is always better to use a little warm water on cotton wool to clean them, than freezing cold baby wipes. Try not to lift up their legs too high whilst wiping them, as it raises their tummies too and they may well be sick! That is why changing at the beginning of a feed is better if possible. But don't leave them in a dirty nappy, as they will get sore.

Breast fed babies nappies are bright golden yellow and very liquid. Variations from this may indicate wind (greenish), projectile and frothy (an infection), or lumpy (baby may be thirsty). Breast fed babies may go 2-3 days without a motion or may be dirty every nappy change. Bottle fed babies tend to go once or twice a day and it is smellier, yellow/greyish and fairly firm. If it is different from this the milk may not be suiting the baby.

If you have eaten anything spicy or acid your milk will make the baby's bottom more likely to get spotty or sore. Exposing it to fresh air for a little while after the feed (again in a very warm room) and using a little Weleda calendula baby cream or other really pure baby product will give protection. Always read the labels and don't use anything with chemicals in it. It will be absorbed.

Often babies demand very frequent feeds in the day and this can be counter-productive. Try if possible to leave 2 hours between feeds at the least, and not more than 6 hours at night to begin with. If you are constantly feeding, the baby gets fretful and tired, you end up sore and tired and nothing is achieved. Also the hind-milk will not be coming through adequately, so this richer formula will not sustain the baby. He will be having little drinks of fore-milk all the time. This is fine if it is very hot, to prevent dehydration though.

How do you know if the baby is dehydrated or getting enough milk? The skull is very soft on new-born babies and the fontanel or 'soft-spot' on the top can be gently felt. It sometimes pulses. If the baby is healthy it should be gently rounded. If the baby is getting dehydrated it dips in.

If your baby cries a lot is it right to pick it up, or are you 'spoiling it'? This is a frequently asked question! Crying is a form of communication and as such serves babies well to let the parents know if they are hungry, wet, uncomfortable with wind or otherwise, or just crying. This last one is hard to recognise, and many parents fret unnecessarily because their child has a cry at a particular time of day. It is best to check when you last fed and consider if they are hungry, check their nappy is not wet or uncomfortable, and make sure they are well winded.

Then if they are <u>still unsettled</u> do 'the five minute trick'. This involves nothing more than putting the child down in his bed, and walking out and shutting the door. Go somewhere where you can't hear him. After 5 minutes (no less) go and listen at the door and almost invariably you will have silence and a sleeping baby until the next feed is due. They can get agitated because you are tense and unsure and very tired overstimulated children may need to cry themselves to sleep. Not cruel, just sensible!

It is the beginning, (or rather continuation,) of your relationship of give-give with the child. If you give in to his every demand he will rule you totally. If you are too rigid he cannot express his own needs. Every parent has a different mix of these two extremes and that is what becoming a parent all is about!

If for some reason you are unable to breast feed, then bottle feeding is the only option, but it is far less good for both you and the baby. Breast feeding will benefit you by losing weight and the uterus returns to normal much more quickly due to the hormonal release as you feed. Some mothers get quite strong 'contractions' as they feed in the first few days. Make sure that you have very good supporting bras, with front opening fasteners, and wide straps. These are not glamorous, but constricting bras can cause problems with mastitis and lumps. They should not press on the breasts or cut in underneath in any way. Bras with drop down flaps and holes tend to press on the delicate areola area too. Buy them when you come home, or get properly fitted allowing extra room for milk production.

In the first weeks as the baby is getting more used to life in the outside world and his tiny tummy is digesting for the first time, he will need to feed frequently. Most breastfeeding mothers tend to 'demand feed' which means haphazard times, so the baby can never be left with anyone else. It is possible to get them into a routine fairly quickly, providing a *full* feed is taken each time. Start your day as you mean to go on, and let the baby feed 3-4 hourly, the same time every day if possible (early morning (6ish,) 10ish, lunchtime, 4 o'clock cup of tea, supper (after yours,) and a late evening one.

If the baby is less than 8lbs you will probably need a night-time one also, about 2a.m, which can be done with minimal stimulation, keeping lights low and not changing the nappy unless absolutely soaked. This way the night/day rhythm becomes established quite early on. This means that sometimes you will gently wake up the baby for its next feed, or keep it going with cuddles for an extra half an hour. This is called 'Mummy demand'! This may sound like very old fashioned advice when most modern mothers are feeding almost continuously, but if you have plenty of rest and fluids yourself and aren't rushing around in the first weeks, it does work. I have tried and tested it many times! Milk reduces if the baby does not suck well, and if you are dehydrated or tired yourself. Good cows rest!

Keeping babies evenly warm is very important. The house should be kept at least 18c and warmer where you change the nappy. Hands and feet may be cool, but their heads and tummies should always feel really warm. Wearing hats has become unfashionable nowadays, but at least 80% of the body heat can be lost though the head, so never go out without a hat in a cold wind. Light cotton caps are available now for new-borns and it is a good idea to use them, especially at night. Silk is also very warm and light.

Overheating may be one cause of cot deaths, so don't pile on the blankets indoors if it is warm, and check the baby's fontanel for hydration. Mothers usually know best, if you are acting instinctively. Babies can happily be put outside in a big pram to sleep in the fresh air, once they get a little older. Make sure you can see and hear them and put a cat net over the pram to protect from insects and neighbour's cats being inquisitive.

If you *have* to bottle feed then try to choose powdered milk that has least additives. Don't give them soya milk unless absolutely necessary because of allergies and check that it is Organic. Many allergies are now known to be caused by GM soya beans. Chose bottles that are most like a nipple shape, so the baby does not suck in wind with a feed. Clean and prepare your sterile bottles and fill the right amount of boiled water into the clean bottles for 24 hours of feeds in advance and keep ready in the fridge. Add the powdered milk in the right quantity when the feed is due, with a flat scoop according to instructions, shake it very well and warm it at least to room temperature in a jug of boiling water. Test the temperature on the back of your hand before feeding the baby. Giving cold milk will chill the spleen and make the digestion less good. Making the milk 'richer' with extra powder may damage the baby's kidneys. Watery milk will develop bad drinking patterns. If you think the baby is thirsty because it is extra hot, then give it just a little boiled water or herbal chamomile or fennel tea between feeds.

A modern trend is to 'demand feed' a bottle fed baby too. This does not make physiological sense, as bottled milk takes about 4 hours to digest, so a bottle fed baby can be very settled and happy on a 4 hour feeding regime. This can be gradually stretched at night as more milk is given to enable both baby and parents to get more sleep. In this case the baby can quite soon be put onto a 5a.m, 8.30, 12, 4, 8, 11.30 routine which suits well, or an hour later if it suits your routine better. The amount the baby takes over 6, 7, or 8 feeds must be divided over 24 hours according to his weight. Check you are not overfeeding, or force feeding. Ask your health visitor to do the sums for you if you're not sure.

Many mothers these days tell me that their baby doesn't sleep. This seems to be a disturbance of our times, with many adults also suffering insomnia. Sleep is the time when the nervous system is replenished and all the cells are renewed with magnesium exchange. We spend about a third of our lives asleep and it is vital for our welfare. On another level we can believe that we go to another consciousness during sleep and we can review the events of the previous day, thus understanding our actions and lessons on a deeper level. Without this we become overloaded with anxieties and life problems and cannot learn our destiny lessons on a deeper level. So establishing good sleep patterns early on is vital for good health in the broadest sense. It is the best way for us to top up our Energy.

A baby soon comes to recognise its own bed and associate it with quiet time, so in the daytime the older baby can be around downstairs for short waking times, enjoying the lights and sounds of the family. But in the first six weeks as the child is still very sensitive to noise, light and stimulation it can be put in its own crib again and again in the bedroom, even in the daytime. Baby alarms are useful to enable the mother to have active times downstairs, or she can take a nap on her bed in the day beside the child. Taking a baby on journeys in cars, planes or into busy shopping malls overstimulates the fine nervous system of the child and means it becomes gittery and probably *won't* sleep! Having the baby on your lap, or propping it up in front of the telly, or working on the computer whilst holding it, will only damage it. I have seen this done often as I worked as a maternity nurse with intelligent loving mothers.

The first few weeks of a baby's life are very vital in establishing physical rhythms and good habits, which will give the child a strong healthy constitution for the rest of its life. Parents need to realise that this is a sacred time of adjustment and keep a protective space around the child at all times. Filling your diary with social or work engagements or visitors does nothing to help keep this space calm and wholesome. It is small sacrifice for the parents in the first few weeks to stay at home and just concentrate on the baby's needs. It is a blessed and happy time if you allow everything else to go on hold and realise that 'maternal absorption' will allow the child to access your Energy and love. Feeling bored and restless is a dis-ease of our current society. Good mothering is still and calm, like a deep pool of water. Learning to just BE is a lifetime lesson, which is enabled by our children when they are very young. This period is actually very short in relation to the child's whole life. Being selfless at this time is the best love you can give your child.

The time after the child first comes home may be totally disrupted by the mother becoming ill herself, with a hormonal condition known as puerperal psychosis. She may stop sleeping and have hallucinations or strange thoughts. This can be treated with drugs, but may cause long-term issues such as pre-menstrual tension and low confidence. Another less defined post-natal problem is depression. It often starts as 'baby blues' but can carry on for some weeks or months and needs proactive attention to resolve it, such as bringing in mother's help, a complete rest or holiday, or social support generally. Drugs are sometimes used in bad cases. Looking at why the mother finds it hard to cope generally may pinpoint a problem from her own childhood or relationship issues, as well as financial or social pressures.

Post-natal infections either in the womb or breast can sometimes arise, so always go to the doctor if you feel 'fluey', have a fever or are experiencing other problems with sore breasts or smelly discharge.

Some women really enjoy these early weeks when they are fully engrossed with their child. Others just live through it, looking forward to having an older and more responsive baby. Until you get there you will not know how it will be. You may be surprised how naturally you take to motherhood.

Chapter 11

The older baby and feeding

Once the child is 6 weeks old, marked by the routine post-natal check of both mother and baby at the doctor's surgery, the child is now settled and more 'earthly'. Feeding is usually into an established pattern and sleeping routines are better. The child has sometimes slept through a whole night too.

You are starting to feel more 'normal' too, getting into a routine with the baby, going out and about a bit more and starting to think about getting your figure back. This might be a nice time to join a mother and babies' exercise group, a drop-in mother and baby group, or even a mother and toddler group where babies are allowed. There are many such groups to be found in towns and villages, and the NCT sometimes has post-natal groups. It is fun to sit and chat about babies with other mothers, and doing occasional swaps of baby care with friends might even allow you some time to yourself.

Your baby is starting to take an interest in the world too, but it is a noisy, polluted and angry world they are entering and the mother still needs to shield them from many of the elements which adults consider 'normal life'. A supermarket can be a nightmare for a young child, with so many visual and sensory stimulations. I sometimes see tiny babies propped up being wheeled around, their eyes nearly popping out in alarm, or else they are screaming. Of course the shopping needs to be done, but how much better to share this task with your partner and leave the child at home in the quiet familiar setting. Similarly with car journeys, visits to far off places in planes, or other major events. "It is so easy travelling with a young baby" I hear you say, but Energetically the child is stressed and disturbed, and vital forces needed for developing organs and nervous system are deprived while the child is stressed.

So try to imagine yourself into their situation and life experience, and only do anything which is absolutely necessary for their safety and wellbeing.

Walks out to the park or in the country are healthy and enjoyable for both you and the child, but keep the baby lying <u>flat</u> until he can sit up unsupported by himself (about 5-6 months?), so as not to put undue pressure on his developing spine. Large prams with hoods are seen as old fashioned nowadays, and have been replaced by modern 'strollers', where the baby sits propped up, often just at the level of the exhaust fumes. They face forwards, so that you cannot gauge how they are coping with the bombardment of sense impressions and they cannot see you, their Mother/Father. Worse still are the double decker style buggies, where one child sits in front of the other. The lower one can see nothing and is almost dragged along the ground; how cruel is that? How often does one see a parent launching into a main road pushing a buggy in front of them? Beware of traffic hazards when you take your precious ones out.

Some parents like to carry the baby close to them in a sling. Again this is warm and comforting for you both, but be careful not to put a very young baby in one for too long, as the upright position is not good for their backs. Better have a sling which supports them sideways above your arm while they are little.

When you go out remember that the baby's head is very vulnerable to losing heat, and vital Energy will be needed to keep warm, so taking away from growth and development. Most mothers are instinctual as to how much covering the child requires but always be aware that *chilling weakens the whole system.* The baby/child is using its Vital Energy to maintain its warmth, thus reducing what it can use for growth, development and later life. How many elderly people does one see in this country with arthritic hips and knees; a fall-back from our habit of dressing boys in shorts when they were little, and little girls in dresses and ankle socks?

When at home with the baby, wakeful periods will mean you have little time during the day to do the chores, unless you establish good habits that the child *can* entertain themselves for short periods. Having a playpen may seem rather like having a cage to some, but it provides a safe and warm environment where the child can be put, near to you while you cook a meal or clean the house. You can lay a rug on the base, and they can spend kicking time in there from an early age, so it becomes familiar and not constricting. Toys can be hung on the sides which they can learn to reach and touch and the baby will learn to roll on to its back if placed on its tummy for short periods, strengthening its neck/back muscles.

It is good to establish a time regularly each day from about 6 weeks old onwards when they are left in their playpen, for example after their breakfast or tea, even when they have learnt to run around. It is *their space.* Not somewhere they are put when they are naughty or if someone comes to the door or if there is a crisis, but somewhere familiar and pleasant. Later on they may like it to be made into a 'den' with cloths hung over it, and some favourite books to look at for 'quiet time' after lunch.

Sleeping routines in the day are still of the utmost importance and when they are sleeping then you can really do some useful work! Having two proper naps in bed, one before lunch (10-12) and one after, (2-4) and a regular bedtime about 7p.m is a good balance for an older baby. The morning nap then can be gradually moved on a bit to combine with the afternoon one, (12-2.30) and eventually just a short quiet time can be established for you BOTH after lunch. Breaking the day up in this way refreshes you both, especially as you may still be woken at around

6a.m for a first feed. Establishing and keeping to sleeping/waking patterns, (without become totally rigid in your demands,) will help you all enjoy more energy and fun when you are awake, and establish a healthy pattern for the whole of life. The rhythms which we instil in a child are vital for good health throughout life.

Food

This is an area of childrearing which is probably debated most amongst young mothers. It is sometimes a fraught subject when the carefully prepared bits of mash you have spent time preparing are rejected by your baby and thrown on the floor! You can feel much rejected in your efforts.

When is the best time to introduce solid food? Your health visitor will tell you the 'proper' time. When mine were little we started at 3-4 months. It is now suggested a bit later. Once your baby can sit unsupported is the time to put them in a highchair. Mealtimes are a *social form* which can be established early on. When both parents sit down to a meal together in a relaxed way they are enjoying communication as well as nutrition. Babies will become part of the family and soon benefit from this social interaction at mealtimes. Mealtimes are not the place for tantrums, spoiling, manipulation, aggression, impatience and negative feelings.

When we eat we are taking in vital Energy to nourish and sustain us, and help us all to grow. Breastfeeding is the first nourishment and should be performed in calm and giving way by the mother; you could even breastfeed your child whilst eating your own meal sometimes, as they get older. Bottle feeding can have a similar mood around it, enhancing the actual cow's milk into an exchange of Energy between the mother and her child.

As soon as solid food is introduced another element is there. The mother prepares the food with Love, hopefully fresh, organic and local, to enhance and maintain the Energy of the earth and sunshine around us in the food. So any microwave preparation, freezing, canning or dehydrated food is not nearly so nutritious in an Energetic way. It has been bashed, kept long, transported on planes and ships, sprayed with chemicals and artificially preserved. Many people nowadays eat this kind of food as a matter of course and survive! But there is a huge amount of obesity in the western world and many illnesses associated with poor nutrition, such as Diabetes. Food which has lost its nutritional value only acts as ballast in our systems. Obesity often starts in babyhood and lays down habits for a lifetime in the metabolism, so it is important to watch your child's weight and visit your health visitor or Dr if you have any concerns. A healthy baby should have some of its ribs showing.

As parents we have an inner longing to do the best for our loved ones. Conscious nutrition is the basis of all good childcare and is badly lacking in this country at present. Even organic packets and jars displayed on the supermarket shelves have little or no real Energy in them. Therefore, if you want the best for your baby, 'bite the bullet' and start buying fresh organic vegetables, locally grown if possible and prepared freshly to enhance and sustain their Energetic quality.

Bottled dehydrated milk powder has little of this Energetic value, with many processes having been done to it. Once the child is old enough to take cow's milk, give it fresh organic milk. Cow's milk has more salt and may stress a young child's kidneys and for this reason alone should be avoided when they are very young. There is always fear about allergies. If you have eaten well in pregnancy you will be far less likely to hand on allergies to your children. Allergies come about by the fact we are imbibing so many unnatural chemicals in our diets, and building up resistance to them. Try therefore to work on your own diet, before getting pregnant at all.

A breastfed baby will start to be interested in your food naturally once it becomes aware that sitting at the table with Mum and Dad is a pleasant social occasion. A high chair put up at the table once they can sit up unsupported means you can give little pieces of cooked fresh organic vegetables for them to pick up and try themselves. Carrots are favourites, but eaten twice a day every day your baby may start to go a bit orange! Try also broccoli stalks, pieces of cooked beetroot (lovely and messy!), peas, beans, celery, and kohlrabi; anything soft and colourful. Fruit too can be tried, raw berries, cooked apple pieces, pears, (local organic are best,) and whatever is in season; this way baby gets to try out lots of flavours and take in the Energy of the local produce. You are <u>training his palate for later on</u>. He does not need extra salt, meat, eggs or cheese at this stage, if he is still feeding from you.

I once observed in a French café a grandmother eating her meal. On her lap was a child of about 6 months old who was calmly eating from her plate too, choosing food that was good for him and just the right amount. The child had a healthy instinct of what was best for him.

As breast feeding diminishes, which normally happens naturally between 8 and 12 months, the solid diet of the child must become more nutritious including some protein, fats and carbohydrates. Self-feeding is the easiest way to introduce new tastes. Some well cooked brown rice or mixed cereal porridge provides both carbs and protein; a little cottage cheese or 'quark' fresh cheese provides calcium, brown bread with wholesome spreads like tahini, nut butter or a smear of Marmite, bananas, other fruit, both dried and fresh, all provide a variety of vitamins, minerals and vital nutrients.

Gradually children will adapt their diets to what you are eating yourselves, and hopefully this is nutritious, fresh and not too salty or spicy. They can have what you have. Young children do not need meat, providing they have lots of other healthy food. Giving them artificial hormones and antibiotics which are found in non-organic meat can be harmful too. They will tell you when they want meat, if at all, but then ensure it is good quality and not just sausages or burgers, fish fingers or chicken nuggets which contain many chemicals and additives.

Finger foods are always easiest to begin with, backed up with a small helping of homemade puree and then mushy food depending on the baby's age and their teeth.

Before your baby can hold a spoon you will be trying to spoon feed him yourself. Beware that this can immediately become a battleground of wills! Pushing food unwillingly does not work and you all feel frustrated. Allow him to lead you and give him the idea that it is pleasurable by sitting down and enjoying your meal undisturbed too. No TV, reading, phone calls, arguments or getting up during mealtimes. No overt attention on him either. He is eating because you are eating. Simple!

Children learn by COPYING. The easiest way to teach them is to do it yourselves! We all want our children to behave nicely when they go out later on. In France and Spain children are taken to restaurants early on and sit quietly while the meal progresses, as it is part of the normal culture to sit over meals. Often children only need a gentle reminder to behave in the expected way. Nagging and cajoling may have the opposite effect.

Often in English families the children are fed early in the evening and put to bed, so that the parents can enjoy a civilised meal alone and discuss things quietly. This is not the best for the children, as they have only their mothers to 'play against' whilst feeding and none of the copying is possible. At lunchtime, when your partner is at work, try having your own meal comfortably sitting at the table, and include the baby as described before.

Running around whilst children eat should be discouraged, as also getting up from the table and making a noise while others are finishing. Conversation, even in the early days, can be encouraged. By the time children go to school mealtimes become an ideal family sharing space. How many families these days have an instant meal on their laps in front of the TV? I was looking after a 2 year old recently who had all her meals sitting alone in front of a large screen TV watching cartoons, about 3 feet away from her. Needless to say she woke with indigestion around midnight every night, crying.

Some children like to express their independence and individuality through food likes and dislikes. It can easily become a fad between older children at school to say they don't like something, which is catching rather like the measles! I stopped this with my children by telling them they had to eat everything, except their one 'favourite hate' which I would respect and not give them. This was allowed to change every now and again, but not frequently. It was a no-nonsense approach that worked.

Food wastage has become a major economic and ecological issue in this country, with most families throwing away nearly half of the food they buy. This is a ridiculous situation which need never arise if we train our children from the cradle to respect and be thankful for what is provided. Saying a grace at the start of the meal may seem very old fashioned but it sets a tone as to the value of what we eat. We do not simply eat to fill ourselves up, but to absorb and utilise Energy from the Universe which is necessary for functioning and growing as healthy human beings.

Growing your own food can become a really pleasurable occupation with young children. An allotment or good sized vegetable garden can provide most of your family's needs. It is cheap, fresh, organic and local; the very best nutrition. Added to this your children will grow up with a sense of the work involved in growing ones food. They can help through the seasons with seed planting, potato harvesting, and pulling up lovely big carrots. They can learn about composting and enjoy worms, slugs and slowworms. Caterpillars turn into butterflies, bees visit the flowers and the connectedness of Earth's cycles is established in a healthy way. It is so much better doing it for real, than watching the inane children's telly programmes which try to show these processes.

My children grew up helping in the allotment. I remember one season in the 'hungry gap' in March when we only had leeks and parsnips to harvest and I was trying to be imaginative with these two vegetables, my daughter moaning "Do we have to eat leeks and parsnips AGAIN, Mum?" It was a nice lesson on how many Third World children live!

Teaching our children to care for and respect the Earth and her creatures is one of the most vital parts of being a parent these days, as otherwise our planet will cease to be there for us. We are destroying Nature at an alarming rate, polluting and raping her, dropping litter, using resources unnecessarily, and unless we change our ways we will find there are greater and greater crisis in terms of changed weather, poverty and food shortages. Instilling a natural *respect and devotion towards all living things* is paramount to good parenting. The next generation will hopefully do a better job than we have.

Keeping animals helps children to realise how important regular habits are; feeding, cleaning and grooming. Even small children can do these things alongside of you, the adult, and learn gentleness in handling and respect for an animal. Keeping hens, ducks and bees will have the added benefit of fresh edible products, and the gritty question of killing and eating home produced meat will arise as the children see the necessity of eating their pets. My mother, aged 8, was served her pet rabbit up for lunch one day out of financial necessity. My children experienced a cockerel and duckling served up for Sunday lunch.

Out of experience we can then chose consciously if becoming a vegetarian is the right option for us or not. There are no hard and fast rules, as each individual has differing sensibilities and physical needs. Becoming a vegetarian tends to make one even more sensitive.

If these practices are to become reality then rearing children in a city environment becomes quite difficult. We are not all blessed with the chance or even wish to live in the countryside, but many young couples do try at least to get a garden for their children to run in, even in cities. It is surprising how much can be grown in a small space if there is the wish to do this. City farms, where children can go to see and pet animals can be excellent learning grounds, and allotments in cities are becoming more available.

Having a holiday on a working farm is a huge learning experience. My father, who was a farmer's son in Dorset, used to take us on holiday to country farms where my sister and I could help get in the cows, help set up the milking machines and feed the young calves with powdered milk. We saw lambs and goats born, and also some die, we experienced how hard the farmers worked and the rhythm of each day. That would not be possible nowadays with health and safety rules!

Not everyone wants to be a farmer's girl though. But the experience of watching kittens being born, of guinea pigs or rabbits mating and the adults caring for their young, of walking a dog regularly or helping to feed a cat, will instil in every child a healthy relationship to nature. We are part of this wonderful planet and as such have a real responsibility to tending it carefully. Children nowadays are more likely to enter the 'virtual reality' of Nintendo games or TV programmes than become aware of the changing seasons and how the trees, plants and animals are developing and growing.

Chapter 12

Life with a toddler

Becoming a toddler must be hard sometimes! Most of us have forgotten the feelings we had then, when the world started to open up for us in a bright new way. We could walk and even run a bit; we had reached the uprightness which is part of becoming a human being. From 9 months to about 2 is the time when so much is happening that every day new things are learnt. It is an exciting time, but also a very wearing and exhausting time for a full-time mother. She must learn patience and yet more patience!

Each new thing learnt must be practiced. Play is work and work is play. Learning to conquer the earthly environment is the goal. Taking saucepans out of cupboards, climbing up onto the sofa, trying to imitate the adult by pressing every electric button in the house, pulling all the toys out of the box and strewing them everywhere, simply to practice putting them away again, or not, as the eyes and mind see something yet more interesting which must be pursued.

Toddlers are wreckers and must be given a safe environment in which to explore and practice their work. They are learning about natural laws, the movement of water, earth and sand. They love to make different noises with things, knocking together bits of metal, wood, and beans in tins; anything noisy. They do not need endless toys bought in shops, with plastic that breaks, batteries that run down or small bits which can choke them.

A large wooden box, preferably on wheels to be pushed around, can be made from recycled materials, painted brightly, and become a treasure trove, containing wooden bricks for building, small logs cleaned with sharp bits removed, interesting stones and shells, things for making noises such as a metal cake tin for a drum, or bells; some soft materials, silk, wool, cotton, velvet, some rag dolls for the older child to talk to and play mothers and fathers. Nothing elaborate or garish or ugly need be in there. Wooden cars and animals can be added gradually as they get older, or a train track perhaps.

We can become obsessed with providing our children with 'educational toys and books'. Children love to have one or two simple artistic books to bring to you for quiet moments, so they can snuggle up on your lap for a bit of Energy. Equally good is a supply of songs and games to share from 'up your sleeve'; finger games, romping and tickling games, nursery rhymes, things your Granny used to do to you. Remember them?

Children at this age are like virtual sponges. They are growing and developing from your own love, gentleness, kindness, patience, humour, firmness, strictness, anger, restlessness or whatever you have inside you. There is an expression "Do as I say, not as I do". How untrue that is! Toddlers learn by imitation and absorbing your finer Energy. If you are calm and happy so they too will be. If you allow them space to breath and express them they will discover who they are and feel confident. If you constantly watch them anxiously and correct them with "No" or a smack they will feel your fear.

Having said that, they need to be kept **safe**, which is your responsibility, so 'childproofing' your home environment is essential. Locks on doors will protect precious items, electric plug covers will stop little fingers getting into trouble, keeping the saucepan handles away from the edge when you are cooking, showing a child gently what hot means, having a stair gate at the top of a difficult staircase and showing the child how to come down backwards.

Nature is very kind and all these things happen gradually. I remember worrying as a young mother about these changes, but they each happen gradually and if you are aware you can always be one step ahead of the next phase of development, and take the necessary precautions.

It is so good for a toddler and young child to see you doing things around the house. Loading the washing machine can become a game, taking the hoover around can be helped with too; making the beds, putting away the clothes, cutting vegetables, making cakes, washing up. All these things can be done with a little companion at your side, sometimes slowing things up, but the fact that they are learning life skills visibly can be a bonus to you the parent. It is nice to have a stool they can carry themselves from place to place to make them taller, so they can join in every activity.

They are learning co-ordination, balance, the measure and weight of material things and to be respectful of things around them. Rather than saying 'No' if you do not want them to explore something, diversion usually works; gently making a game of taking something precious off them and saying 'Thank you', rather than snatching it away from them fearfully, will keep them peaceful.

The 'terrible twos', when children have tantrums, are often an indication of the relationship with an overanxious or controlling mother. There can be moments where the child's will crosses your will, but a child who is constantly thwarted and prevented from doing things will learn to scream to get their own way. Spoiling children is not done by being too lenient but by being too strict where unnecessary. A happy child is one who knows the boundaries placed for safety, but can be free within those boundaries. This stands good for all ages of children and those boundaries need to be in place early on for the child to feel secure and loved, but also appreciated as an individual. So as a parent be very clear of your boundaries and consistent always in your approach and the child will become more confident and self-assured as they mature.

Watching the programme 'Super Nanny', where things have gone wrong in parenting, it is often obvious that the parents have not set those boundaries clearly enough. Bad behaviour is often like a cry for help of a child who is fearful.

Potty training often becomes a huge issue in mothers' minds. It is usually much easier than you were led to believe. Timing is the most important thing. Many children start being aware of when they pee as young as 7-9 months old, especially girls. As soon as the child is mobile and crawling you can introduce the new potty into the bathroom. When you go to the toilet you might put the child on theirs, just to show them that it is the same. Only leave them on it for as long as they want, as forcing it will have the opposite effect. Seeing their pee or poo for the first time in a pot may be astonishing! Let them look at it too, but no major handling. It stays in the potty.

Putting them on it often and praising when they do something is likely to be most effective. Also knowing when their natural time for passing stool is and watching their faces, you might be lucky to catch something! It is always easier in the summer time too, when you can let them run around naked in the garden. They are then aware of when they pee, but it doesn't follow that they will want to go to the potty there and then! Praise and patience usually wins in the end. Children will not be wearing nappies at school (although some I know went to Kindergarten in them), and boys are generally slower than girls, as in most developmental stages. There are books written about this subject and you can become almost obsessive. It is much better to remain relaxed and happy about what is achieved day by day.

The same holds good with speech. Often a child who has had to cope with stresses along the way may be slower learning to talk. Don't allow them to continue using baby words instead of the real ones if they can articulate and say their vowels and consonants. Sometimes it is an emotional ploy to remain in the baby stage. At other times it may be glue ear and poor hearing, so it is always worth checking with the health visitor if you are concerned. Speech is learned by listening to the mother and father talking and singing, so make sure you do lots of that from day one. Television watching together or listening to story tapes does not have nearly the same effect. Babies soon get to know the tone of voice. Making babbling sounds to the baby such as BBB or MUMMUMMUM can make them more conscious of their own mouths as they watch and copy yours.

Life with a toddler can be great fun! Apart from the household chores times and the quiet alone playing times, as a parent you can develop a little 'programme of events' which you both enjoy. A walk every day is a good idea as it allows the child to develop their legs and stamina, their circulation and balance. Often children spend hours riding around in cars and are expected also to sleep in them during the day. On such a walk expect to look at each stone and flower and pussy cat, to walk into each puddle or climb onto every hillock. Go at the toddler's pace and enjoy seeing the world through their eyes; an exciting new experience. It is important to hold the child's hand firmly, and in areas with busy roads to have a reign attached to your wrist too, in case they launch towards something interesting. It is not cruel to keep them safe! It is a privilege on a sunny day to be able to leave the chores behind and take a picnic with some friends to the park or a beauty spot, with run-around space, maybe some ducks or animals or swings and enjoy the fresh air and freedom.

On cold wintery days a music and movement group or an outing to the swimming pool might bring some adventures and new friends. Babies start to be aware of others at quite an early age, but they do not play as a team together until they are rising three. Therefore finding other mothers with children of similar ages is a huge bonus, for you more than the child initially, but gradually children start to play together rather than alongside each other. There are many such groups to be found in towns. Taking a child to nursery and leaving it there may be sanity break for you, but do not kid yourself that the child *needs* it, until they are of preschool age. It is much better that they know you are near and you accompany them to groups and activities until they are at least three. Some nightmare church halls can be found, full of plastic toys, with toddlers running round and round becoming totally zany and unhappy. Try to choose a toddler group with smaller activity corners, quiet times during the session for a story or group activity, and a more peaceful atmosphere. Playing alongside your child helps them to learn, but allow them to leave your side too and explore this exciting environment.

Art and craft activities can be fun. You do not need to worry about the end result. It is the doing of it which is important. Make a game of putting everything out ready, putting on protective clothing and clearing up at the end, so the whole process has a beginning, middle and end. These early disciplines will help the child later to be more organised and tidy in their approach to work and to respect and value all materials. Have an organised system of storage too, so that as the child gets older they know where to find everything themselves and that everything has a home to go back to. Nowadays there are endless storage boxes and drawers for sale in bright colours.

Some parents worry that their children are becoming clingy. The truth is that they are deeply in love with you and need that bond which usually is at its strongest around 9-18 months. They may even cry when you go out of the room at times. Showing them your love and laughter when you come back in, rather than being upset by their tears will help. Don't allow the tears to stop you doing things, or else the baby is ruling your life. Again it is give/give in your relationship.

Sometimes night waking is a problem around this time. Toddlers do appear to get nightmares (?) sometimes and may wake up and scream. Check back in your mind what they did and ate the previous afternoon. Was there a rich supper, a TV programme, an excitement beyond the normal routine? Usually you can find the answer.

Pick them up for a cuddle briefly, then put them back in bed and do not allow them to come out of their room or into your bed, unless you want company for many months to come! Again gentle firmness and a confidence of what YOU need and want will help them to find their equilibrium.

An evening routine that never varies is a good idea to help settle children to sleep. A calm supper, some gentle play, tidying up the toys, then a warm (not too hot) bath with some water play will relax them. Into the bedroom and cosy night clothes (cotton only) and no getting overexcited for the next bit. Then once in bed a candle can be lit and a bedtime story told. Children love repetitive simple stories with a rhythm to them, such as the gingerbread man, chicken licken, or the old woman who swallowed the fly. It is the sing-song voice you use and the calm tone which makes them sleepy. I used to sing a bedtime lullaby and say a prayer every evening too. A goodnight kiss and firmly closing the door so it is dark completes the routine. The children if they have had a happy active day will very soon be asleep and stay asleep until morning.

Usually problems with settling occur from babyhood. No routine, bringing the baby down into the adult world of lights and TV for the evening, giving too much rich food as the evening meal, having a hot bath straight after supper, getting cross and agitated because you want them packed off to bed fast, trying to contend with cooking and taking phone calls during the settling routine, giving children ugly or frightening images from books, and keeping the door of the nursery open and light coming in. Children need to be warm in bed too, so a sleeping bag is useful if they tend to throw off the clothes.

There is nothing more lovely than seeing a child peacefully asleep. Seeing your offspring thus, you really can imagine they have gone to the angels. There is such a vulnerable innocence about them. It is us and our fears that spoil them. Be careful not to impose these on your children. They are pure and good and can remain so for many years to come.

Chapter 13

Living with problems

This is an important aspect of parenting which I should like to mention in a positive way. What happens if there are problems either at birth or as the child develops? Because it is such a dangerous journey into life, birth damage can occur, or there may be inherited congenital birth defects, which leave the child less than 'perfect'. These problems come to light as the 'normal developmental milestones' are assessed by the paediatrician, health visitor or GP and it becomes obvious that the child may have some difficulties with mobility, sight, hearing, mental function or may need total on-going care for the rest of their lives. Life expectancy may be shortened too.

The first question every parent askes the midwife at birth is "Is it alright?" Midwives have a responsibility to carefully check the baby after birth for the most obvious problems, and a paediatrician will usually do another check before you leave the hospital. The GP again checks the baby at 6 weeks and health visitors are specially trained to do the developmental checks at different ages, for language development, hearing, mobility, sight and general functions.

Parents themselves often worry unduly about their babies, but it is most likely that if something *is* amiss the parent will already know instinctively before it is picked up by the medical professionals. Is the baby a bit floppy, does not feed well, or as it gets older does not learn to smile and recognise you or gazes at you unknowingly, sleeps a lot and does not follow you with its eyes? Parents know if something is wrong. But facing it and accepting it is quite another story. Sometimes a friend or close relative may pick it up too and comment on it.

You may be very full of worries and anxieties, depressed or feeling guilty, or actually in total denial. The truth remains though that at some stage you start to feel acceptance that your child is not clinically 'perfect'.

Having a disabled child is of course an enormous physical, emotional and also financial challenge, but is often compensated for by the huge amount of love that you feel for the child. Because they are especially vulnerable and needy of your Energy, you are able to give far more day by day of your own Energy to the child than might normally be the case. It sometimes feels as though you are in a space of 'grace' where you are experiencing the opportunity to give and give yet more unconditionally.

You may become very tired and worn down if the experience is a long-term caring one, but will find pools of strength you never imagined you had.

How does a disabled child experience the world? Simply through the LOVE it receives, and also is able to give. I have observed older children with severe cerebral palsy laughing and giving joy to all those around, also children with Down's syndrome, and even autism, where they may be more 'distant'.

Our society does not generally accept things which are not perfect. Going around with a disabled child you may experience stares or embarrassment, or lack of co-operation. But I think attitudes are changing. In the olden days abnormal children were kept locked away from society in homes, but nowadays they are much more fully integrated and some even are able to attend schools normally.

The destiny of a child incarnated into a less than perfect body is a very unique one. They are learning soul lessons this lifetime which cannot be learned in other ways so easily; patience, perseverance, giving out love, accepting help and care, enabling others to learn these lessons too. We cannot start to know how this plays out in the big scheme of things for that individual. Seen from this perspective alone it may be easier to understand the *choice* of the child on a higher level to be born like this. You may totally disagree with this, but it may be worth pondering on.

Practical help is obviously an issue with a disabled child. Because the child may be helpless and like a baby in its needs, you will need to ask for and get lots of help from other loving adults. You become a 'community of carers' around the child. Fathers will need to be fully involved emotionally too, even if they are the breadwinners. Other siblings will be affected by having a disabled brother or sister, and I have known families where the children have become exceptionally mature and loving in this situation.

Even if the child does not have a very long life for medical reasons, they come in and join your family in an extremely special way and 'touch you' so that when they are gone again you will always think of them with love and joy in your heart. Being the parent of a child with special needs is a great privilege.

I hope any parents who are feeling fearful, guilty or angry reading this will forgive my observations, which I have made having worked with many such children in different circumstances throughout my life as a nanny and nurse.

Chapter 14

Working and having a family

This subject has been touched on before in this book, but the decision to have a family and become a mother is such a huge one that it warrants a special chapter. Our 'class structure' in Britain reflects very much the outcome of how family life begins and continues through to school age.

Traditionally working class families have lived close together. You still find areas in Britain where Mum or a sister or two live within walking distance or a short bus ride. It is therefore quite natural that the <u>extended</u> family can become involved in childcare. This is perhaps the optimal arrangement as the same cultural standards of behaviour are then passed on to the children. Cousins grow up together and aunts and uncles become familiar to the child, as well as grandparents.

In less developed countries, for example parts of Africa, families live in groups and share the childcare. Often grandmothers are left in the huts to tend the babies while the mothers work around the village complex, harvesting and preparing food or collecting water. This seems to work very harmoniously and gives the Elders a task to do in their declining years.

In this country working class mothers have often worked part-time on low wages and have had to juggle childcare with their working hours. Employers are still loath to take on mothers full-time in responsible posts, as children can sometimes fall ill, or need to have their Mums. Also further pregnancies will mean gaps in employment. New laws have now made it much easier for mothers to hold down full time employment and fit a family around their own work needs. There have even been some recent experiments of children attending the office/ work environment while the mother tries to work. Not to everyone's taste and some mothers must find it hard to concentrate. Working from home is also a way forward now the computer age has arrived, but again concentration when you are trying to 'multitask' is an issue.

Middle class mothers, who generally have moved away from their home town to take up a career after university or college, often decide to continue work fulltime whilst having children and take a maternity break for some months and then have to find suitable childcare for their older babies. This can be a daunting task! It may involve heartache and guilt too. I see many advertisements in the Nanny Agencies for 'part-time' care starting at 7a.m and finishing at 6-7p.m with even some evening babysitting. This means that for almost all the child's waking day, except at weekends, mother and father are not there. Children are being cared for by trained nannies that may never have been mothers themselves and may be straight out of college with only academic knowledge of childcare.

Keeping a child in its own home environment may be a more expensive option but at least there is flexibility in its daily routine, the child gets to go out to the park and has more freedom of movement. Live-in nannies/au-pairs may be possible for some with a large house, but then the family are sharing their space and life intimately with a stranger.

Nurseries also fill this need for full-time childcare and you see children being unloaded out of big cars into these places first thing in the morning as the fraught parents rush off to work. At lunchtime they are lined up in a row to be fed; they have to comply with the 'rules' and routine of the day, and are surrounded by noise, bright lights, plastic broken toys, and minimal playground time. Coughs, colds and tummy upsets are common, creating yet more stress for the parents when their child can't attend. Granny then gets called from afar to help care for a sick child! These scenarios I have seen again and again with working parents. Having worked in a reputable nursery myself, I would *never* recommend them to a young mother!

Well-to-do and aristocratic families with a high income have no worries about paying for childcare. Historically they were perhaps the least able to provide a stable loving environment for their children. Fathers were often absent, mothers had wet nurses, full time nannies and then governesses and the children often had their own domain in the nursery and only came down to see their parents once a day. The nanny then became their true mother, and often one reads how important this person was in their lives. Sometimes they would be there through two generations.

Today's rich and famous still have children and do not look after them totally. They can sometimes become almost a status symbol! At birth or soon afterwards a maternity nurse will be employed to do the night feeds. These mothers believe it is possible to breast feed in the day (to be *seen* to be doing the right thing) and the maternity nurse will bottle feed at night! Do I sound cynical? I have experienced this scenario several times at work.

Physiologically the milk will soon start to dry up as the breasts need constant stimulation to produce enough milk at each stage. After a few weeks with the maternity nurse, a full-time nanny or au-pair is then employed who usually then changes from time-to-time, leaving the little ones confused and bereft. Then as soon as possible they are sent to expensive nursery school, prep school and then public boarding schools. No wonder that many of our 'upper class' show a 'stiff upper lip' and have little real connection with their emotions. Our country is run by such people, who are often extremely emotionally/spiritually deprived.

I have spoken quite strong words which may be offensive to some, but just because society at large <u>accepts</u> something as normal, it does not mean it is necessarily a healthy way of going about things. I have worked for many wealthy families in London and the Home Counties as a Maternity Nurse and have quietly observed what happens when people have 'more money than sense!'

Nowadays we have a wonderful welfare system which allows parents to stay at home, albeit with a reduced income. How much money do you actually need to survive? We have become accustomed to a certain kind of lifestyle, and housing. Many families who have one good income will compromise the second income for the sake of their children for a few years. It becomes a conscious decision. Fathers nowadays are much more likely to take an active role in childcare and may be willing to go part-time or even become a 'housefather' to enable their wives to maintain a career, a childcare share situation; or Granny may give up her work to care for a new grandchild regularly.

Speaking from personal experience, I had this conundrum. My ex decided he couldn't compromise his career for the home situation and I also wanted to work part-time. I would not get a nanny, or go to child-minders, having explored the local options. Thus we parted company and I became a single mother and a fulltime one, because I truly believed my children needed me at home. My daughter as a teenager once said "Mum, why don't you just go out and get a proper job?" Little did she realise the sacrifice I had been making over many years to sustain the family unit well. I had a badge once which said 'I'm a full-time working Mum'!

Single mothers do not HAVE to work, although they are encouraged to do so now by the government. Many single parents at home on benefits are criticised by others as being a drain on society. Parenting is little valued! A child with only one parent is already emotionally disadvantaged as the Energy which it receives from both parents in normal circumstances (both male and female Energy) help to build up its vital organic structure. If the father is absent then the child will have to get its 'male energy' from elsewhere. This may show in illness much later in life, particularly weaknesses of the abdominal areas. Realising that many, many parents are now separate, one can ask what ways we can address this in our society?

Feeling guilt and stress, in <u>whatever</u> you decide to do, does little for the Energy you give the children. Instead you are filled with fear. You are financially stressed and unable to TRUST that you are being a good parent and enabling the next generation to develop harmoniously. Try to get to the point where you KNOW INSTINCTIVELY WHAT RIGHT IS FOR YOU. Then it will work. There is no right and wrong way. But at each stage ask yourself the question, "Is what I am doing here, the most LOVING and ENERGY GIVING thing that I can do for my children?" Your heart always knows best, so take a little while meditating and your answers will come to you, from that deep intuitive space that as a parent is so valuable.

Chapter 15

Siblings and bigger families

Thus far I have written as though you had just one child but of course the majority of couples decide that they want a little brother or sister for their loved one, so they get pregnant again.

If you decide you want to stick at one child there may be reasons for this. You may be getting older and feel that you do not have the Energy to give to another one; you may have had a very frightening and painful labour or other complications the first time, so you have been put off any more for ever; or your emotional and financial circumstances have changed, so you can't 'afford' another child. Some people just feel that because of the exploding world population they will stick at one child. Whatever the reasons either way you should be pleased with what you have. Many childless couple would give their eye teeth to have a child at all.

Having two or more children is the most natural thing in the world. If you decide to have an only child you are ensuring that it will be more strongly connected to you, the parents, as it grows up. Everything it needs, its emotional life and Energy, have to come from you. You will need to provide extra friends to come and play, so it does not become very socially isolated. The world will revolve around it, and as it grows up this will colour its attitude to life in general. Selfishness has nasty connotations, but a singleton has none of the experience of sharing and quarrelling that two or more children will get. It expects to be, and knows it is, number one!

When you have had one child for maybe 2 or 3 years it is very difficult to imagine how you will be able to share your Energy between two children. I often hear this with second time pregnant mothers. 'How can I love the second one enough?' Love is without limits and you will be amazed at how easy it is. Each child is also a totally different personality, so it is rather like having two friends with you at the same time. You may react differently to each one, as their personalities demand. And it is amazing how different they are, too!

Pregnancy the second time is very different too. You will be involved with life full on with No1, and to give the space and Energy to the coming child will need your consciousness and dedication. You should try to find a time each day, hopefully when your eldest is having quiet 'alone time', to spend with your approaching child, to get to know them a little and give them some Mummy time.

Pregnancy probably goes more smoothly, unless you are overdoing things and getting overtired. Early nights, and afternoon rests are important even if you feel radiant.

The labour and birth is also totally different, so don't expect anything. Be aware of all the variations of the starting of labour as before, but as we midwives rather crudely say it is a 're-bore' so the second stage of labour will be MUCH easier too. The baby often does not engage fully until the contractions are strong so occasionally there may be problems with a twisted cord or a presenting arm, hand or head bent backwards. The midwives can sort that all out! The more babies you have the looser the uterus is and the more irregular presentations and lies are likely.

There is a slightly higher risk of a post-delivery bleed too if there have been many births, as the uterus does not contract down so well, and for this reason alone some doctors will not give permission for homebirths after 3 babies.

There is unlikely to be the need for a cut or episiotomy either and afterwards second-time and subsequent mothers usually get back to health quicker and with more confidence. Feeding is easier and the baby may well be more settled.

Nature is kind, as everything is more natural and easier, but you still have another child to care for.

How do you prepare a toddler or young child for the shock of having a little sister or brother? In all my years' experience I have never seen a first child who has not had <u>some</u> small reaction to the new-born, however well prepared they were.

Teaching the child that Mummy has a baby inside her tummy is all very well, but where has she suddenly gone to when the hospital admission happens? Who comes to look after them and how this goes is paramount to an easy transition. Try to prepare your child for this separation in a positive way. They are going to be at home to look after Daddy perhaps?

When Mother first comes home with the new baby it is important to give the eldest child extra attention, include them in everything and make them feel responsible and special. Buying a little present for them may offset the jealously of seeing mountains of gifts and cards arriving, and friends will often do that, but at the end of the day it is mother's ENERGY they are missing.

So cuddles in bed while you are feeding the baby, special story times, keeping to a settling routine at bedtime, not palming them off too often with other friends or relatives or nursery, will all help them acclimatise to sharing you. Expect the unexpected! Wanting a bottle at bedtime, getting into the baby's crib, reverting to nappies when they have been potty trained, going off their food, spiking a temperature even or waking at night, all these are symptoms of a disturbed and fearful child. But don't worry, it is NORMAL and if you deal with it calmly it will soon disappear. Feeling guilty, or trying to make up to the child unnaturally will only condone their behaviour and make matters worse.

Fathers can be wonderful at this busy time and take the eldest child off for special treats, and one-to-one-time, so getting time off work is doubly important with second and subsequent children for this reason. They may have displayed some jealousy themselves when the first child was born, depending on your relationship and where they come in the family. Subconsciously they may look to you as a mother figure and go through their sibling jealousy themselves.

Your parents and parents-in-law can enjoy being involved around the time of the birth and afterwards, but only invite them to stay if you have plenty of space and feel really comfortable with them around, as being on 'best behaviour' for them can be doubly stressful at this busy time. Whoever you trust to help you after the birth, make sure that there is *someone* who can take the practical strain in the first couple of weeks so that you can concentrate on the dynamic of two children and give your energy to breast feeding if possible. The best friends and helpers are those who can without asking rustle up a meal when you have forgotten to eat, hang out the washing and make sure you have enough dry spares around, pop out to the shops and walk the dog, which is now the bottom of the pecking order. (Even pets can become disturbed and stressed by a new arrival and should be given some extra TLC!)

As the weeks go by, routine in your day is a good way of ensuring sanity! Try to think around the programmes, feeding and sleeping times of both children and get a routine sorted out in your mind. Do you need to do a school run in the car? Does your toddler have a special dance session you don't want them to miss? Lift sharing with other parents, swapping play times, and allowing your eldest to go off with granny or a special friend, can enable you to give a quiet special space to the new-born. Each child benefits from alone-time with you, and your youngest, although very 'portable' will remain much more settled if you don't have to take them everywhere in the car. See if an elderly neighbour might be willing to wait in with the baby for ten minutes while you rush your child down to playgroup, rather than bundling them up on a cold morning. People love babies, so trust others to help you!

You may sometimes get things right and the day will go smoothly and sometimes it will be a nightmare and you will think you are a terrible mother! By 5p.m you may be at snapping point. Rather than losing your cool and smacking your beloved child and shouting at them when they are 'naughty' yet again, remove yourself somewhere quiet for a few minutes, take a few deep breaths and count to twenty, or whatever helps. Then go back in with a smile on your face and enjoy the next bit.

It is hard work being a mother and none of us are saints, so if things are not going so well <u>get help</u>. Don't feel you are a failure. Not everyone is a calm 'earth mother'.

Join a toddler group and share your anxieties with other mothers, get swaps going so you have a bit of personal space, talk to your husband/partner and see if they are willing to give you some hours to yourself at the weekend.

Many mothers find their sanity by going back to work. As previously said, unless you *have to,* this may be the greater of two evils. Where will your child find their vital Energy for growing up strongly? You are their chosen mother and as such are always the best person to care for them.

Siblings themselves will soon rely on each other for Energy. Large families survive this way, as the younger ones are looked after by the older ones. Some very happy family units are found thus, providing there is enough to eat and housing is not too cramped.

There is a trend at present for larger families again in Britain. There doesn't seem to be a logical reason, especially with welfare cuts.

Some practical tips about going out and about with two babies; some very good buggies are on the market at present which have two seats, both of which can be lowered almost flat so the young one can remain lying down. Ensure when you are choosing a buggy that the child's weight is still alright for the strength of it, and that the wheels are large and easily manoeuvrable. There is nothing worse than trying to go up a curb or into a shop with small cheap buggy wheels which do not turn easily. Look after your back and abdominal muscles too!

Because pushing such a weight can be stressful on the mother's physique, it is doubly important to do post-natal exercises after second and subsequent births. Carrying a baby around on your hip can also put a lot of strain on the pelvis and lower back, and even lifting a heavy toddler out of a cot every day can strain your back. So give yourself time to get fit; swimming, water exercises, post-natal exercise classes, Pilates classes, and yoga are all good, as well as the gym, but make sure you have a personal trainer who knows you have just had a baby.

The pelvic floor is stretched by birth, so this is the most important area to concentrate on and can be started straight after a normal birth. Pulling up the muscles inside gently and frequently is the essence of this exercise, but get a midwife to explain it if you're not sure. Try stopping midstream when you urinate and you will know how you are getting on. Many older women suffer from incontinence because they did not do their post-natal exercises long enough or hard enough.

The abdominals are the next set of muscles to start working on. Lie on the floor with your knees up and gently pull in the lower tummy and release. Sometimes pregnancy splits the abdominal muscles apart then you need to do special and extra exercises.

Gradually build up your stamina and strength, as mothering is physically challenging. There are many mothers who suffer long-term problems or back injuries after several children. Making sure you are in peak condition before getting pregnant a further time is also a good idea.

Losing the extra pounds you put on with a baby is important, so eating the right foods, lots of fresh vegetables and not snacking on high energy sweet stuff is important to get your figure back each time after the birth. Whist you are breast feeding you need a few extra calories, but this will also help you to lose weight if you are eating healthily.

Loving and pampering yourself can be difficult when you feel very tired and so fully occupied. An occasional massage or spa, a nice haircut which is easily manageable, a few new clothes to suit your changed figure (bigger at the top and maybe a little bigger all over?) will make the world of difference when you are tired and hormonal after the baby.

When you feel right, relaxed and fulfilled in your role as a mother, the babies know that and enjoy life. A happy mother will mean happy healthy babies. It is as easy as that!

Chapter 16

Growing into school

As a parent it is so easy always to be anticipating the next stage, and this can be particularly so between 3 and 4 when you may be longing for some 'me time' and getting the child to school seems the dream of a lifetime! I often hear mothers discussing their plans for this stage and wanting to plan ahead, rather like organising a holiday. However the stage of preschool can be absolutely delightful and should be savoured as a special time before your child rushes off out into the world.

After the long difficult days of having a young toddler who has to learn the parameters of life, it can be a treat to spend time with a little person who now speaks, understands right and wrong, and can bring initiative to each situation. They can become little companions to you, especially if you have a young baby too who needs looking after. They will want to help you in all that.

Around their third birthday the child will start using the word 'I' in a conscious and correct way. Prior to this they may refer to themselves by their Christian name or a baby nickname. They do not have a conscious separation between themselves and the world. They do not think logically and imitation is how they learn. And they have learnt a huge amount by then, depending on how much time and Energy you have given them.

Now at 3 they are ready to be their own persons, playing with others in a social way, interacting and bargaining with other children. Games become highly imaginative, including mothers and fathers, shops, policemen, firemen, train drivers, builders, farmers or whatever other area of life they have seen and experienced. Their world is like a small mirror image of the adult world they have been brought up in, but their likes and dislikes are now given full expression.

They learn to hop on one foot, dance, sing in tune, retell a story, undress and dress themselves and their dolls or teddies, construct quite complicated things with bricks and tracks, play hide and seek and other guessing games, and are busy from morning till night. A happy 4 year old is a charming sight.

As every parent knows they go through a 'why?' phase. This is a form of communication with you and should not be ignored. Nor do you need to launch into a deep scientific explanation about every subject. Suffice to express wonder at the beauty of the world around and how magic it is.

Apart from continuing the routines of household tasks, baking, cleaning, washing which they love to help with, having their own little brush, spade or whatever tool is involved, it is also now time to have playmates. So a gentle nursery environment for a few hours a week or swaps with other children are ideal.

Having a 'nature table' at home can become a focus for the seasonal changes going on outside. Children can collect treasures on their walks and enjoy keeping the table as a special place with sometimes a little surprise appearing on it as well.

They can also now practice being on their own in a chosen social environment with 'friends'. These connections can deepen further as they go to school together, or may fade. Staying overnight with Grandmas can be an exciting adventure now, rather than daunting.

Many parents get very hung up on introducing letters and numbers at this stage. A child's brain is like a sponge and a child of three can learn to read if given the right stimulation. Proud parents encourage this often and may spend much time introducing toy computers, educational telly programmes, puzzles and books. Charts fill the bedroom walls, so that the child is absorbing their letters and the fridge door inevitably has the jumble of bright letters on it, as well as all the pictures they have painted and drawn.

But how necessary is it to introduce these academic aspects into a child's life at this point? The body and brain are still growing rapidly and the body needs to be stimulated and encouraged as much as the brain, especially in our world today where so many trips are done by car and children's bodies do not get as much normal exercise as they used to.

So running to the park to climb and swing, clambering up trees, helping with digging and planting, swimming, and playing in sand are all vital activities for this age, rather than spending hours watching TV or sitting doing puzzles and looking at computers. There is plenty of time for all that later on.

In Britain children start school the year they become 5 which means that some children, depending on their birthdays will only be just 4 when they start. At this age a whole long day in school, being expected to 'conform', sit down and listen, learn to read and write and do numbers is totally exhausting. I do school pick-ups and see many children coming out of reception class white and drained by their day, and by the end of term they are getting sick with coughs, colds, tummy upsets and may even get upset when they leave their mothers in the morning.

We take all this for granted, and do not ask WHY the children are getting sick! The immune system is stressed by the wrong kind of education. The body, brain, spirit and emotions of each child need to be addressed together, not just the brain. Education at this age needs to be more craft and activity centred, with shorter hours to allow the child imaginative free play.

In Europe, in some countries such as Germany, children only start school when they are 6-7, with the big changes physically shown by the change of teeth. And even then they are home again by lunch-time to enjoy an afternoon with their friends playing outside in the fresh air.

Our British society encourages mothers back to work as soon as possible. Families can become stressed if a child is ill from school or during the holidays, and a nanny has to be employed. Children often have to go to school in the dark in winter for 'before school club', even to have their breakfast, and do not get fetched home till late with 'after school care'. This is becoming quite normal and accepted as ok for children. We may well see the results of these actions much later on in health issues arising in middle age, when young children have been stretched to their limits and have had to use their own vital Energy to survive these situations.

Children DO survive. Humans are innately adaptable and able to cope with stress of different kinds when young. But long-term this will have an effect on our growth, the strength of our digestion, our brain power and memory, and even our bone density. We need to build up our children's bodies to be fit and strong, not only by feeding them the right fresh food but also by enabling them to breath out and play imaginatively for as long as possible.

Some parents feel totally bereft when their child goes into school on their first day and are unwilling to 'let them go'. This is not a healthy scenario either, as a child must and does grow away from the parents in different amounts at different stages of childhood, but when a child is READY for school then it is right and good to let them go into this new stage of life.

Chapter 17

Ideas for new eating habits

Having mentioned diet several times in this book already, a section on changing your own diet when you decide to get pregnant for the first time (and you are eating at home more of the time,) which can be then <u>maintained</u> and adapted for the whole family, so that your children grow up into healthy adults without obesity, seems appropriate to include here.

Avoiding toxins totally is never possible in our modern day and age, but the thing we *do* have control of is what we put into our mouths and also into our children's. Teaching them healthy eating by educating their tastes from babyhood will be the biggest educational favour you can do for them, and allowing them to understand your reasons for choices also, as they get older and meet other children who are not so fortunate.

As previously mentioned as soon as the baby can take solids, they can eat what you eat, with only small adaptations, but introduce new foods gradually and don't expect your 6 month old to eat a raw whole-food high fibre diet! Use your imagination and common sense and your instinct will tell you what they can eat.

Look into your kitchen cupboards, get your partner to agree with the principles (he can always have a rubbish binge out at work!) and prepare to throw out or give away all your rubbish foods. A good starting point is the following list of basic ingredients. You may like to then browse the whole-food shops and have a few extras, but don't be tempted to get anything 'naughty' as it's easy to slip back into old habits of eating.

This list is based on a healthy mixture of carbs, protein, good oils and fruit and veggies obtained if possible locally and in any case organic. Think about food miles and pollution on the way to your plate. Think about sustainability and our responsibility to the planet as a whole when we support unethical cash crops in countries struggling to feed themselves. Do you know whether your foreign food is fairly traded? How many aeroplanes are used to bring food to your family?

Have you got the space outside (even on a balcony or roof) to grow some of your own food? Can you at least have some fresh herbs on the window sill to add to meals? Remember the process of collecting Energy from the Universe to sustain ourselves. Get rid of the microwave and only use the freezer if you have one to store a few emergency essentials.

Many people nowadays are becoming intolerant of gluten and there are many processed foods on the supermarket shelves which are now 'gluten free', but are still high in sugar, salt and additives and probably also contain GM soya, and corn syrup, both of which have been found recently to cause severe health problems. GM foods have been found to stick to the lining of the gut and prevent healthy absorption of vital nutrients and they gradually build up in the body.

The gluten intolerance problem often seems to arise when large quantities of inorganic wheat are consumed at an early age and your body becomes toxic with the sprays which are more concentrated in wheat kernels than in other grains. Leaving out all wheat will make you much better, and you may then be able to reintroduce organic spelt wheat and oats after a while. Better that you don't give your children these toxins in the first place.

This list is not inexhaustible but contains all your basic needs to create healthy meals for all the family.

You may find it worthwhile to get a bulk order of basics delivered from somewhere like Suma, and share large quantities with other families. You can save £'s this way, getting good food at cost price. Most companies are happy to have private customers, providing you buy a minimum amount at any time.

DRY STORES (all organically grown), to keep in stock

(No added sugar, low salt, no colours, preservatives, gluten free if necessary. ALWAYS READ THE LABELS.)

Porridge oats; course is best for porridge.

Muesli; make your own mixture as liked, in a large bowl, and store in an airtight container (with no seeds for young kids), including fine oats, barley, rice, quinoa and millet flakes, ground almonds and an omega seed mix, fine ground. Add a few raisins or sultanas, chopped dates or apricots, fresh fruit in season after you have soaked it in warm water for at least half an hour.

Rice cakes, without salt

Oat cakes, also available with ground pumpkin seeds

Flour; wholemeal spelt, gluten free brown, buckwheat

Baking soda and yeast for making your own bread

Pink mountain salt or 'low salt'

Cinnamon, turmeric, cumin, cardamom, allspice, mixed herbs, curry mixture

Tinned 'Whole Earth' baked beans, without sugar and salt but tasty, other organic tinned beans if liked, chickpeas

Tinned chopped tomatoes

Olives in olive oil

Olive oil (extra virgin), sesame, walnut, almond or hemp oils as liked or UDO'S CHOICE which balances omegas 3, 6 and 9

Lentils, brown rice, barley kernels, quinoa, wholemeal cous cous; all useful for soups and stews

Wholemeal, or gluten free, pasta coloured and different shapes for the kids

Small jars of pasta sauce with vegetables and low salt (for emergencies only!), usually make your own from fresh.

Herb teas, not fruit teas which contain additives

Grain coffee (Caro, barley cup or No-Caf)

Real organic cocoa powder 100% pure (you can't live without healthy chocolate!)

Agave, rice, or date syrup, good local honey, all alternatives to beet sugar, but use sparingly

Dried fruit; including apricots, mango, dried banana, sultanas, dates, prunes (useful high energy snacks for hungry kids, but still containing loads of fructose and therefore 'fattening' and bad for teeth

Nuts (kept in fridge to prevent moulds growing); almonds, pine nuts, macadamia, cashews, walnuts. Freshly fine ground for young children, providing alternative protein and fat

Organic fruit puree, a useful standby for young children, but not for every day, as 'fresh is best'

Sugar free fruit spread

Small organic bananas

Yeast extract and low salt bouillon for flavouring soups etc.

Vegetarian pate, olive spread, pesto, tahini, savoury alternatives to cheese to go with bread, refrigerate once opened

IN THE FRIDGE

Fresh locally grown organic veggies in season, including onions and garlic. Go very easy on potatoes, they are not essential. Eat everything while it is fresh, except root vegetables which can be stored a bit longer. Think about ordering a weekly box from a local farm scheme.

Organic salads in season, try not to buy vast amounts flown in from Spain

Lemons, oranges, apples, and pears, all organic

Other berries in season (not winter strawberries.)

Eggs, free range, organic if possible as feedstuff for hens has antibiotics added

Milk; whole organic milk, cow's or goat's, for children; skimmed or semi-skimmed for you, or alternatives like coconut, almond, rice or oat milk. Soya has a mixed press, always drink organic because of GM problems and see if the high oestrogens suit you.

Yoghourt; cow's or goat's, or coconut, (newly available); just natural with no sugars or fruits added. You can add your own when you serve it.

Quark or fromage frais, a very healthy 'young' cheese which is easily digestible and can be incorporated into cooking or served as dessert.

Cheese, essential for growing bones and teeth, but dairy may create extra mucous or eczema in some children. Goat cheese is an alternative. Cottage cheese is low fat, as are one or two other cheeses. Better to choose these varieties, and avoid processed cheese altogether.

Bread; some families eat a lot of bad processed white bread. Only eat organic brown and try making your own varieties with soda and low salt.

IN THE FREEZER

Freezer to microwave cooking has become extremely popular in recent years and has added to our nutrition problems. Get rid of your microwave as they have now been proved to be unhealthy for us and our food. Do not store ready meals, unless your husband needs them for comfort!

If you still have a freezer below your fridge pack it up with cardboard or polystyrene bits to partly fill it, but keep just a few 'emergency essentials' for a very rainy day or if you come in late and have nothing in the house. These could include:-

Pieces of fresh caught and then frozen fish, which are usually stored frozen anyway, such as salmon (organic only), cod or mackerel. Avoid breaded processed varieties.

Beany burgers, or veggie sausages, not those made from quorn which are fungus based. Check the ingredients of these, as they may contain a lot of salt or sugar. Use sparingly

A bag of frozen peas, useful if anyone gets a bruise too!

Organic oven chips in healthy fat, again a treat because everyone likes chips, but not a frequent meal

Homemade ice lollies, from pure organic fruit juice. Only allow this occasionally as the acid can damage little teeth. Ensure a glass of water is drunk afterwards

Booja Booja ice cream, which is expensive but totally delicious, made with cashew cream and agave syrup, so no dairy, sugar or nasties in it. The chocolate variety is probably best.

Frozen cut up bananas and mango pieces, which make basic home-made ice cream when put in an electric mixer and whizzed up with some cold milk. Other fruits can be used too, like strawberries or currents. No extra sugar needed

Small tubs of leftover homemade soup, pasta sauce or veggie stew, which when thawed at room temperature and heated on the cooker can make a quick meal, or if you know you are going out late. Having one or two things like this can take the pressure off, but remember that the vital Energy of frozen food is much less than fresh.

And so you have your basic ingredients for your family's food needs for the next 20 years! There are thousands of tasty ways of combining these natural ingredients to make healthy meals. Become inventive and share ideas with your friends too.

Just to start you off, I have included a few ideas here. Just choose one option:-

Breakfasts 7-9 a.m.

- Porridge, made with chunky organic oats and water, cooked long and slow; add some ground up Omega seeds, some blueberries or other seasonal fruit, a drizzle of agave or date syrup and some cold milk. Satisfying and healthy before a cold start in winter.
- Home-made muesli; mixed grains soaked in water with milk added, also fruit in season, or dried chopped fruits, and some yoghourt.
- Wholemeal toast or bread dipped in a boiled egg (aged 2+) or with tahini, fruit spread or a smear of honey. Butter is better than margarine.
- Natural yoghourt or fromage frais mixed with fruit.
- Cottage cheese and mashed banana or fruit puree, good for tinies.
- Pancakes as a treat, buckwheat flour is best, with maple or date syrup, and lemon juice.
- In hot summer a fruit smoothy, made freshly with mixed berries, and natural yoghourt. You can add some ground omega seed mix in too to make it healthier.

- To drink you can have grain coffee, herb tea or Roibosch tea, and children can have some warmed milk. Don't serve it ice cold as this stresses the spleen, as does frequent ice-cream.

Mid-morning snack 11ish

An important meal for toddlers and busy preschool children, you can join in too for a relaxing sit-down and a warm drink.

- Thin slices of apple, well washed with the skin left on.
- Segments of orange or Satsuma
- Dried fruit and nut mixture (avoid peanuts, sweetened fruits, yoghourt coated fruit and nuts)
- A rice cake and fruit spread
- Plus a warm drink of herb tea, e.g. mint, rosehip, chamomile, no sugar added. Children will learn to drink this if given early on.

Lunch 12.30 -1 p.m.

This should become your main meal, warm and satisfying, but no pudding is necessary. We only crave pudding because we have been brought up to expect it. Children will know no different.

- At least two thirds of your plate can be covered with vegetables, fresh varied and seasonal. Try to include as many colours as possible, as minerals and vitamins are found in diverse foods.
- Limit your potatoes. As a nation we eat large amounts of these, but they are not necessarily the healthiest option. Once or twice a week at most.
- Grains can be used in imaginative ways to provide bulk, and protein can be given as cottage cheese, grated cheese, poached eggs, or ground nuts.
- Beans and pulses also contain minerals and proteins if combined with grains or seeds/nuts.
- Fish can become a regular meal, but stick to small oily fish, or plain white fish, and beware of where they are coming from. Are you eating sustainable fish?
- Chicken, turkey or lamb if you want to eat meat occasionally (about once or twice a week) but make sure it is organic and from a good source where the animals are humanely killed.

Afternoon snack 3.30 - 4 p.m.

When your child wakes up from their nap a small snack can help the child to 'incarnate' again, so a piece of fruit or an oatcake and a drink of water may help them to bounce back. Teaching your child to drink ordinary water rather than sugary drinks, which are full of empty calories, is important and starts in the first few months of life. Don't take 'no' for an answer. Plenty of children are taught to drink water.

Supper (no later than 6p.m)

This can again be a warm meal in winter, as the 'high tea' used to be, or in summer can include some raw vegetable sticks or salad stuff and humus or cottage cheese. Chewing is important for children so don't be afraid of giving them some raw food from time to time, once they have all their teeth.

Some ideas might include:-

- Vegetable soup with bread or some added beans, lentils or grains.
- Pasta with vegetable sauce, home-made, including garlic or onion, and fresh herbs
- Oven roasted vegetables with melted goats cheese on top
- Baked beans on toast with some salad
- Cheese on toast and salad
- Wholemeal macaroni cheese and salad
- Bread fingers with savoury spreads, pate etc. and vegetable sticks
- Rice pudding or quinoa pudding made with milk or almond milk, sweetened with a little fruit spread or honey. Comfort food for a cold day!
- Home-made pizza base, using spelt four, olive oil and a little water to mix into smooth dough. Cook for a little while 'blind' before adding your toppings.

Juggling the needs of children with husbands coming in late may be tricky, but don't hang around to feed the children as they get overtired and don't digest their food well before bedtime. But aim for your evening meal to be eaten together as a family if possible.

As said before you should eat and enjoy the same meals as the children. Giving them instant 'appealing meals' like fish fingers and chicken nuggets or bought pizza with chips is a trap that many parents fall into, so that by the time the children start school they are eating rubbish food from the freezer, or instant quick things and their pallets are spoilt.

Once you have children in school fulltime it may be easier to do a healthy packed lunch, which should include some raw vegetables, (e.g. carrot, broccoli or celery,) protein such as cheese or nuts, some carbohydrate in the form of bread, rice or oatcakes and 2 fruit snacks for them during the day. Chocolate bars, crisps and white bread sandwiches which most children take to school are to be avoided.

Everyone can then eat a hot family meal together by 6p.m. Avoid heavy puddings or rich meaty dishes. Save any things like this for a lunchtime meal at the weekends. Make the meal a sharing sociable experience for everyone.

Peer pressure becomes huge as children get older. I remember my daughter at 14 rebelling about her 'healthy lunch' as she was the only one in her class to have such food! Instead we negotiated that she would take money to buy a jacket potato or piece of pizza for lunch, but she still had her veggies at supper time. Young people are growing up into an unhealthy world, but may be more able to cope with such things if they have some discernment. It is the parent's task to instil and form their basic eating habits and explain why other types of food are less than healthy. Hopefully once they are adult they will find their own healthy path.

Healthy eating not only gives you less food wastage and a stable weight without obesity problems, but it also safeguards against illness at a later stage in life. It gives you much more Energy to live well. Illnesses such as cancer, diabetes, high blood pressure and arthritis can be avoided if you change your eating plan and follow a balanced and energising new diet, which is suitable for all the family. It becomes cheaper in the long run to avoid processed and fattening foods, and spending a little more on fresh organic food week by week is an investment well spent. The government is trying to educate people into this line of thinking too, and putting up the cost of soda sugary drinks is one way they are trying to teach us. How successful it is remains to be seen!

Having a baby for the first time is a huge life change in itself, so it is perhaps a good oportunity to look at your own diet afresh at this special time and decide if you can make that commitment to your loved ones to nourish them with the very best food available.

Chapter 18

Qualities of parenting

Becoming a parent is an adventure! It is not a path to be taken lightly as we have heard, but it is also the simplest and most natural thing in the world, the continuation of the human species.

Some new mothers/fathers take to the new life they have chosen 'like a duck taking to water' and are complete natural parents, others take longer to grow into it, and for some it can be quite a struggle and challenge and they may feel failures on occasion when they lose their patience or their children are turning out very differently from how they imagined and dreamt.

Learning to accept the other human being and LOVE them is part of the path of initiation of parenting. I call it INITIATION quite deliberately, as the lessons one learns on the way are life lessons indeed.

These lessons may include:-

- selflessness,
- love,
- letting go of control and trusting,
- courage,
- humour, and fun
- patience,
- gentleness,
- fortitude,
- organisation skills
- financial budgeting
- learning to receive affection and love from another,
- physical skills; climbing, jumping, dancing, hopping
- cooking and other domestic skills
- craft and art skills
- music and rhythm
- teaching
- academic skills, reading, writing, science, history and maths
- acting
- first aid and nursing
- intuition and instinctive behaviour
- meditation and relaxation
- Many other things!

Childcare and midwifery are jobs which are desperately needed at present, as many parents and the government are failing to understand the value of them. Caring for another's life is a huge responsibility.

All the above listed things and more you can learn as a parent. They become part of you as each situation asks something of you anew. Some of these skills and life qualities you will have been taught by your parents. You may feel gratitude to your own mother and father as you gradually realise the things they have passed on to you which you absorbed quite unconsciously from them as a child. Good parents create more good parents through the generations.

You may suddenly hear yourself saying a phrase which your mother used to speak to you! This can be disconcerting at first but it is totally natural as we have absorbed their speech as we learned to talk. You will treat your child as you were treated, UNLESS this was less than good, in which case you will have to revisit that area consciously and decide for yourself what is appropriate.

In the bible it states that 'the sins of the father shall be passed down to the sons, through seven generations' and this can be seen clearly in families where a history of abuse, alcohol or other addictions, mental illness, violence or marriage break-up become the 'norm'. What happened to your grandparents or parents need not necessarily be taken up by yourself when you become a parent. Genetic inheritance can be tempered by consciousness, as in the debate of 'Nature or Nurture?'

If you do not like the way you were brought up, then look at your own childhood again and decide which bits you want to reproduce and which bits were not worth copying. Thus development of the human race continues, hopefully always onwards and upwards.

Remembering too that the 'soul' or 'being' of the child may have been here many times before and that they have chosen you as their 'tool for learning'. This may help you to understand some of the challenges that they bring with them themselves.

We are not here as parents to meld them into clones of ourselves, or what we would like them to become, we are here simply to help them to 'find themselves' and to lead them gently into an independent life of their own.

Ultimate love is allowing and enabling the other to become their own person in the greatest form imaginable.

Chapter 19

Caring for sick children

'Illness' is a nasty word and has certain connotations of pain, hospitals, being out of control, visits to the doctor, taking nasty tasting medicines, and life generally stopping while we sit tight to make sure we don't die!

Our life experiences colour how we feel about this word. We may ourselves have had a nasty bout of illness as a young child and the dreamlike memories of fear, pain and concerned adults, with maybe even a separation from our parents, give us a sense of foreboding or fear.

Just for a moment stop and remember your own 'childhood illnesses' or accidents, which you felt were major events on your journey through childhood.

Do you remember being afraid? Where you perhaps rushed off to a strange frightening hospital? Or was it pleasant to stay at home off school with your Mum, Dad or Granny taking care of you and bringing you perhaps bowls of jelly, thinly sliced bread and butter, or a special piece of fruit. Were you allowed to watch a special TV programme or snuggle up in your parent's bed, or look at a treasured book to while away the long hours? Do you remember being delirious from a fever, or taking nasty medicines?

These experiences and memories will strongly affect how you deal with your own children's illnesses and health problems. If I am opening up some skeletons in the cupboard it is for the very reason that our FEAR will influence how we can deal with and help to heal our children.

Young babies come into this world with no expectations of life except those that have been inherited via the genetic makeup and those felt in utero during pregnancy from the mother. I make a strong case that any major trauma occurring during pregnancy WILL have a subconscious effect on the unborn child at some level. Therefore, again, remember what happened during the child's development in utero. Were you as a pregnant mother happy and fulfilled, or anxious and unwell with lots of major life upheavals? This will have a bearing on your child's ability to cope with any events in the future, and whether they associate 'stresses' with fear.

I would like to bring this pondering one stage further and take a stance which you may like to encompass or reject outright as ridiculous! That is, that we come to earth many times and our previous memories are held deep within us at an Energetic level.

Reincarnation, as this is known, has been accepted by many people all over the planet for many thousands of years. There are modern anecdotal instances of children remembering a past life and traumas and if this is so, it may also colour the relationship they have to their body during this incarnation, and what they experience in this life as 'lessons' on a soul level. I leave you with this thought!

Another aspect you may become interested in is the idea that all Energy in the Universe is interconnected, and therefore at conception, and also at the baby's first breath, this pattern of Energy *imprints* itself on the child as an influence of Cosmic Energy. This is known as a birth chart and is unique to each individual. Patterns of the planets and fixed stars have been studied for many thousands of years and are known as Astrology. If looked at and read in an intuitive broad way they can shed light on many difficulties, gifts and qualities which make up the child's destiny and character.

So here you have the full picture of the influences on your child's development;

- Chance!
- Genetic inheritance
- 'Nature or nurture'
- The mind/body connection
- Karma, or the influence of our deeds in a previous lifetime
- Astrological influences

You can decide which of these aspects is meaningful in your path together with your growing child. This will also colour how you think about illness if it occurs.

The 'meaning of illness' is an area which is now being explored more and more by general medicine, as the mind/body connection becomes more accepted.

Thus 'We create what we are and have, in terms of life patterns and illnesses'. So illness is nothing more than an expression and reaction of the body to what has been happening around it in the previous weeks, months or years.

However as a parent, experience brings untold wisdom and when something happens that you cannot understand you may be led to ponder it more deeply in order to understand its meaning.

The body has the innate ability to come to a point of BALANCE and does this by creating a state of illness which then gives the organism time and energy to come back to that central point of balance. Illness is the means by which we become whole again! It can therefore be seen as a helpful blessing rather than an ill-fated wind.

For each individual this central point of balance will be a different place, which means there is no 'correct way' of dealing with, for example, the common cold, as a tall thin sensitive person will deal with it differently from a short fat fiery person.

We are all constitutionally unique and therefore there is no ideal human being, or 'perfect health'. What works for one will be wrong for another.

In Chinese medicine, Ayurveda medicine and other Holistic approaches, such as Homeopathy and Anthroposophic medicine, the WHOLE PERSON is carefully observed before any treatment is given.

How this 'Balancing of the Life Energies' is going to be supported by natural remedies is the science of these aforementioned approaches, and as such can be respected, once one understands that the whole human being is being treated not just the symptoms, as is the case in allopathic medicines which you get from the GP or the chemist.

Therefore searching out these alternative treatments for your children not only ensures that they do not have to suffer the poisoning side effects of drugs given to them, but their bodily processes are supported naturally when their own bodies are trying to heal themselves, coming back to that unique point of balance, which for that individual at that particular time is health.

Conscious parenting is the most fulfilling and interesting path, and has huge consequences on the future of the planet as our offspring go out into life as strong healthy individuals. A healthy society creates a healthy future for our planet.

Chapter 20

The Immune System

What do we understand by the Immune System? It is the most vital aspect of remaining healthy.

Over thousands of years our human bodies have built up a way of combatting foreign invasion of microbes, bacteria, viruses and fungal organisms which can be found around us in the environment and also within us. Put in simple terms we carry within us 'good' and 'bad' organisms, which often only become bad if they live in the wrong place in our bodies, or start to multiply massively creating an 'Illness'.

Within our circulating blood are cells which have developed specifically for fighting these invading inappropriate organisms, including white blood cells, specifically T cells, and others. They often have the ability to engulf and swallow up malignant organisms, and it is during this process of 'fighting infection', (or foreign cell activities such as cancer,) that the body reacts in a particular way.

Heat is engendered during this; an inflammatory process which we know as FEVER. During the course of a febrile illness, the temperature (which is normally between 36-37degrees centigrade) can rise as much as 3 or 4 degrees. The body also responds by using its lymphatic tissues, or glands, situated in the neck, armpits, abdomen and groin areas, to filter out the dead or infected cells and cleanse the body; a wonderful mechanism! The foreign organisms are literally 'burned out' by the body's heat.

In a simple febrile illness caused by a virus such as influenza there are other symptoms also, such as muscle achiness, headache, sore eyes, sore throat, perhaps sickness or diarrhoea. The whole body 'feels ill' and our first response nowadays is to suppress the fever with paracetamol or aspirin or some such drug, and try to stop the symptoms

The whole body is working hard to combat the infection and the only way to heal it fully is to work with it.

Rest, fluids, an alkaline diet (of which more later) and sleep will help the body to overcome its crisis and balance itself again. The usual course of a febrile illness is that the temperature drops again after a day or two, and even goes below normal for 24 hours, and the body will gradually rebalance itself and the symptoms will diminish, leaving the person weak but renewed and cleansed.

Time is the one factor which our modern society deprives the body of in this healing process. The body needs time to heal. If we rush it, by using antibiotics, anti-febrile drugs and pain killers we leave the body in a weakened state for the next invasion of bugs, rather like a defeated army being attacked again!

By allowing the body to heal itself, the body also becomes strengthened. It has produced antibodies to the particular bacteria, which will protect it if this invades again in the future. This is known as a Healthy Immune System, where the person builds up natural immunity to common illnesses and the bacteria which can often be found, particularly in wintertime, in damp or muggy crowded spaces.

Common colds are perhaps the exception to this rule, as we can catch them frequently, but if we are healthy and unstressed we do not catch colds, even if people sneeze in our faces. We manage to overcome the ingested virus before it gives us symptoms with our immune system.

Mothers pass their accrued antibodies on to their children, in utero, and more particularly in the first breast milk, known as Colostrum. It is very important that babies get this milk as otherwise they are much more likely to contract the common illnesses in their society, such as flu, coughs and tummy bugs, and also any of the 'childhood illnesses' which their mother has had herself. Genetic inheritance is an important aspect of illness and when a homeopath or doctor takes a full history, they always ask in detail about the parents' and grandparents' illnesses, particularly things like cancer and TB.

As children grow and become more mobile they will naturally contact bacteria in the environment, as in dirt and soil, and will start to build immunity against these. A healthy child will be naturally immune to many illnesses by the time it starts to mix with other children.

But something is not right here, I hear you say! We are told to cleanse and disinfect things to stop infection. Keeping everything squeaky clean has been found in recent studies to increase our chances of catching common illnesses, as natural immunity does not get the right stimulation to develop.

Nowadays we are being told to have our children immunised against many sometimes fatal illnesses. Otherwise they may die of horrible complications or get brain damage, or go blind or deaf.

The government's immunisation programme starts ever earlier and small babies are now receiving multiple injections to stop them from getting these diseases. They can have as many as 35 injections, starting at 6 weeks or even earlier.

In England there are strong financial incentives from the government for GPs to get a 100% take-up for childhood vaccinations.

But what about the claims that there are side effects?

It is claimed that since the '80's, when the government programmes were fully established, the numbers of antigens in vaccines has been reduced considerably, making them ever safer.

The arguments about the causes of infantile autism go on! It is now thought that the mercury used in producing the vaccines may be the main cause of autism.

As a discerning parent how does one start to take the very important decision as to whether to have your child immunised against all these diseases, or to refuse this service or to make a compromise with just a few of them, and if so which ones?

It is one of the first major decisions that one makes for the child after birth, (other than whether to breast or bottle feed), and has far reaching consequences on the health and life of the child right up into adulthood.

Finding out as much as possible about the different illnesses and how prevalent they still are in your area is an important starting point. One could argue that this is a selfish standpoint to not vaccinate, as the disease only becomes 'extinct' if you do 100% vaccination programmes. The aim of vaccination programmes is to obliterate these diseases!

But a strange phenomenon can be observed here. New diseases come along in the place of the old ones! It is as though the bacteria or virus develops its own immune system and fights back to survive.

Recently there has been a new outbreak of measles and the government are urging all parents to get their children vaccinated, in a panic wave hitting several communities. Parents had chosen not to protect their children for a reason. Now the parents are queuing up for the jabs! Such is the power of FEAR!

The same is the case with the use of antibiotics, which since the last world war have become used more and more to fight the multiplying of bacteria in the body. There are now more and more 'superbugs' to be found in hospital environments, and some professionals are warning that antibiotics may become useless in the future as a new generation of bugs are born. Bugs have learnt to survive too!

I believe that if too many immunizations are given and too many antibiotics used, the Energy of the child and their Immune System becomes severely compromised and this can give rise to illnesses in later life, such as ME, Chronic Fatigue and Fibromyalgia as well as an increase in allergies.

Interestingly vets recognise a condition known as 'Vacinosis' in animals, but it has yet to be recognised by the medical profession. I suspect there is too much financial payoff at stake for them to take this seriously at present.

With my own three children, my husband and I decided only to give them Tetanus vaccine, which is active in Gloucestershire in the ground. We had an allotment and the children spent a lot of time playing out in the garden and fields. It was MY FEAR which made me go that route. I only started the course once they were fully mobile and playing outside, at about aged 3.They had all the childhood illnesses, (whooping cough, measles, rubella, mumps, and chicken pox) and I nursed them through them

All three of them travelled widely as they became adults and we discussed which jabs were essential for each country they were visiting, and they had only those absolutely necessary. Some of my friends and colleagues think I did a disservice to the general immunity of the population by not giving them their jabs. The debate continues!

Chapter 21
Acidity and alkalinity

I would now like to mention specifically the work of Dr Robert Young, an American biochemist whom I have met. He has researched over many years the life of blood, cells, bacteria, viruses, fungi, cancer cells and microbes in the blood under different environments of acidity and alkalinity. His popular book, the pH miracle, describes what happens in the blood when we eat particular foods and act in certain ways to create an over-acidity, which in turn encourages the over multiplication of 'malignant' cells of different kinds. If you put those same cells back into an alkaline environment they revert back to healthy cells, and the symptoms of illness disappear. There is a lot of further information about this approach to health on the website www.energiseforhealth.com which is an English version of the American www.innerlight.com.run by Dr Young.

These research facts become an important key to understanding all illness and acting upon this knowledge can help keep us healthy. If we can stay alkaline we have a much higher chance of combatting infections, cancers and other chronic conditions such as Candida, Diabetes, Arthritis and Fibromyalgia.

Having virtually cured myself of fibromyalgia over several years, I can vouch that if I become acidic because of stress, anger, eating the wrong foods or tiredness, then my body becomes acidic (as proved by urine pH tests) and my symptoms reappear. I am also much more likely to catch a cold. I have been doing research over several years on this, using my own body!

We can discover what we can do ourselves to improve our immune system, keep fit and well and avoid the many common viral infections which seem to attack those with a weak immune system, particularly if one is stressed or unhappy or it is cold and damp.

Returning to the gritty problem of whether or not to follow a full immunization programme with your children, try to understand the immune system in terms of Energy. A healthy supply of Energy from the Universe in the form of good food, right exercise, right thinking and a healthy emotional environment, enough sleep, avoiding many common toxins in today's environment, will give your child a strong start in combatting infections and will vastly reduce their NEED for immunisation.

Only you as a parent know whether you are strong enough to give your child these health-giving Energising elements in their day-to-day life, and whether you can overcome your FEAR of disease sufficiently to protect your child in other ways. Do not underestimate the role of fear in any disease! Fear stimulates the adrenals to produce cortisones and this in turn creates more acid in your blood.

The blood itself is extremely good at maintaining 'homeostasis', (or an even acid/alkaline environment,) but it does this at the cost of the body's organs, cells, joints etc., which can then become overly acidic and create illnesses. Therefore acidity does not show up in blood tests, unless one is seriously ill.

Ask any parent and they will naturally want to do 'the best' for their child, but much ignorance exists today as to what a healthy lifestyle consists of, which will enable children to develop healthy immune systems and fight off diseases themselves.

By taking full responsibility for your child's health and refusing immunisation programmes, you will also have to take the responsibility for providing an excellent diet, a relaxed happy lifestyle with fresh air, exercise and love to give the child the best start in life and build a healthy immune system.

Chapter 22

Nature or nurture?

This question has become something of a cliché in our society, but it begs the question how as parents do you give your children the 'best environment'?

If children are asthmatic or have eczema, for example, this may be from a long line of genetic inheritance and it may be a 'family weakness' which is already known about before conception In this case it will be doubly important to address it consciously during pregnancy or even before you get pregnant, and decide whether you will adopt special exclusion diet during pregnancy, cut out all alcohol, wheat, diary, caffeine, sugar and artificial additives, if you do not know what the specific allergens are. If there is a family history of nut allergy, for example, you can omit these. The process which produces allergens is complex but often starts in utero.

Being aware of inherited family illnesses, from both sides of the family is therefore important in preconception and pregnancy care. It may be wise to see if the treatments you are getting for an 'Illness' yourself can be modified during pregnancy so that you do not have active symptoms. Try to cut out all medications if you can and go to a holistic practitioner for help and advice. This might be a Naturopath, Homeopath, Acupuncturist or Ayurveda practitioner.

You may have a stomach weakness of some kind for example, IBS or a tendency to ulcers. This could also be inherited, so it is important to look again at what upsets your stomach and change your diet accordingly.

Nervous conditions are very common, and anxieties around childbirth may highlight something that happened at your own birth, so addressing that with the help of hypnosis or counselling may be a good idea.

If you are unfortunate enough to have suffered from a cancerous illness this could also be due to your lifestyle or environment in some way. Are you living near an environmentally polluting nuclear power station or overhead power lines, or near a motorway or other disturbance? Is it possible to remedy this in some way before the pregnancy is too far advanced, by moving house?

Look carefully at your own lifestyle and diet. Are you smoking, which has been proven to cause bronchitis and asthma in infants? Do you use a microwave and eat only frozen ready meals, which have little Energy in them? How much organic food can you source and eat?

Remain alert to environmental, dietary and inherited problems as the child grows up. Have you missed a vital clue as to WHY they are creating these illness symptoms?

Stress is probably the greatest cause of illness in our modern children. It comes in many forms but is a sad fact of our modern lives. We travel around in cars, planes and trains, we sit for hours in front of moving images on the TV, Nintendo or screen games and computer, we have many financial stresses which may well be 'absorbed' unconsciously by our children.

Relationship problems often go along with all these things, to the extent that 2/3 of children nowadays may have to cope with a divorce situation, step parents, or half-siblings, and two homes. Often one or other parent may be absent completely and many many children are partially brought up by nannies or child-minders or in nurseries because our society and government is currently encouraging all mothers to go out to work. This may be a financial necessity for some, but society 'norms' are hard to go against.

All these things have a bearing on our children's health. In the 'bad old days' there was lack of health-care, schooling, lack of sanitation, cold damp houses, extreme poverty and hunger, even the dreaded workhouse.

Fortunately many of these things have improved (although the current financial situation in Britain means that many families are again going into poverty). If a child does not have enough good food, light and exercise and most importantly a sense of security and being loved, then they will start to show signs of illness.

These signs of stress may appear first in small ways like poor sleep quality, poor appetite, bedwetting and then go on to show more serious things such as restlessness, bad behaviour, disruption at school, increased coughs, colds and tummy upsets, abnormal fevers, glue ear or headaches. The child may even become depressed or suicidal or may go on to develop some major symptoms such as severe asthma, epilepsy, childhood arthritis, diabetes or cancer.

Major illness does not just happen! It is the final outcome of a situation which may have been developing over several years and as such can be traced backwards by a discerning parent or practitioner. When and how and most importantly WHY did these symptoms start? Why has the child been stressed, or was it neglectful diet or lifestyle which pushed the child into illness?

As parents caring for children we need to stay alert at all times as to how we have been acting with and treating our children. Many illnesses can be avoided by simple changes in diet and lifestyle, and if you are not coping with life and things are getting too stressful this can have a direct impact on the health of your children. It may seem obvious that a happy secure environment is also a healthy environment, but what changes can YOU make now to improve it yet further and ensure that your children stay as healthy as possible not just as children but into adulthood, because as parents this is our ultimate responsibility; to ensure a healthy and happy future generation.

Whatever inherited problems are encountered it is still possible to help the child to heal and grow strong through healthy nurture.

Another simpler interpretation of Nature and Nurture can be based around our most basic human needs.

These can be listed as;

- Good nourishment
- Light and fresh air
- Protection from adverse climatic conditions and enemies
- Enablement and love

I will take each of these elements for survival and thriving and elaborate on them. We take much of this for granted but it is helpful to go back to these basics from time to time to see where we might be going very wrong in modern society.

Good Nourishment

Taking the idea of there being Universal Energy in ourselves and all around in Nature a step further, one can understand how taking in food is in fact taking in Energy from plants and animals and *transforming it for our own needs.* This, which we usually call digestion, is a magic process, far more complex than just the digestive enzymes which we learn about at school. The gut has a huge surface area and also 'intelligence' and if it becomes sick or inflamed it is the first thing which causes illness in us. It KNOWS what the body needs and can sort out the fine substances from the rubbish which we eat, and absorb just what the body needs at any particular time.

How stressed our intestines must be at present with all the rubbish that we try to put down there; chemical additives, large amounts of gluten, sugars, poisons off the land, even pollutants such as chlorine and fluoride which are added to our drinking water! Our poor gut is working extremely hard but in many instances becomes inflamed and the tiny Villae are damaged by too much of the wrong foodstuffs, even from an early age. If the gut is unhealthy then illnesses will follow.

Thus in fact we may be living with malnourishment when we think and hope we are eating 'healthily,' but not taking enough care of <u>what</u> we eat. We do not then have the capacity to absorb the right amounts of minerals, vitamins, proteins, good fats, carbohydrates and pure water into our systems and we suffer from food intolerances, obesity and other serious illnesses as we get older.

In the western world this has now reached epidemic proportions. In other parts of the world, where there is severe lack of food, the digestion has not got enough good food to imbibe and therefore also suffers. Parasites may also be a huge problem.

If you want your children to grow up into healthy active adults then nourishment is the core factor of bringing them up. Spend time researching this subject even before you decide to have children, and resist copying the 'norm' of how we feed our children in the western world.

School meals have recently been in the press. Huge improvements are still needed here. It is much safer to provide your child with a healthy lunchbox which you can oversee.

A simple totally organic diet, taking the plant as the basis for each meal, is a good starting point for providing a healthy balanced meal. Each part of the plant has a different way of producing Energy.

1. Roots (carrots, beetroot, and parsnips for example) have stored Energy over the winter, and are therefore high in sugars and carbohydrates for energy.
2. The stem and leaves of plants give a balance of vitamins and minerals and are essential to health. They also absorb much light when growing, and therefore much Energy (e.g. cabbage, celery, salads)
3. The flower comes at the peak of the Energetic life of the plant, and usually in the time of greatest warmth. Its Energy is therefore huge. Plants such as broccoli and cauliflower are therefore most nutritious.
4. The seed or fruit is the Energy held ready for the next generation and as such also contain sugars and proteins. They are readily available as apples, grapes, citrus fruits, berries and so on (containing large amounts of instant Energy as Fructose) and nuts and seeds, which contain a lot of protein too. Grains also come into this category, and are used widely for their sustaining Energy (carbohydrate).

If one can create a balanced meal containing all of these 4 elements as shown above, from the plant world, then one has a good start in life and a much better chance to remain healthy.

A healthy lunchbox might therefore include some carrot sticks, celery, lettuce or watercress, raw broccoli, nuts or seeds or wholemeal bread with seed spread and a fruit! How often do you see a child eating this? If you start right, when children are first experiencing new tastes, it is easier to go on in this way. Meat and fish, eggs and cheese and other dairy foods can be added in moderation to bring variety, but they are not as essential as the right vegetable/fruit mix.

If meat is eaten then it should be of a good quality and organic, locally reared and humanely slaughtered, as the meat industry is currently very suspect in adding hormones and antibiotics to animal feeds. Most animals are slaughtered in a fearful environment after long journeys, and the meat contains many stress hormones from that. Added to this problem are the other things like preservatives, and antioxidants, not to mention the ubiquitous horse meat!

Fish may be sourced from unknown highly polluted waters, and may contain heavy metals. Small fish, caught locally, are best. Try to buy fish that is sustainably caught. Fish contains good Omega oils, but these can be taken from seeds as well.

Dairy foods, including cheese, unless organically prepared, are nearly all full of growth hormones and may contain other additives, and they may also create a lot of mucous, so are best avoided if your child has a blocked or runny nose, asthma, coughs or ear problems. Alternatives to milk are coconut, almond, soya (but no GMO), rice, oat or goat's products, all organically grown. Always read the labels for hidden ingredients.

We still assume that milk is the most important food for young children. That *is* the case with breast milk of course, but why do we assume cows are able to provide best nourishment for our children? Their milk is created for their calves!

Eggs can be eaten sometimes but chose those organically grown; again the feedstuffs for chicken normally contain loads of artificial chemicals, antibiotics and hormones.

Grains, which make up a large proportion of our diet in the western world, should only be eaten in their original wholegrain form, as refined flour which is found in pastas, biscuits, white and dyed brown bread, cakes and pancakes has little nutritional value and can even cause obesity and diabetes. The **GL diet** which is based on how quickly foods are digested is a good one for daily living and will ensure you get enough of the right nutrients and reduce the fat-forming foods.

Oils are necessary for building up cell walls but they should be good quality olive oils, or other plant oils such as hemp or almond. Oils also can be found in fish. Omegas, found in oils, are essential for brain power. Consider giving your child omega supplements, but ensure they contain 3, 6, and 9 in the right balance.

Food of organic/biodynamic quality may be hard to come by and more expensive, but it is the best start in life you can give your dear ones. Several companies are now available online providing healthy locally grown organic food, and this can be delivered as a weekly box or separate order. Try to buy as locally as you can to avoid food miles.

All this advice may sound extreme but only by demanding unadulterated food will things start to change for the better and our children will not have such obesity problems and be overall healthier. YOU can vote with your feet and put pressure on governments and farmers to begin to grow healthier food for us all. This will, in the longer term, also benefit the planet's health, as the soil will become richer, and food will again contain the vitamins and minerals it used to. Currently many supermarket vegetables have little nutritional value! It is not just about large crops and cheaper prices!

Thinking about other aspects of agriculture, one can also muse on the difference in the health of cows kept in overcrowded conditions on factory farms, producing large quantities of milk, or the health of cows on mixed farms, where animals, grains and vegetables are all grown together in a balanced way.

A good example of this type of organic farm is Highgrove, in Gloucestershire, belonging to Prince Charles, where the land is sustained with organic muck and the crops are balanced, without the use of chemicals. It is the very hard labour-intensive methods which produce the best results, and we seem to have lost the ability to honour hard work in this country. Our children are being educated to sit in offices in front of computers! Rates of pay reflect our society's priorities.

Having your own garden and growing your own vegetables is not only satisfying and fun, but also produces the best food! It is grown with love and your Energy. You and your family are relating to a local patch of the earth and are caring and sustaining nature throughout the seasons. This is healing in itself both to the planet and us. The allotments in cities have become more and more popular in recent years, which is a sign of hope for the future.

This is nourishment for our children which we can become proud of! Fresh is best.

"Pick 'em and eat 'em", straight off the plant if possible! Learn to forage for wild plants too. There is plenty out in nature fit to eat. Make sure you are well informed about what you are finding out in nature, especially with fungi.

Light and fresh air

Strangely this is an issue which is much less spoken about, but equally as important as nutrition in maintaining good health generally.

When we go outside on a sunny day and run around we are soaking up the oxygen and sunlight into our bodies and this will act as an Energetic 'sponge' for growth and Energy. Notice how quickly your hair and finger nails grow in a warmer climate.

Interestingly there are some people on this planet who have become so spiritually developed that they no longer have to eat food, but can survive on Light alone! This proves the phenomenon that we do absorb Energy from the sun, and can even live off this, taking in no food whatsoever. It is not to be tried out without proper preparation and training however!

Strangely we have become so frightened of the sun that our children are in serious danger of not getting enough of it. We are scared of skin cancer and we wrap our children up in plastic when they go out in summer, putting on thick sun block creams and plastic playsuits on the beach to 'protect them'. I am NOT saying that children should be allowed to burn, far from it, but a little and often is the best way.

When we have sunny days in early spring or autumn it is so important to get out for a play or walk, and not sit around indoors or in school. A daily walk in all seasons to and from school is healthy and good. How many of our children now are taken by car everywhere and rarely go into the countryside to play, or run around in the garden, even in winter?

Exercise encourages good blood and lymph circulation and exchange of oxygen in the cells. It helps excretion of waste products too and maintains our weight and muscular strength. It enables bones to stay strong and not become brittle and is health-giving in every sense of the word. It relaxes the mind and enables us to de-stress, concentrate and learn better too.

Daily exercise is a vital part of remaining healthy. Muscles start to deteriorate after only 6 hours of not being used.

Children are naturally boisterous and enjoy running around and moving as soon as they are able to take an active part in the world. Firstly as babies they learn to wave their limbs around, especially when naked, to roll over, and sit up, then they come up onto their knees and pull themselves up onto furniture or an adults hand, and then one day, having walked with help for some weeks, they suddenly 'take off' independently and become toddlers.

All baby animals have this natural instinct. Watch a young lamb, goat or calf, just after it has been born, and see the effort it takes to totter along on trembling legs. Within hours it is steady and soon will be jumping and gambolling amongst its friends out in the meadow. The Levitation and Energy of this movement is a joy to behold.

Watch young children in the park playing chase with each other, or running and jumping into puddles. It is natural for us to move in a healthy state.

Try staying absolutely still for some time and you will begin to feel how the cells and blood are still moving within the body. Movement is LIFE. Life is MOVEMENT.

As parents we can encourage this movement in a healthy and harmonious way. Non-jerky non-aggressive dance is wonderful to do and watch. Why do modern dancers do this popular jerky movement? Is it because we are losing touch with this natural harmony of movement and we need heavy beat rhythm to stimulate us to move at all?

The Olympic tradition of the Games can indeed be encouraged amongst young people as running, jumping, throwing, swimming, riding, jousting and others are all natural easy movements which if practised in a non-forceful way can bring us into a healthy relationship with our bodies. In health we are at ease with our bodies. We enjoy the movement. Team games can also encourage this.

So as soon as you become parents think about what exercise you do yourselves, and how to incorporate a healthy life-style into life as a family. Can you take a country walk at the weekend; ensure you have holidays with plenty of sunshine and running around, with not too many hours in the car? Can you take the children out every day to a park or countryside area, without car fumes, noise and danger? Much better to incorporate something natural than rush the kids off to the mini-gym after school in the car.

Many people nowadays live in cities, but planners know our physical needs for exercise, space and green parks and they are always to be found somewhere. Even walking around an estate can be a time for observing the changes in the gardens. Walking in nature can become a fun family time.

When our children were little we used to go out at least twice a week for a good long walk in the woods, or hills and now they are adult they still practice this.

Protection from adverse climatic conditions and enemies

This may sound an obvious thing in our society nowadays, but it is the most basic form of security for a growing child; to have a home which it knows and loves, which can become its own creative space and haven.

In our current society in Britain many children are living in temporary accommodation, bed and breakfast establishments, or with grandparents, as there is a real housing crisis, caused by over-inflation of house prices, high rentals and lack of council houses. This has become a political nightmare for many, and now the Government is planning to build over many acres of England's 'Green and pleasant land', destroying the very thing which keeps us healthy! What a short-sighted crazy idea!

At the same time there are thousands of empty properties around the country, under-occupied houses, (as many people now live on their own) and many 2nd homes which stand empty for much of the year.

Greedy landlords are allowed to push up rentals much higher than mortgages for equivalent properties, and mortgages are very hard to come by, as a self-employed person, or first time buyer. We urgently need new legislation on these issues.

This state of affairs has meant a lot of stress for poorer families, which has had a direct effect on children's health.

'Enemies' can also be interpreted as danger and criminal offences on our streets, caused by social deprivation, very mixed races and classes within communities, who rely heavily on the welfare state for survival and high unemployment in these areas. Things seem to be getting worse at present with government policies.

A way forward can only be found when communities themselves start to take responsibility for their own members and act together as a whole to upgrade empty houses, grow food on community allotments and city farms, become more neighbourly and loving, and act strongly in order to discipline destructive youths, who are bored, frustrated and angry with this degrading society.

In other countries 'enemies' are real life-threatening terrorists, or worse still government soldiers, who are heavily armed by us in the west. The only way forward towards peaceful solutions and health for our children worldwide is by banning firearms and ammunitions, in fact ceasing to produce them at all, and helping communities to rebuild their lives from total destruction. This may take several generations of loving care and guidance to achieve. Wars could cease, if we all believed strongly enough in non-violence. Idealistic? No, true!

'Adverse climatic conditions' are affecting most countries of the world in some form nowadays, as we seem to get more extreme weather patterns, with no immediate solutions. Until we learn to balance our own lives and live in a more ecological way day to day, reducing the use of cars, using less fossil fuels, and polluting less, our planet will continue to be 'sick'. Our children are the next generation and can be taught about the problems which we have created for them and some possible solutions which are emerging from are cutting edge scientists, designers and ecologists.

Schools take an active role here, but enlightened parents can also guide their children towards a better, healthier future.

Enablement and LOVE

This last thing on my list encompasses the real meaning of parenting. What do I mean by Enabling? It is allowing the incarnating child to develop into a strong and confident human being with unique gifts and qualities, which may appear 'out of the blue' or seem to be inherited from a parent or grandparent. Children, if given love and guidance in the right measure, whilst also being given firm boundaries, will develop into individuals with minds and souls of their own, to go out into life and develop into strong adults

How does one do this as a parent? Becoming ever less selfish, fearful and controlling, and more loving is the obvious path of development of a parent, but sometimes a hard School of Life. Nowadays there has been a swing towards more freedom and less discipline both at home and in the classroom. Is this necessarily the right way forward?

I sincerely believe that children with firm boundaries are more secure and will have fewer behaviour problems than those who are allowed to argue and get their own way when they have a tantrum, be that as a baby or teenager!. 'No' simply means 'no'! This starts in the cradle. How one treats a baby will then reflect in the toddler, in the preschool child, the school child and then the teenager. Start as you mean to go on!

Decide what rules are important in your household and practice them YOURSELVES and stick to them. This requires self-discipline, courage and humour, and most importantly a partnership in parenting. When parents have different attitudes in parenting and discipline, things can go awry.

Within a simple framework of rhythm and consistency the child can develop as an individual, be praised and encouraged in all they do creatively and lovingly, find their own means of expressing who they truly are and work through their own issues which become apparent as they mature. No human being is perfect and getting along with your children, warts and all, is as important as getting on with your partner!

This may all seem so obvious to you that it is hardly worth reading about, but you may come across a screaming child in a supermarket whose mother is about to abuse it verbally and physically, and a quiet encouraging word may help disperse the situation, or you may have a friend or relative going through a tough time with discipline or marital difficulties. We can all learn to help each other.

Keeping families healthy is a community affair. In African tribes if a couple is having a problem, a ritual is created where the whole village stands around the couple who are placed into a 'magic circle' and they listen and give advice and ask for the wisdom of the ancestors to come and help them.

In western society we can also perform this important task of listening and standing beside someone in a crisis. It is not necessarily about giving advice and trying to sort out the problem as just BEING there for them in a loving way.

The last word to be mentioned in terms of healthy living is LOVE.

"Love the Lord thy God and love Thy neighbour as Thyself" was Jesus' commandment to us. If we can understand this in its broadest context we have the 'recipe for a healthy family life', to enable our children to grow up and develop into happy healthy adults. This is a Christian Ethic, but can be applied to any creed or religious belief, or even Atheism!

It is NOT about beliefs and details of cultural traditions, but about acceptance and love of the rich variety which we have created as the human race. Here in Britain we are particularly diverse in race and cultures, so perhaps we, as the country from which I write, have a task to show the whole world how it is done?

Chapter 23

Caring for a sick child at home

We have already looked at WHY a child may become ill, and avoidance of stress and overtiredness is of course the ideal. But children DO sometimes get poorly and need an environment and time for their bodies to rebalance and heal.

Keeping a child at home, where they have their own bed, familiar things around and the Energy of a loving mother and father is the very best thing you can do for a sick child.

Nowadays there is increasing pressure for women to go out to work and therefore this becomes the first problem when a child is 'under the weather'; who is to look after them?

Grandparents, if they live close enough, can perhaps act as a help in this scenario, and many young working mothers resort to this in a crisis. Nannies, who may already be employed, may act as 'surrogate' Mum in this situation and provide a calm and healing environment in the home.

The worst scenario is probably to send an unwell child off to nursery or school when really they should be kept quietly at home. 'Kalpol', children's Paracetamol, is often used in this situation to keep the child going, and suppress any fever which may develop. By doing this the child has to work even harder to heal and often the natural healing process is suppressed.

Chronic conditions then may develop, such as ear aches, chesty coughs which don't clear up, croup, tonsillitis, tummy aches, and headaches which keep recurring throughout the winter months, or towards the end of long school terms, when most children get more and more tired from long days spent indoors with little or no play/creative time.

The child is then taken to the doctor who prescribes antibiotics and the 'bug' is temporarily suppressed. The immune system however has been weakened by this treatment, and the illness may go to a deeper level and create allergies, chronic asthma/bronchitis, IBS, chronic fatigue, or even Rheumatoid arthritis, or cancer.

If a child is tired and stressed it will easily 'pick up a bug' from school or nursery. This bacterium or virus may already have been in the blood or tissues of the child for some time, but as the acidity of the child rises from stress the organism has the perfect environment to start growing and multiplying, causing symptoms.(refer back to acid and alkalinity in part 1.)

This may also happen to you as an adult when you 'keep going', seemingly healthily, but when you stop or go on holiday; then your body has the time to be ill, or rebalance itself. It happens commonly in people who push themselves too hard.

Any treatments given and home remedies for children should always be aimed at alkalising the system. The following tips will hopefully give you, the parent, plenty of help without resorting to drugs.

The common cold and its complications

Colds can easily be 'caught' as our antibodies seem to forget how to protect us, even though we may have several colds in one year. They usually start with a sore throat, feeling tired and muzzy headed, and then the runny nose, sneezing, blocked sinuses and cough develop. At the beginning the best treatment is an early night, so the body can alkalise during sleep. The changes that occur in the cells during sleep ensure renewal and healing.

Lemon juice is an alkalising agent, strangely enough as it seems so acid, but a squeezed lemon in warm (not hot) water with a spoonful of good local honey, which contains healing enzymes stirred in and sipped slowly will ease a sore throat and reduce acidity.

Plenty of fluids are needed too, to help detoxify the body. Warm water is best, made into herb tea (peppermint, chamomile, sage are all good). Encourage children to take these drinks from babyhood and they will learn to accept them. Don't put sugar in as this is too acid. Rather use natural low GI sweetness, such as rice syrup or agave syrup if they do need a little sweetness.

All fruits and vegetables will help to alkalise the body, so try to offer as much of these as possible while the child is suffering from any kind of illness, in the form of vegetable soups, fruit puree (apple with berries is nice), or fresh fruit, cut into small pieces. Fresh stewed fruit is always better than the convenient sachets of fruit puree now widely available.

A super quick natural ice-cream can be made with chopped banana, put into a container in the freezer to harden. Berries and other fruits (mango and pear work well) can be frozen too to add colour and flavour. Put them into a food mixer with a little coconut or almond milk and whizz up until it is ice-cream texture.

Maybe a Smoothie made with a few oats, fresh fruit and seeds will go down well.

You can also offer little bowls of raisins, unsweetened dried mango or pineapple, with cashew or almond nuts, and pumpkin and sunflower seeds for them to nibble. Young children should not be given whole nuts/seeds.

Children will love these special treats.

Try to make food special and appetising without resorting to crisps, sweets, fizzy drinks, or chocolate. Meat, eggs and fish are not necessary when a child is congested. Avoid sugar, wheat and cheese as much as possible. Milk shakes are not a good idea as milk is mucous forming.

Although having a cold may make a child less interested in food, it is a good idea to encourage a light healthy diet during the course of a heavy cold. It will keep their Energy up and always ensure they have plenty of liquids.

Garlic is a wonderful natural antibiotic, and antifungal. It can be put into soup and vegetable stews, or stir fries but as it has a very strong flavour don't force it on your child in a raw state except in very small quantities. It may be palatable raw with some honey and cider vinegar mixed with it, once it is well crushed. Give a small teaspoonful of this like medicine, just taking the juice.

Manuka honey, from New Zealand, is full of healing enzymes, and though expensive to buy, can be spread thinly on rice cakes as a treat when the child is poorly.

Elder, as found in hedgerows, with white flowers in the late spring, is a wonderful treatment for colds and coughs. You can try making your own Elderflower cordial, using honey as sweetener. Dilute a little of the cordial in warm water with a slice of lemon. It makes a cold clear up quicker and loosens mucous. Elder Berries can be collected in early autumn and a cordial made by steeping them in hot water, honey, ginger and cloves. The rich purple syrup makes a great cough mixture. You can find quite a few different recipes on-line.

Root Ginger, though rather an adult taste, is very cleansing to the system and stimulates the warmth of the body to overcome the bugs itself. It can be chopped up finely in soups or a slice in hot water can make an interesting drink with lemon and honey.

Vitamin C is well known as a remedy for colds/coughs. It boosts the immune system. It can be found in fresh fruit, especially oranges/ Satsuma etc. and also fresh vegetables not overcooked. Taking a supplement of Vit C throughout the cold winter months can help keep colds at bay. Get a good one from the local health food shop, especially for children, and ask the assistant for help on dosage.

Echinacea is becoming better known as a winter remedy to boost the immune system. It can be taken by children and is most efficacious as drops. Again check with the assistant about the best dosage for your child.

Mustard sounds like a real Granny Recipe, but can be very good at times. Put a deep bowl of hot water on the floor on a towel, add about a dessertspoon of mustard powder, and get the child to sit still with their feet in the bowl. Sit beside them and read a story. Once the skin begins to pink up, gently dry off their legs/feet and massage with nice oil and put on woolly socks. This can be a super treatment for a tired cold child who wants a bit of TLC (tender loving care!) and helps with the stuffed up head feeling as it draws the warmth down. Try it yourself if you have a cold.

An older child can have a steam inhalation.

If the cold becomes really heavy and sinuses are painful and blocked, steam can be used to help clear the passages.

Great care must be taken with this, and the child must be well supervised.

Boil a kettle of water and pour into a large basin. Add a chamomile tea bag, or better still a few loose chamomile flowers. Also Vick, eucalyptus oil or Friars Balsam can be used in small quantities for really blocked sinuses.

Settle the child down next to a table so they can lean over the hot bowl. Put a towel right over their heads, so that the steam comes up onto their face and get them to breathe deeply, let them stay under the towel for at least 5 minutes, longer if they will.

Afterwards dry their face and make sure they do not go out into a cold atmosphere for a while. They can also have a good blow with tissues, as this loosens the mucous.

The steam is very soothing and healing to the inflamed sinuses.

With a young child, setting up a steamer in the bedroom can be really helpful at night, especially if they are prone to croup, which is a spasm of the throat, and can obstruct breathing and be very frightening to both the parents and child. Herbal oils, such as eucalyptus or lavender can be added to ease the congestion.

If your child is unfortunate enough to get ear problems these can also be eased using natural methods. Firstly ensure that your child wears a good woollen hat when they go out with a cold. Cold air onto an already inflamed system will create more inflammation.

Ears and the tube between the throat and ears may get blocked with mucous and middle ear infections may occur. These are incredibly painful and a screaming child may need to be held and comforted in your bed or on your lap. Giving Kalpol for this is not unreasonable as earache is one of the worst pains.

An extremely useful treatment may be done with a large onion.

Cut the onion into fairly thick slices and store in the fridge. Take one large slice, wrap it well in a cotton handkerchief and place it over the painful ear. Put on a hat or head scarf to keep it in place and encourage the child to rest quietly in bed lying on the affected side, with possibly a warm hot water bottle as well placed on the ear.

The onion actually 'draws out' the inflammation and this may avoid a ruptured eardrum or glue ear developing. Glue ear is when the mucous becomes sticky and sucks in the ear drum causing hearing loss. It is treated most often by inserting grommets, small 'pegs' which break the vacuum between the outer and inner ear.

If the child is obviously ill, with a temperature, delirium or the pain is not subsiding it may be a case of needing an antibiotic, but try an onion first as it often works!

Chest complications after a cold are also fairly common. The cough, rather than being loose and tickly will become heavy with a rattle. At this stage a fever may develop.

Observing your child and allowing them to rest quietly at home may avoid further problems and they will gradually improve with a good diet, fluids and care. However if they get a fever, or the cough is much worse or they are breathless, you could try a chest poultice. The easiest is made with lemons.

Cut up a large lemon (organic) under warm water until the juices of both skin and pulp are running. Get a large cotton handkerchief and put into the water. Wring it out well, so it is not dripping and place right around the child's chest. Cover immediately with a layer of warm wool, and get them to rest lying down for at least 2 hours. Remove the poultice and repeat as necessary. The lemon draws out the inflammation.

This can also be done with old fashioned kaolin poultice, as bought in good chemist shops, or with curd cheese. German 'Quark' works well for this. It is a well-known treatment in Germany.

Resorting to antibiotics is a fairly frequent scenario, but before you get some from the GP try to establish if the infection is viral or bacterial. Antibiotics only work on bacterial infections.

Many antibiotics nowadays are becoming ineffectual as bugs are becoming 'superbugs'. Therefore giving them unnecessarily only makes this problem worse. I have read that antibiotics may become a thing of the past in a few years' time.

When you have a cold you feel rotten and so this is NOT the time to be sent to nursery or school. Many parents take the attitude 'Oh, it's ONLY a cold' and children will be sent off with streaming noses or coughs. Much better to keep the child in an even temperature for 24-48 hours until the worst symptoms have passed. Catching a cold is an indicator that the immune system is under stress and the child needs a bit more 'Mummy time'.

Our present government is pushing for all mothers to be able to work. They are supporting financially those who want to send their children to nursery.

I recently read of a Swedish research project which studied older children who had been brought up in state-run nurseries. They consistently showed more psychological problems, more addictive behaviour and more depression and violent tendencies than those who had stayed at home with the parents.

It is hard to stick out against the 'norms in society', especially when there are also financial incentives to do otherwise.

'Grannies remedies' did us well for many hundreds of years and we may well have to resort back to them again in the future, when nature is the only cure.

The very simplest and best thing you can do for your child is make sure they stay WARM when their bodies are in an inflammatory state with a cold or cough. Allow them to rest more and reduce their activity programme to a minimum. That way only does the body have a chance to rebalance and heal itself; as it surely will, given the right environment.

Fevers

The next stage on from a cough or cold is a full-blown fever. Fevers can be due to a bacterium in the blood or an acute viral infection such as influenza, or a so-called 'childhood illness' or a complication of a cold such as ear infections or bronchitis. A small child with a high fever can be a very frightening thing, as they go quickly into a state of crisis. Other symptoms are usually present to give a clue as to the nature of the illness.

The child may well want to sleep. They look very flushed and may also become delirious. Their breathing may become shallow, they may be a little blue around the lips, or they may have a febrile convulsion. This is a serious side effect of high fever in young children.

Taking the child's temperature is necessary to recognise the severity of the illness. This can be done with an oral thermometer in older children, or up the bottom, or under the arm in younger ones. The best easiest temperature gauges are those that simply go on the forehead and give an almost instant reading. These can be bought in chemist shops and are an essential part of any family's first aid kit. If you are caught out without a thermometer a good instant check can be done by putting your hand on their forehead. It will feel much hotter than usual.

If the child has a fever of 1-2 degrees centigrade (no higher than 39C) then there is no need to panic. Make sure the child is dressed in warm cotton/wool clothing and try to get them settled somewhere where they can lie quietly. This could be a sofa in the lounge where you are sitting quietly, a little bed in the dining room on an inflatable mattress where they can see you cooking or washing dishes, or it may be their own beds, providing they are given a little bell to call you, or you pop in and out frequently. Children do not like to be left alone when ill, and should also not be left in case the fever rises sharply. Just sitting and cuddling them for hours can be the most soothing beneficial thing for them. Ensure the house is kept a warm even temperature and that you have someone else to do the school pickups, shopping or whatever needs doing out and about. Your prime task is to create a 'Huelle' (a German word meaning a wrapped up cosy space), within which your child can relax and feel totally nurtured and safe.

Time heals and your child will be busy healing whatever the problem, given the right environment.

Ensure they take enough liquids, as a fevered body quickly gets very dehydrated, and offer only fruit puree or small pieces of fruit for the first 24 hours. The digestion probably needs a rest too. Giving them some ice to suck on can be soothing too, but avoid cold ice creams at first. As the temperature goes down you can start a light diet as offered for a cold, with no sugar, wheat or dairy, or additives whatsoever.

If the fever is rising above 39-40c and the child is beginning to look ill, getting a fan to cool them down can help. Also gently sponging them down with a sponge dipped in lemon water (as made for cold compresses above) will bring down a fever. Another good way is to bring the temperature down to the feet by wrapping the calves up in a cloth containing either quark or squeezed out lemon clothes. The child must have these on for several hours and they can be changed regularly. Not all children will have a fit if the temperature rises. My youngest son had a temperature of 43c once with no ill effect!

However use your powers of observation and instincts to know whether the process is sustainable or not. Calling the doctor might set your mind at rest or might involve an antibiotic injection or even admission to hospital

Some things to look out for, at which you will need to call medical help

- A febrile convulsion or fit
- Severe headache
- Stiff neck or sensitivity to light,
- Extreme dehydration from vomiting/diarrhoea.
- Any unusual rashes which are not explained as measles, rubella, chickenpox.

Check out the symptoms of the childhood illnesses if you have decided not to inoculate and the child may have been in contact with them, so you know just what you are dealing with. Measles must be carefully nursed as the secondary meningitis infections; ear or eye problems may cause difficulties if you do not keep the child quietly resting. Most problems that one hears about are due to poor nursing and pushing the child back to school too quickly.

New varieties of childhood illnesses are appearing as a result of mass inoculation, which means that symptoms may not follow a very typical pattern. In this scenario your doctor can advise as he knows what is going around, and the illness picture which is presenting.

Young children will often spike a temperature if they are teething. This needs rather different treatment, as the work the child is doing changing/cutting their teeth is a fundamental development, which needs space, time and understanding. Some children sail through this, others become quite ill and restless. Giving homeopathic Chamomile drops in a little water, or granules will act as a soothing help for this process.

Using Homeopathic remedies can be incredibly efficacious when a child is ill. Knowing what to give when and how each remedy is suited to a particular child can be confusing initially. If you become interested in this deep subject it is worth taking your child to a qualified homeopath and asking them which remedies would suit them for a fever. There may be other developmental issues which can be really helped by giving these little sugar pills or drops. They have no side effects and can be surprisingly potent.

A common one used for fever, when the child's face is flushed and the eyes look glazed is Belladonna, but this will not be the remedy of choice for all children.

Whatever else happens, remaining calm with a sick child is of the utmost importance. Put your life on hold for however long it takes and try not to have selfish restless thoughts about what you are missing of REAL life! Life is real enough for you in the sick room and it is the very best most important thing you can do for your child. It teaches you patience by the bucket load!

Accidents and injuries

Before I start on the practicalities I am going to say a strange thing; "Nothing happens by accident!"

By this I mean that the child will become involved in whatever trauma that befalls him/her and on a deeply subconscious level will know why this is happening to them. They may need the 'stop' that an accident brings and any lessons they learn from going through this experience will be valuable to them on a developmental level.

They may be craving more love and attention; they may have become over-restless and inattentive to what their bodies are doing. Or there may be a deeper level on which this occurs which we cannot even start to judge or understand. These may seem callous and strange words indeed, but ponder them and glimpses of understanding may start to appear. I do not believe in an angry God who punishes, but that everything in the world has a natural pattern of Energy flow.

Some children are very accident prone and always breaking bones and going off to E and A, to the extent that some parents have even been accused of neglect by the hospital staff.

I am not intimating this at all! Having had one son who was often in casualty, it 'just happened'; but WHY?

The first reaction of a parent in an accident is usually huge shock and fear. Try if possible to learn to trust a process and remain calm in the face of the pain of your loved ones. That way you can give more love and support. What is your biggest fear? Always ask that question and face it. Many conflicting emotions may be present too. Guilt, anger, blame, shock, disbelief, but the greatest one is fear.

Make sure you know what to do in any given situation. The role of the parent often involves being a first-aider and practical skills are sometimes important. Get a good book and study it or go on a paediatric first aid course.

In your first aid box you should have not only the normal selection of sterile dressings and plasters, but a bottle of Bach's 'Rescue Remedy'; herbal drops in brandy which you put on your tongue every few minutes if necessary and can also give to your child. It can also be put on the temples or wrists. This is calming and helps you feel more in control.

Arnica D6 is a well-known homeopathic home treatment for shocks, bruising and tumbles. The little white pills can be bought in most good pharmacies and should be sucked under the tongue until dissolved. You can give these immediately and then continue for a few days after the accident until the child is more steady and less traumatised, taking it 3-4 times a day. It also comes as a tincture, which can be used diluted in boiled water as a compress for bruises and sprains, or as a cream to be put on bumps and bruises. Never put arnica on an open wound or graze, or use it when the skin is broken.

If the child has a dirty graze or cut, clean it very well first under running water or bathe it gently in cool boiled water that has some Calendula lotion added. This is made from marigolds and is a wonderful natural antiseptic. Diluted Witch-hazel is also good. It is important to remove all the grit and dirt before putting on a dry sterile dressing. Calendula cream is also available, or use a mild antiseptic cream without too many additives.

Keeping a frozen pad in the freezer to put onto sprains and bruises is a useful thing. Frozen peas are almost as good!

Sometimes it is hard to know if a wound needs stitches. As a rule of thumb try to bring together the edges of a wound as tightly as you can using 'steristrip' plasters. If you are unsure, or the wound is jagged or in an awkward place, or near eyes or mouth, take the child to be sutured professionally. Scaring will develop from a badly healed wound, which they will not thank you for in the future.

Burns, if mild, should be treated by running under cold water immediately. I keep an Aloe Vera plant on my kitchen window sill and the juice from a leaf broken off can be smeared directly onto a burn or scald and works really well. It can also be put onto burned tongues after hot liquid! Any large or severe burns need professional care.

If glass is involved in an accident never try to remove it from the limb but take the child straight to hospital. Taking the glass out might cause serious blood loss.

If you think the child has broken a limb try to keep it as still as possible strapped to their body. You can improvise a sling or splint with a scarf or tea towel.

Shock, when the blood pressure drops and the child is white and semiconscious from blood loss or trauma is serious; always call emergency help if the child has lost a lot of blood or seems to have an internal injury.

If the child has a head bump observe them carefully for several hours afterwards and don't let them go to sleep in case there has been some internal damage. Uneven pupil size or drowsiness needs immediate medical attention.

It is often difficult to assess if you need to take your child to hospital. Children get bumps and bruises as a normal part of growing up, but a child's cry will often indicate how severe their damage is. Sometimes there is a horrible silence after a fall and then you know that immediate action is needed. If the child is very upset emotionally don't over-fuss but give them diversion or calm cuddles and it will soon pass. You know your child best and instinct is often the best guide.

If you think the child has broken something or may need surgery of some kind or an anaesthetic, don't let them eat or drink anything until you are sure. Delayed treatment because the child has eaten within 4 hours can be crucial in the healing process.

Remember that any trauma will shock the child on a deep level. This means that they will need rest, quiet and your healing presence to help them recover. This may take a few days. Sometimes a child will even get a temperature after an accident, as part of the shock to their system. A light diet and a few treats will help to make them feel special and loved and recover quicker.

Your own Energy as a parent is transferred to them when you give love, cuddles and comfort. You are acting as a Healer to your child and this action cannot be underestimated.

Giving Love unconditionally at such times is the greatest gift to your children. Fear is the opposite of love and feeling fear prevents you from giving your full love, so work on overcoming your fears to help your child when they experience trauma of any kind.

Tummy upsets.

These are very common in young children and are usually caused by a 'bug' or virus which the child has come into contact with. Washing hands before eating and after using the toilet is an important lesson to teach a child from an early age and will minimise the risk of catching an infection. Tummy upsets may occasionally be caused by food poisoning and the suspect meal needs to be traced if possible.

Allergic reactions to certain foods can also induce tummy upsets, which can be quite extreme. Keep a note of any repeated episodes, and ask your doctor/health visitor if you are concerned.

The strengthening of the immune system through good general care and diet will help also in fighting off any bugs which are going the rounds at nursery or school, or mean that the infection will pass quickly through the system and leave the child little affected by it.

Conversely a weak child may become very ill quite quickly if they lose vital body fluids through vomiting or diarrhoea and this may then become a medical emergency and admission to hospital for rehydration may be needed.

A young baby can quickly lose fluids, and this is obvious by lassitude and the fontanel (soft spot) which is caving inwards. In this case call a doctor.

Normally the child vomits as the body's natural mechanism to clear the system of toxic waste; as is also diarrhoea, so it can be seen as a cleansing process. The child needs to be supported in this in the same way as with any illness, with quiet rest and sips of water. It is best to rest the digestion completely to begin with and only give a rice cake (with no butter) of the child says they are hungry.

How long should you starve them? For 24 hours after an acute attack of sickness or diarrhoea only give water or herbal tea, (chamomile is especially soothing and should be made weak with no sweetening) and then gradually introduce a light non-fatty diet, like some vegetable soup or fruit puree, or some porridge.

If the child is sick again, reduce the amount of food given and wait and watch! If a tummy bug lasts for more than 2-3 days and there seems to be no sign of improvement you should contact medical advice, as a child may become dehydrated. Giving sachets of rehydration powder, containing vital electrolytes can sometimes be a good idea if they are very sick and weak, but don't ignore the symptoms if they go on longer than a couple of days.

The symptoms of appendicitis are worth being aware of. Tummy ache which can be severe is usually felt across the middle of the abdomen, around the umbilicus. It may also cause sickness. If the child complains often of tummy ache of this kind or has a temperature with severe tummy ache, don't ignore it. Burst appendix is not uncommon and may be life threatening.

Tummy ache can also be a sign of emotional tension. Some children are more prone to it than others. Having wind pockets or just sore feelings in the abdomen may indicate nervous tension and a digestive weakness. Helping the child to be calm at mealtimes, with no toys, distractions, TV or rows and to sit down throughout the meal may help a nervy child to digest better. Massaging the abdomen gently can be very soothing in this scenario, the child may like to lie down on their front with a pillow under there tummy.

Recurring tummy aches can also be an attention seeking ploy, so look at things like relationship issues in the family, school bullying, or general unhappiness for some reason. A sympathetic chat at bedtime can often sort out problems of this kind and make the child feel more supported.

In normal good health we are not aware of the digestive tract and its workings. Only of there is inflammation or disease do we become aware of what is going on in this highly complex and important part of our bodies. The subconscious metabolism then becomes conscious; hence if here are emotional, nervous issues these can also be felt in the abdominal area.

In this section I have tried to cover all the common problems which may occur day by day when one has a young family. There are detailed and excellent books available on first aid and childhood illnesses, and having a small reference library will help you to diagnose and treat these common problems yourself with more confidence. The GPs and health visitors are there as back-up for you if you are concerned or the child is not recovering spontaneously. Have trust that young bodies do heal spontaneously and well, given the right calm environment and diet. Your task as a parent is to support that natural process with intuition, calmness and love.

Rhythm and warmth

The child's Energy is closely associated with MOVEMENT and LIFE. The pulse, which we take so for granted, is the sign that the heart is alive, and it maintains a steady and unwavering tempo throughout our entire lives. Only when the heartbeat stops are we dead! The heart muscle is the strongest in the body and starts to beat even before the heart as an organ is fully formed in the embryo. This is a strange miracle worth pondering. The beat is there before the organ; in fact the organ is formed BY the beat!

Another miracle of life is the sustaining of warmth. The warmth of mammals has developed gradually over time. Dinosaurs, fish and birds have a very different kind of heat mechanism. The blood sustains and nourishes every cell in our warm bodies, and pulses with life throughout every cell, renewing and sustaining our processes.

Without warmth we quickly die. If we get too hot we can also die. We take these things for granted, but it is worth thinking about if you are a parent responsible for maintaining the warmth of a baby or young child, or even a teenager!

The surface skin area of humans is covered with sweat glands and fine hairs, which help to even out changes in temperature, but in our fickle climate we also have to wear varying amounts of clothes and have heating in our houses. If we ignore this need we can soon become ill.

The head has a large surface area and as much as an eighth of your body heat can be lost rapidly through your head. If a child gets cold regularly they also have to utilise their own Energy to maintain body heat; Energy which should be going towards growth and development in a young child.

From this perspective one can begin to understand how some of the British habits of the last century of dressing children in shorts and ankle socks throughout cold winters may have contributed to the large numbers of elderly people now who have got arthritic knees and hips in this country! The Energy which should have been used to develop strong limbs went into keeping them warm, thus weakening the child as they grew older.

How often does one see babies with bare heads nowadays out in the cold wind? Yes, they survive but at what hidden costs? How often can you hear a young child crying from cold on a windy day down by the sea? Keeping our children warm is rather like keeping a precious plant in the green-house. If you put it out in a cold draught too early in spring it will curl up and die, but if you keep it indoors on a hot day it will become lanky and yellow and eventually die also. Our children are no different. We need the right balance of warmth and wrapping to keep them healthy. Overdressing will not allow them to move and use their limbs, but underdressing, which is the bigger problem, weakens their Energy and can cause illness and frailty later.

Clothes made of natural fibres which breathe and allow the child to sweat naturally with layers of cotton and wool is best. If artificial dressings are put into the clothes to 'keep them fresh' this also may affect the ability of the skin to act as a natural organ of excretion, which it is. Nylon, acrylic and other artificial fabrics are best avoided altogether.

Rhythm is an interesting topic as it is largely hidden in our bodies, but every process has its own rhythm. There are rhythms of the liver and gall bladder, the hormones, the sleep mechanisms and many other bodily systems. Everything gyrates together in harmony rather like a huge 'Dance of Energy'. From a parents' perspective it is therefore helpful for your growing child to sustain and maintain these natural rhythms.

Bedtime should be at the same time each night, preferably early for young children, as sleep is vital, mealtimes should be regular, the pattern of the week can also be developed with special things on special days, so the child comes to recognise the 7 day rhythm which is also not just incidental.

The seasonal rhythms can be celebrated also. These are ancient points in the year when certain rituals were done, dating back to the Druids and even earlier, when people knew intuitively about the cycles of the sun, moon and stars. Our modern Christian festivals are loosely connected to the cycles of the seasons. In Mediaeval times the rent was collected on quarter days. The Celtic festivals recognise these dates also, with midsummer, midwinter, spring and autumn equinox. Harvest, All Souls, or Halloween and May Day are all markers of these yearly cycles.

Doing fun and creative rituals, appropriate to each age group, on these festivals can help the child to connect more strongly to the natural seasonal changes. Their awareness of the earth and its seasons helps to strengthen the body's rhythms also.

A healthy child is one who connects in a natural way with its environment and its cultural inheritance. It absorbs this unconsciously in the early years from its parents and wider family. If this is disrupted or not recognised the child can feel unsettled and not have a deep connectedness or sense of 'home' to the place on earth where it is brought up. In later life this can show as restlessness, many moves and a weakening of the natural rhythms of the bodily functions, such as sleep, which may then cause illnesses to develop.

Rhythm in the widest meaning can also be found in music and beat. Children who have an early environment where music is heard and practised develop their sense of natural rhythm. Dance is another way to do this. Research has shown that children who play an instrument and sing have a higher IQ and find concentration easier. The brain develops more fully when natural rhythms and tones are introduced early on.

Sleep disturbances.

I would particularly like to mention here the ever increasing problem of sleep in our modern children. Having initially been invited to take part in the TV programme 'Bedtime Live' recently, but then declined, I watched with horror some of the scenarios which were being tackled by the 'experts'.

A child, who has natural 'organic' rhythms (i.e. who during the day eats good food regularly, plays in a calm environment, has plenty of fresh air and exercise in the right amounts, who is kept the right temperature and dressed well, who has plenty of contact with their parents in a relaxed happy loving space and who has had a normal relaxed birth with no complications, and has been breastfed well,) will normally go to bed happily and sleep for up to 12 hours a night!

Problems with sleep often start very early on, and then may need professional help to sort them out later. If a baby is carried downstairs and stimulated in the early weeks every time it cries, its night/day rhythms will not get well established. Because food is a new experience to a baby's body, the timing, quantity and quality of feeds helps to establish these natural rhythms. Therefore complete demand feeding as has become popular is perhaps not helping our children to sleep. Chemical cow's milk formulas may also have a bearing on sleep quality as it is digested differently, and car rides and TV watching must also overstimulate the child's nerve-sense system.

Rigidity in a parent is not good, and anxiety is even worse! Many children will settle happily with a grandparent or nanny but will play up over-anxious parents. This is not just a statement from my personal experience but also the tales of many of my older female friends which leads me to write this! Fashions in childrearing go in cycles, and we seem to have experimented a lot with our children in the last 20-30 years.

It is helpful to have a bedtime routine to enable the child to wind down after a busy day. Many children cannot sleep because they are overtired and overstimulated.

The routine could include a warm bath, with some lavender bath oil to relax them, and some water play. Mum or Dad must always be there calmly enjoying this time with their children. Rushing off to cook a meal, answering the phone or whatever disrupts the child.

The child's evening meal, with a parent eating too, must be taken early with just a warm drink at bedtime, as the digestion needs time to settle before sleep. Waiting up for Dad to come back from work and then bouncing around in play can disrupt the settling.

Getting into bed, without any TV or radio in the room, with a soft cover and some special cuddly toy, but not too many bright garish stimulating pictures on the walls or covers, one can then tell a story, simple and repetitive for young children, imaginative, while you cuddle them gently or perhaps a book read each night for an older child; then a brief chat about the day, some sharing time or perhaps stroking the child's head gently, until they are ready to let you go downstairs. A song and a candle to create a quiet atmosphere can also be calming. The light goes out and the door is shut, from an early age, with no arguments! Minimal fuss or anxiety or going in and out after settling will give the child security and a strong message that they don't play up! If you are sure in yourself that the child will sleep it invariably will.

Occasionally a baby may have had a traumatic birth, as in a caesarean or forceps and then a cranial-sacral osteopathic treatment may be helpful. This is a very gentle and non-invasive treatment that encourages the cerebrospinal fluids to move more harmoniously. This happens at a normal birth, but may become disrupted if there are birth delays or no natural passage through the birth canal. It can have a dramatic effect on settling the baby into a calmer routine.

Another time that sleep may become disrupted is if the child has an unnatural separation from the parents through a hospital admission of the mother or child. In this case quiet perseverance using gradual separation techniques can help an anxious child to settle again. Patience and love will be needed, and a set pattern which never changes.

If you want your child to sleep in your bed, you will allow it too, but don't expect it to suddenly disappear again! Set the rules you want from the outset. Children just like animals can be trained providing you stay calm and focused. Talk about problems with your health visitor and make sure you have a united front with your husband/wife.

I had a son who did not want to stay in his cot at the age of 14 months. It took 3 nights (and my husband being persuaded by both the GP and health visitor) to get him not to stand up and scream, but after that he slept perfectly, and never played up again.

Finding your boundaries with a small child is a two-way process and involves much patience, humour, insight and love. The path of parenting is a path of personal development.

Emotional problems

Holism, the subject of this book, is about the WHOLE PERSON, which includes not only their body and mind, but also their emotions, social environment and their path through life which we can term destiny. It is the higher energies, explained in various terms by religious and spiritual practices, which concern us also. Who we truly are and what affects our health in the very broadest sense is Holism.

Our society reflects very much what is going on in each and every home throughout the country. Bringing up healthy emotionally balanced children is the basis for the next generation and how they create a future community, both in terms of work, ethics and morals, and also as future parents themselves. As parents we are constantly learning from our children if we can remain alert and open to what they innately bring. We do have to help and guide them however.

Any routine and rules are part of the relationship you create with your child, which starts early on in utero. How much do you demand and how much do they get their own way? There seem to be two extremes and society tends to swing like a pendulum between these two.

If a child is over regimented and not allowed to express its uniqueness and grow into its own being, it will become tight and unable to express its natural gifts. It may suffer from constipation or nervous stress in later life, or be unable to initiate things and feel low self-esteem or depression.

A child who does not have any consistency or rules will suffer as well. Many children in our current society are in this situation, offspring off the '60's kids'. Parents do their children no favours with a totally 'laise faire' attitude, as boundaries give children a sense of security. These children may grow up trying drugs or over-binging on alcohol, and may find it hard to hold down a regular job in later life, or take responsibility for parenting themselves.

One of the keys to nurturing a young child is to help them to feel a sense of wonder and devotion to all things natural and beautiful. The world is a beautiful place with huge diversity of creatures and plants which we have a responsibility to care for. If we drop litter, squash flies, kick the dog, disregard and neglect our patch of garden, use foul language and get angry easily we are giving strong messages to our children. We are literally teaching them aggression and lack of love.

It is not just a 'class distinction', how we talk to and treat our children. Every human being has it in them to be loving, gentle, kind and patient. Nowadays one of the greatest negative influences on our young children is the constant bombardment of ugly and aggressive images from the television. Even cartoons like Tom and Jerry (fun as they may seem to an adult) are aggressive and distorted. The animals are not true animals, but are distortions of human beings. If a young child, who acts as a complete sponge to everything around them, watches television, not only is their concentration span diminished as they watch constantly flashing changing images, but they are taking in on a deep level the distorted image of the human. Huge eyes, little legs, enormous mouths, angular 'disabled' bodies. Watch some children's programmes and you will see it for yourself!

For parents TV is a wonderful 'babysitter'. A child will sit quietly for hours not disturbing you while you chat to a friend on the phone or make a meal, or even work at the computer! Instead of talking and relating to you, their parent, and learning about the skills of life and attitudes and love, our children are put into a semi-conscious state (the same part of the brain is used for watching TV as when we are unconscious) and given the equivalent of pornography to watch! These may sound strong words, but I have seen time and time again how children react after they have watched some television. They are restless, maybe flushed, cannot concentrate and start acting out the aggressive behaviour they have been watching.

Multiply this by hundreds of hours over the years and we are breeding a generation of brainwashed children who have short concentration spans, learned aggressive behaviour, lack of communication skills; and a sense that the world of 'illusion', especially from the electronic games they play, is in fact reality.

What are we doing it for? Simply to respond to peer group pressure? Or to keep them quiet? Or to 'educate' them? If you are experiencing ANY disturbance or problems with your children's behaviour or sleep, the very first thing to try is to 'break' the TV! Make it disappear (maybe up to your bedroom, in a cupboard, if you are still addicted).Keep TV, electronic games and computers absolutely out of their lives and you will be amazed at the gradual changes that occur!

Sure, you will have to supply other games and pastimes. Perhaps a large sandpit for a young child in the garden, some pots of paints, baking times, hide and seek, cutting and sticking, a climbing frame and swing, regular walks, a pet to learn to care for, some beautiful story books (not a repetition of the distortion from the TV characters!) or some building materials. Children between 3 and 7 love to build houses and camps, play families, even play with dolls. The child learns by acting out what it sees around it. They COPY everything and then practise it. That is their work!

If you sit all day at a computer the child will want to do likewise, if you bake something interesting, the child will want to copy you. If you sew and knit, the child will soon want to learn. If you make lots of tea and chat to your friends, the child will play this out in their Wendy house. This may seem obvious, but YOU are the measure of their world to begin with. They are busy from morning till night learning how to be like you.

That is the greatest compliment you will get as a parent, and you will soon perceive how they have 'absorbed' you. Do they drop litter or pick it up, do they say thank you and please, do they sit quietly at the table and eat their food, do they take an interest in visitors and smile and greet them with confidence, do they keep their rooms tidy, do they go to sleep easily at night, do they show an interest in nature and animals or plants? All these attributes are learned by COPYING.

You cannot expect your child to be polite if you shout at them to reprimand them. You cannot want them to be concentrated and peaceful if you are restless and easily bored; you cannot tell them off for quarrelling with their brothers/sisters if you quarrel with your partner!

Just as they are learning so too you are learning from them. If you hit a big problem, and there can be many as the years go on, first look at what is going on in YOU, and see if you can change that first. If you are anxious or depressed find out why. What is your fear? Are you unsupported, lacking self-love, angry, low in self-esteem?

No-one is perfect and neither are your children. The personality of your child, their unique gifts and qualities and also their problems are obvious to you if you really observe them from a very early age.

As a parent you can adjust your attitudes and parameters to suit each child. Listen to what they are telling you, even in their first cries, and demands. That is not about giving in to their every demand, but understanding their pain of being human too. You can feel in empathy their frustration and fear, you can try to overcome that same frustration and fear in yourself.

This may all sound very idealistic, but it is the ground on which you build your child's future emotional health. Listening to advice from others can be very confusing as each person carries their own fears, built in from childhood, and the best way to help your child in their problems is to look inside yourself and use your intuition to understand what is happening.

Sometimes sharing your own growth with a close friend or counsellor may be helpful. At each stage of childhood and parenting the child can show us another aspect of ourselves. Some people love caring for babies. They are naturally maternal/paternal and enjoy the demands and cuddles needed.

Others will find this stage challenging and boring and long for the baby to become a little person with whom they can talk and play. Other people prefer a school age child who is exploring the world out there, and comes back from school with new knowledge. Others find the challenges of teenagers stimulating and interesting, as the young person flexes their emotional muscles ready to 'leave the nest'.

Whatever stage you enjoy and whichever bits of parenting you personally find challenging, sharing your journey with others, your partner, teachers, friends and family, can be a support and help.

Having experience of being a single parent of three children myself, I cannot say too strongly how support is helpful and necessary. We were not intended to live in isolation, as nuclear families. If you observe all indigenous peoples (and also apes etc.) you can see how family/community support is part of growing up healthily. Grandparents are important to enable children to have a sense of history and continuum, and they can develop a unique relationship with their grandchildren. Other friends with children of similar ages can provide extra 'siblings', particularly if you have an only child. Doing swaps during the holidays and weekends can bring new dimensions into your family life and also give you a few hours to yourself when needed.

The assumption that parents have the greatest educational input in their children's emotional wellbeing is greatly challenged nowadays by societies' and the governments' pressure for parents to work outside the home. Homecare and childcare is totally undervalued by our current society, reflected in the minimal wages that nannies and housekeepers are offered. It is seen as much more important to sit at an office desk all day staring at a computer screen.

So our children are neglected and brought up haphazardly in nurseries and by child-minders, who sometimes (as experts) do a better job than the real parents. Why do we have children? Is it just a status symbol? With the rapid over population of the planet we have to seriously ask whether we are worthy of becoming real parents! The continuation of the human species relies on good parenting and also good education, whatever we take that word to mean.

With a risk of alienating you, or sending you on an unhealthy 'guilt trip', by what I am saying, I would like to point out that we have a very grave problem in our present age. Children are emotionally deprived throughout all of society and differing income brackets, because we do not give enough importance to giving our children our time and parenting skills on all levels. Earning money has become a greater priority. Only when this fact changes will we start to build a healthy society for the future of our planet.

One aspect which needs to be mentioned is the early sexuality which children are experiencing. There are several factors which may be influencing this. Children experience early stimulation with our modern environment. They are encouraged to use their nerve/sense systems more than in previous times. They are forced to sit up earlier, have long car and air journeys and have less sleep. Their diet may well influence this too, with meat containing growth hormones being fed to the animals.

Toys show sexually developed figures (such as Barbie dolls) and TV is constantly showing precocious tinies acting up (as in Hanna Montana). Children's clothes are now like baby adults ones, children wear makeup and bras much earlier, and generally children come into puberty earlier and earlier.

Children are literally being ROBBED of their childhood, a time of dreamy imagination, of play and learning about natural laws and social interaction. These lessons are being missed out on, as we rush our children headlong into an adult world of ambitions, material needs, technical and academic achievements and money making.

It may be no surprise to hear that degenerative illnesses, Alzheimer's disease and dementia are becoming ever more common at earlier ages. We do not have the oportunity to build up our physical bodies as children sufficiently and we are therefore weakened and this shows itself in later life as illness and early aging.

Future generations may well suffer greatly because of what we are doing now to our children. Despite all scientific predictions, the average lifespan may in fact start to shorten in the future, despite all the innovations of modern medicine.

Chapter 24

Teenagers

That confusing time from about 9 to 21 we loosely call The Teens. It is certainly a time of many changes and parents will often, in retrospect, joke about having 'survived' it unscathed!

In my work as a nurse, midwife, therapist and teacher, and most importantly as a mother, my most interesting and challenging times certainly have been when I was with this age group. As adults we observe the new birth of the next generation. It can be fascinating and uplifting, or threatening and frightening, depending on you and your insights.

My rich and varied life has given me opportunities to interact and spend time with this age group. I have been a single parent of my own three children and their teenage friends, supporting as best I could their emotional and educational needs, whilst juggling shared care with my ex-husband, and working alongside this as a practice nurse and self-employed massage therapist.

I had the wonderful oportunity to work as Matron for the National Youth Orchestra for two years, during their intensive holiday music courses, overseeing the physical and emotional wellbeing of up to 180 young people between 13 and 18. They were not only highly motivated to perform to their highest standards musically, and highly intelligent as well, but emotionally vulnerable trying to keep up in a big group away from home and working under huge pressure.

I briefly stepped into the role of Matron in a public school, where I noticed the behaviour and emotional needs of children in a boarding school situation, away from their parents for long periods of time, surrounded by the rules and rhythms of an institution.

As a massage therapist I have treated very disturbed and abused teenagers at a home-school, where physical touch was immensely therapeutic but also threatening.

From time to time I have also been involved in teaching 'normal' teenagers in small groups in the classroom situation on 'moral issues', including sex and childbirth, getting them to think deeply about their maturing bodies.

More recently I have enjoyed teaching English to foreign students aged between 13 and 19 in holiday language schools, again vulnerable as they are away from home and coping with many new challenges.

Working as a live-in nanny, or surrogate parent, from time to time, I have cared for some very vulnerable and deprived children, some over several years, and watched them come into puberty and grow into lanky teenagers. I have seen how early damage from neglectful parents, using drugs and alcohol, can have lasting effects on these young people.

My many nephews, nieces and now great-nephews and great-nieces from around the globe appear on my doorstep intermittently and I am always amazed at the physical transformation each time I see them, observing their emerging personalities and how their gifts and life skills develop.

I also meet young people in a local drama group; highly motivated and interesting teenagers, spending their leisure time as an integrated part of an adult performing group, gaining self-esteem and confidence in doing so.

Last but certainly not least the local school children from a council estate pass my kitchen window each school day and I can observe unnoticed at close range how they interact with each other, the fads and trends of each year group and the problems they sometimes overtly show.

All these varied experiences have enabled me to ponder deeply the processes of growing up, from a helpless infant to a lively innocent child, dependent largely on its parents for guidance and nurturing, to a lethargic gangly awkward teenager, who relies heavily on its peer group for support, but still maintains the spark of individuality which enables them eventually to find their life purpose and go out into life as an independent adult.

For many 'incarnating souls' nowadays these transformations can be painful and jerky, as our society, like many before us, seems to think that teenagers are 'stroppy and difficult', and our sensitivity towards the processes involved has become somewhat blunted by our modern way of life.

My hope in writing this book is to enable us to perceive the 'beautiful white swan' that is about to emerge from the 'ugly duckling' and to support this process more consciously as mature adults, to which the teenagers look for their role models and inspiration.

Each new generation brings particular qualities to enrich and transform the world. New ideas and feelings bring leaven into the earth's Energetic field and adults may feel threatened by these changes. After all "We are the mature adults and we know best how things are done, don't we?"

If we can learn to listen to what lies behind the teenagers stroppiness, we can perceive an ideology which can breathe new life into our dying earth existence.

Our acceptance of these new ideas will make it easier for young people to grow in maturity and experience whilst still keeping alive in them as adults the freshness of youth. We have a responsibility to the next generation to enable them to heal the sicknesses of the Earth we have created.

Today we hand over a very sick planet to the next generation. There is massive climate change, pollution, overpopulation, extinction of many species of creatures, and a lack of moral fibre, as we all strive for a more and more comfortable material world, where attaining money seems to become the highest ideal and life goal.

Young people are inheriting this world as their place of work and learning; as a place to have their children and continue the human species.

As young children we 'dream' our way into existence, accepting the things we are presented with unconditionally. By the time we are teenagers we begin to question and challenge what we find as the 'status quo' and bring our own ideas and imaginations to the whole. Often there is a huge gap between what we perceive around us and our hopes and ideals.

We need also to break free from our parents in a healthy way in order to find our OWN way forward. We need to REJECT our parentage for a while in a healthy way before we can accept it again and integrate it into our personality. That is the big challenge.

Small wonder that young people are 'Stroppy'!

Chapter 25

Growing up

New-born babies come into this world innocent and unspoilt; ready to absorb all that is around them, both positive and negative. We copy like sponges the essence and Energy of our parents, totally reliant on their nurturing care.

As children we defer to the adult world with respect, as the 'grown ups' around us guide and teach us all we know. We love and watch our parents as they provide us with the role models of whom we are to become. We imitate their behaviour and absorb their moral fibre and habits. It is a natural process, starting as a helpless infant until we can care for ourselves. It occurs also in the animal world around us as young calves and lambs, for example, learn to eat grass, wash themselves, go with the herd, and whatever other processes are innate to them.

Children are taught to conform in school also by their teachers. They have to line up in the playground, stay quiet in assembly, and put their hands up to ask permission to speak and all the other conformities we expect of school children.

At about the age of 9 some big changes start to happen as the faculty of individual criticism is born. Prior to this if a child criticises something it is as a copied action, but at about this age the child starts to feel separate from the world around.

Mood changes or sulkiness may be apparent and the child may start to argue or question their parents. This has to do partially with intellectual development, but is also an emotional separation which is starting.

At this age too there are the first signs of hormonal changes which we describe as puberty. The sex hormones of oestrogen and progesterone in girls and testosterone in boys start to be produced and this kick starts the massive physical changes which then take place over the next 5 years or so.

Initially in girls there are the subtle changes of hair starting to grow in private places and the first signs of breast tissue development. Girls are usually proud of these changes and may spend hours in the bathroom gazing at themselves, or comparing themselves with their friends. They look towards the womanly changes with eager anticipation and discuss these at length. They are rather like rosebuds about to open! They become shy of their bodies and self-conscious for the first time.

Parents will observe that these changes are happening earlier and earlier to their children now, due largely to the growth hormones which are added to animal feed which passes in the food chain in meat and dairy foods to the children. I suspect also that early mental and sensory stimulation may activate these processes too.

Food is a definite factor in defining when puberty starts and also how easy this will be for the youngster. Diet will be talked about in a later chapter.

In boys development may be a bit slower than in girls. They may still be acting as little boys in the playground in year 5 and 6 of junior school, whilst the girls stand in huddles, not wanting to charge around or climb trees any more, talking about boyfriends, make-up, and pop idols. Some may even have started their periods before they leave junior school nowadays.

The next changes happen quite quickly. The limbs start to grow longer, as the child has a massive growth spurt. Their noses grow, the soft cartilage becoming longer and bonier and the facial features may change quite a bit. Milk teeth are usually changed by now and the large back molars are cut; the lower jaw also grows. Their hair may become greasy and hormonal acne spots may appear on their faces. Breast tissue develops in girls and they start to need to wear a small bra for support.

Boys will be proud of the development of their penis, and hair, and may want to show these off in games with the other boys. One day their voices will be childlike, the next they can only produce a squeak and then suddenly they growl in deep tones. This change of voice is the biggest sign of 'manliness' and can take some months before it settles. Facial 'fluff' appears and boys have a first try at shaving. It can be a confusing time for a young teenager who is going through all these massive changes.

Because these major things are happening physically there is a huge emotional shift too. Children will hang out together in groups, copying their peers in terms of dress style, choosing favourite idols which become the focus of their 'love' (usually pop stars), staying for long periods in their rooms just listening to music or fiddling around.

Their rooms become a haven and usually a tip! Parents often have issues over this and may storm in and try to 'clear up', or threaten loss of pocket money or other privileges, or cajole the teenager into some sort of compromise situation. The teenager is actually asserting their right to their own 'cave' which will become their adult space.

Some teenagers may dislike their bodily changes and stop washing, and only wear clothes which are tatty or torn. They may think they look 'cool' walking into town with virtually nothing to cover up with, on a freezing cold day, wearing the trendiest local fashions. All the norms of their upbringing are thrown out!

Parents may get stressed out by all these normal changes. The delightful child who was biddable and happy has become a morose, grumpy, smelly, disobedient teenager. What has happened to their little darling? The creature who appears late in the day for food, having slept like a baby for hours and hours, wearing outlandish clothing and loads of makeup, who grunts an answer to a question and then goes out without telling you where they are going is a typical teenager! It is hard to love such an imposition in your home. It is hard to stay connected to the 'real person' who is emerging from all these chaotic changes!

And then gradually another change occurs. The young person starts to express their own ideas on things; they listen to adults again and can start to debate; they are less abrasive and more thoughtful; they start to take an interest in looking clean and tidy as they spruce up for an evening out with a new friend; they shave and come out of the bathroom looking fresh and intense, with a concoction of wonderful smells around them; they start to want to earn their own money and take some responsibility for their wardrobe and other expenses.

Choices start to present themselves. What to do after school and where to find further training or work, or University? The young person is preparing to leave the nest and create their own life. They are making their own life choices and starting to find their LIFE PURPOSE. They are growing up!

As parents we can support and observe this whole process, and marvel that the child we knew has come through the chaos of the teenage years and is still the person we loved and nurtured as a baby.

The 'Essence' of the individual remains the same, and is recognisable in the different stages to the perceptive and mature parent, from the first cry of the baby, to the wave goodbye as they leave home. Enabling this 'Essence' to become visible in a healthy way is the path of parenting.

"Our children are not our children. They are the sons and daughters of life's longing for itself...." quoted from K. Gibran, spells out the fact that we do not possess our children. We cannot control them. We can only enable them to become themselves, help them to find their own life path, and treasure those moments when we let go of expectations and perceive the true essence of our gifted children.

Chapter 26

Who am I?

This is a question which at some stage will be asked by each one of us, usually during our teenage years, sometimes subconsciously, but at other times uttered very clearly by a maturing young person.

How do we find out who we truly are and connect to our true nature and life purpose when we are surrounded by so many role models, false images and trends? It is hard to stand out from the crowd if you are unsure which part of you it is safe to expose.

I believe this to be the reason why so many teenagers act like a 'flock of sheep'. They are frightened of their own immense power, personality and gifts which lie just beneath the surface, and therefore negate these for a bland 'lookalike' image, which means they do not stand out from the crowd.

They are catching glimpses of their true self as they begin to mature and they cannot yet work with it fully. It is easier to try out different things which are the 'cool' thing of the moment.

Each generation has its fads and fashions, its trend setters and its icons. From the 1950's we had people like the 'Teddy Boys' and Elvis Presley, then the Mods and Rockers. The 60's had the Beatles, Flower Power and Hippies. In the 80's the Thatcher Kids and Yuppies started to emerge; the Boy Bands and things like the XFactor and Big Brother have influenced more recent teenagers. There are more and more urban tribes.

Then there are the favourite TV programmes which every generation latches on to; the Apprentice, Friends, Neighbours, Hannah Montana etc., etc.; the 'must sees' which are discussed at school next day.

Clothes fashions rate highly too. These are often linked to TV stars, or the latest dance routine or hair styles. Young people are under a lot of pressure to have the latest brand of trainers or the most up-to-date school bag even.

As parents it can be exasperating and extremely financially draining to have to provide all these latest fashion items; consumerism also seems to be penetrating into younger and younger age groups. How do you control the vast sums which can be spent on clothes, make-up, mobile phones, bags and shoes?

Apart from looking alike, teenagers nowadays need to communicate constantly with their friends. They do this via mobile phones, I-pads and Notebooks which they all seem to need to possess. This means that they spend more and more time looking at screens and writing short messages to each other. This can also eat up hundreds of pounds.

It is a phenomenon of our time that young people do not want to be alone. They constantly have to have the reassurance of others of their age group, even if this is not always positive, as happens in text bullying for example. To spend time alone is to have to face ones true self.

So all these devices and outer coverings of clothes, make-up and trappings are really a ruse young people have to avoid spending time with themselves and getting to know who they really are.

Young people are Soulful, i.e. in touch with their souls and deeper emotions. Life is ruled by the emotions, as a teenager, and these can either be black or white. It can be a little like living with someone with bipolar disorder at times! There are the sighs and sorrows of first love, especially if it is unrequited. Other emotions are felt strongly too. Anger, happiness, loneliness; and these pass across the countenance like the ripples on the sea on a stormy/ sunny day. It is never dull living with a teenager!

Poetry and music or acting becomes important as an outlet for these emotions. Sometimes school productions of plays can be deeply moving. It is healthy to channel and enable these strong feelings to be understood and worked with. If they have no recognition they can become bottled up and clinical depression or eating disorders may start to appear.

As adults overseeing this age group we can be aware of these stormy emotions. They may ricochet off onto us and cause hurt and arguments which are not of our doing. It is important that adults keep a calm overview of any situation, and do not descend into these emotional storms with the adolescent. Practicing equanimity is the path of enlightenment with teenagers around!

Often there is not only emotion but also rejection of the parameters which have been set in previous years. Pushing against the boundaries is very common and this represents the teenagers wish to be in command of their own destiny.

It is a betwixt and between stage with one foot in childhood and one foot in the world of adults. It is a transition time, which if understood well can be exciting and educational for the adults as well as the youngsters.

It is more than anything a time when the true self of the person is being born. That can be through the <u>intellect</u>, the <u>emotions</u> or the <u>will,</u> or healthily a combination of all three.

The intellect and brain has the greatest oportunity at this stage of development to absorb new knowledge. The academic 'squeeze', which the majority of young people go through in our schooling system in England, with the taking of state exams, is a recognition that the brain is at its most active. It can absorb facts and figures and regurgitate them onto the exam paper. It is a learned skill which some become very proficient at, getting excellent results at GCSE and A level.

Other pupils may function very differently; using other parts of their brains, and may not have the ability to process these facts. Instead they may be extremely creative and artistic and need outlets which reflect these gifts. All schools need adequate facilities to encourage these children/young people. If they do not get these opportunities they become stultified and starved of creative outlets, and may suffer psychological problems as a result.

The third type of person is the doing/active type who enjoys sports, making things out of metal/wood, engineering or land work. These students may be streamed into the bottom group as failures, or taken out of school and put into some sort of college environment, or be offered apprenticeships for future work.

Most secondary schools currently do not provide adequately for all types of people. No-one is better than another; people are just different!

As a young person goes through secondary school they will be exploring 'Who am I?' in many different ways. It is important that there are sufficient outlets and variety in the school system to enable each young person to discover their own strengths and weaknesses. Not many schools in this country can boast that true diversity. It is often left to chance or supportive parents to find the right environment to enable the student to fulfil themselves completely.

After school activities such as team sports, swimming or music lessons are often fostered by parents at an early age, but then drop by the wayside and are considered 'uncool' as the child becomes a teenager.

At home teenagers may be surrounded by all kinds of influences and difficulties, which are part of their inheritance and will need to be worked through also, in order to come eventually to a place of freedom and individuation.

Such difficulties may be from inherited traits such as addiction, poor health, low IQ, poverty, or marriage break up. Nowadays there is also a trend towards the 'absent parent', when both parents are out working fulltime to pay for a nice house and everything that goes in it! This can be a form of real emotional trauma, which unfortunately has not yet been recognised by society at large or the government who financially encourage all parents to work.

Top earner's children may suffer the most emotional deprivation, as the parents are totally work/money focused with little time for the family. Children may be brought up by maternity nurses, nannies, prep school matrons and then boarding school masters, with little daily contact with the parents. It is assumed that these children will learn to 'cope' and will perhaps become our country's leaders. Emotionally they are often crippled. They will primarily have trained their brains in intellectual thought, with little emphasis on their true gifts. Once they become 'adult' they have been trained in intricate thought and opinion, but emotions have never had time to mature or ripen, and be worked through in a healthy way.

Teenagers need a parent to refer to almost more than a toddler does, although if firm foundations have been laid in babyhood and young childhood and the growing child feels secure and loved with non-anxious parents available and listening when they need them, then a mature teenager can feel a natural growing independence and cope with coming in from school alone, or being left to their own devices on some occasions.

'Who am I?' might also include an aspect of caring for a disabled or unwell parent. Many young people are silent carers who manage to do domestic tasks before and after school, and give emotional and physical support to a parent in a very adult way.

These children tend to become independent and resilient at a younger age, and very practically competent, but they can miss out emotionally on the sharing and fun of the teen years and may also suffer isolation and a feeling of being different as they grow up.

Watching the TV programme about the Millennium Children with Professor Winston, one can observe some of these fascinating traits in a group of children who were all born at the same time, but from very different backgrounds.

Some parents in the last TV programme, looking at the 13 year olds, described a huge sense of LOSS, as their children become independent teenagers. They wanted to keep the closeness of childhood and did not want to LET GO of the young person stepping into their teens, with their new interests and secret lives.

Whatever sort of relationship you have had with your offspring as a child, expect big changes in this relationship as the teens start. There may be battles, or withdrawal, or manipulation to win points, or, more positively, a growing closeness almost like that to a sister, especially between mothers and daughters. Sharing clothes is a sign of this new relationship.

It is important to try and create one-to-one 'special times' when these new relationships can be fostered. An activity holiday or long weekend away may heal rifts that have developed and create a new mutual respect. Either parent may feel the benefit of these special times away with just one teenager.

In African tribes, the young men go with their fathers and the other men into the bush for some time and learn the hunting and warrior skills which were needed for survival. They go through a ritual of circumcision and after that do not share a hut with their mother or the other women, but become young warriors themselves. This is a true 'Rite of Passage'.

In our society we can also try to find new Rites of Passage for our young people; appropriate rituals which can mark the end of childhood and the beginning of the 'going out into life' phase.

When I was 13, I went to confirmation classes and was prepared to take my first communion as a Christian. This service was a Rite of Passage, recognised by the church. Each child had a special gift and witnesses of family and friends at this occasion, and a special meal afterwards.

In some schools the first ball or dance is celebrated with much colour; limos, special dresses, and photos in the local paper!

A forest, 'boot' or cadet camp or the Dartmoor Ten Tors expedition can give a youngster such an experience too; of entering the 'world of men'. Their strength is being stretched to the limit.

My parents also sent me across Europe alone on a train on my 13th birthday to stay with a German family for 6 weeks. This may seem dangerous nowadays, but at the time was not thought to be so. I had to learn a new language and cope with myself in a totally strange environment for the first time. It was a very growthful experience which I still vividly remember! I was learning about the 'Who am I?'

Love is a loosely used word nowadays but in the context of parenting it is this above all else which enables the young person to answer the question of 'Who am I?'

By feeling real acceptance of the young person, 'warts and all', and not constantly criticising or putting them down, but really encouraging and praising them, they are more easily able to learn to love others, and feel self-esteem, or self-love. Without this sense of love, or self-worth they will not develop into whole healthy adults or discover for themselves 'Who am I?'

Chapter 27

Physical Care of Teenagers

When we look after a baby as their parent they are completely reliant on our nurturing and total bodily care (refer to my book 'Natural pregnancy and childcare'). As our children get older, as parents we teach them how to care for their own needs, by instruction and copying. By the time they are teenagers mostly all physical needs are now independent.

However this is not a process which just happens naturally but must be gently encouraged and the parent must be conscious at all stages of *how* they teach the basic skills of washing, grooming and keeping oneself healthy. It is ultimately the parents who will help to instil good habits which will last a whole lifetime and ensure that the body which they helped to produce is a worthy 'temple' for the entire lifetime of the individual.

I use the word temple intentionally as this is a House of God. Whatever our beliefs or religion as we grow up, as parents we can help to instil a sense of self-worth in the body itself. It is the tool which as an integrated part of us enables us to fulfil our life purpose and learn and grow through all our experiences.

Reverence for material matter seems to be disappearing from our culture. It starts with reverence for our own bodies. If we hate our bodies, as many young people do, then how can we care for them, nourish them and use them adequately for our life's work? Sickness will be the eventual outcome of these negative feelings.

As a baby/small child, parents can play with and admire the physique of the child, encouraging them to use it in many different ways. Washing times should be regular and fun, without neurosis or concern.

Caring for teeth, finger nails and hair is equally important with young children. To make it a part of every day or week routine bodily care, parents instil those habits gradually into the children. Without becoming overly conscious children can feel happy with how they look before going off to school. They can have their lovely clean long hair braided or put in a pony-tail; they can have lovely natural shampoo to wash it, which smells good and doesn't sting their eyes. Hair washing can be made fun, with games. If the parent always dyes or perms their hair this gives a strong message to the child that nature is not good enough somehow. Using natural tints (e.g. Naturtint) not only is healthier for the body, but better for the environment. These can be suggested to a teenager wanting to experiment.

Teenagers *will* want to try out the latest styles and fads and one's reactiveness (or not) to what they have done, and an HONEST response as to how it looks, may enable them to choose wisely in the future. Many heads of hair get ruined by chemicals during these years, because the parents are either stroppy themselves, or not caring about their own appearance.

Make-up is used increasingly from an early age in our society. Without seeming to be 'old fashioned', teenagers can be encouraged to use natural products which not only are better for the environment, but also keep natural young skin healthier. The skin is an organ which balances the toxins in the body. If it is blocked by chemicals then the body cannot excrete adequately and may become more toxic which could lead to sickness.

One example is the use of spray deodorants which are very popular in young teenagers. They contain aluminium (and also propellants which are bad for the environment) which if used long-term causes heavy metal toxicity and can clog the underarm pores, even leading to breast cancers. Instead of this, one can encourage the use of a crystal stick, which can be bought from good chemists and health stores, which simply neutralises the sweat and stops odours.

Hauschka, Weleda and several other good firms, produce make up with purely natural ingredients. They are expensive but a little goes a long way, and you could buy your teenager some as a birthday present.

Without meaning to offend, go back to your own teens in your memory and think about how you cared for your body. Did you copy your parents in everything, or did you try to do the opposite? Were there rows about how you looked, what you wore, or what you did to your hair, or how much makeup you put on? These memories may give you a clue as to how to respond now; with equanimity!

Teenagers also suffer from Spots! These are usually on their faces but can break out anywhere on their body and can be itchy or full of puss, or 'blackheads'. Many creams exist now to counter these unsightly break-outs, which are primarily caused by the changing hormones.

However the approach which can be more helpful is to heal from the 'inside-out'. Fresh fruit and vegetables, especially eaten raw, contain vitamins which are healthy for the skin, and eating plenty will enable the skin to balance itself. Drinking plenty of fresh water too will help excretion. Taking a walk out in the fresh air at least once a day will help skin, and a twice daily cleansing routine will be important.

Firms such as 'Lush' which are fun and trendy can help with advice on 'face scrubs' made of natural plant ingredients. Hauschka products are excellent too.

Eating garlic regularly may also help to cleanse the system.

Things to avoid if you have spots are;

- Sugar, including sweets and chocolate
- Tea and coffee
- Lots of dairy foods, strong acid cheeses
- Using lots of make-up, cheap creams and lotions; cover up creams, which only clog up the skins pores
- Environmental pollutants; putting your dirty hands on your face, chalk dust, felt tips or inks, petrol fumes

If the spots are extreme a deep balancing with acupuncture or reflexology might help the hormonal balance of your teenager.

Care of nails and teeth is equally important. Instilling the twice daily habit of teeth brushing, using suitable size brushes and a natural children's toothpaste, will give your child a message that it is good to do this as part of life. Often teenagers have to have elaborated dental orthodontics and this can be a danger for teeth if they are not precise with their cleaning habits. Many teenagers start to have fillings from eating too many sweets and drinking Coke, (a tooth left overnight in Coke completely dissolves!) and the amalgam fillings can cause long-term toxicity of mercury in their bodies. It is better to pay for white fillings instead, if possible.

Children can be taught how to clip their own nails too and clean them out, and not bite them. Nail biting is most often a sign of an anxious child and needs to be observed and helped, not criticised or condemned. A happy fulfilled child will usually stop the habit naturally. Painting the nails with lacquer will weaken them long-term and stop them 'breathing' naturally. This has become very popular recently; especially nail art and extensions using glues. Schools can help here, by forbidding the wearing of nail varnish.

Feeling their genitals, and getting pleasure from doing it, is a natural thing for young children to do. I have seen parents spank their child and tell them it's dirty! What sort of message does that give to a child naturally exploring their bodies' sensations for the first time? It should be mentioned though that you don't do it when Auntie is there; or maybe not in the school playground! Exploring your body is considered a private thing in our society.

Teaching your growing child about the sexual changes which are pending is one of the most important things to help them through this time of change. If it is done too early, which tends to happen at present, then the child will have an unhealthy absorption with sexual things too soon, but if left too late, a young teenager may be left with important questions and have to cope with the hygiene essentials of having their periods, and embarrassing situations may occur at school. Parents can watch for the signs of mood swings, breast changes and body hair and the monthly menstruation will not be far behind. Buy your daughter some good body-shaped towels, which will not leak, which she takes to school in a pretty little bag. Sometimes early periods can be very heavy. Tell them about washing, and showering more often when they have a period and how to cope at school. Dried blood can smell strong and needs to be dealt with to avoid your child getting teased. Blood on school dresses can be agony, so taking spare underpants and even a dress to school may sometimes be necessary.

If your child gets bad period pains these can be helped with a hot water bottle and lying down for a couple of hours. Some children never have these problems, while others suffer badly. Herb tea, made from Melissa (lemon balm), can help the cramps, and other homeopathic medicines can be prescribed to suit your child's constitution.

Having a period is not an illness though. It is a wonderful maturing process and means the young teenager is potentially a woman. This could be marked in some special celebratory way. My daughter was allowed to have her ears pierced when she got her first period. A friend's daughter had a party!

Boys equally go through big sexual changes, and it is best if their father or another close older male friend can tell them about things like wet dreams and sexual urges. It is amazing how strongly the hormonal influences can drive young lads. My son, while studying psychology at University, informed me proudly that boys in their teens suffer the same as acute, constant Pre Menstrual Tension! Testosterone can make boys feel pent up, aggressive and restless. Physical outlets such as sporting activities can help this pent up energy be channelled in a good way.

If your teenager goes through an 'allergic to water' phase, as some do, especially boys, it is a good idea to bargain a minimum amount of cleansing, for example a shower and hair wash on two nights a week, which is adhered to strictly. Again one can ask oneself what is going on that the lad does not want to care for himself, or love himself at all. Being firm and consistent early on will avoid battles of will over these issues.

It is lovely to see young children exposed to light and fresh air in a natural way, playing by a river or at the seaside, or in the garden paddling pool, without any self-consciousness. Our society currently tends to cover children up at all times to prevent burning. This may mean that your child is not getting the necessary light to build strong bones. Rickets used to be a problem, but apparently can also affect modern children.

Check out the air quality in your area and how long the burning time is. Apply a good natural cream regularly and allow your children to enjoy the freedom of nature, as we used to. Never allow your child to burn though. Wearing sun hats is almost more important than creaming, as it is the head which suffers from too much sun and overheating.

A mention must be made of a more negative aspect of childhood, and that is abuse. If we are trying to enable children to have a loving, natural relationship with their growing bodies, what sort of damage does it inflict when another human being abuses them, often in a sexual way, using warped emotional tactics to do so? Their bodies are no longer revered and sacred, but are the object of another adult's sick impulses. Physical abuse has been around for as long as we know and is often found in close families, not only done by sick people out in the streets. It is a sign of LACK of LOVE towards that child. Those closely associated with it are often in denial, which makes it all the harder for children to share this pain within the family.

As a society we need perhaps to rethink the punishment for those adults who are sick. Instead of feeling extreme anger and despising them, should we not feel huge compassion for an adult who has so little respect for their own and others' 'temples'? Can we help them to learn to love themselves more? In any case society should be protected from reoffenders. Many child abusers are walking around free in our cities with no supervision or follow up after early prison discharge. Is our current prison system the best treatment?

The child also will need much healing after having this experience. Often the truth only comes out as an adult, so therapy will be about learning to self-love. If left untreated the abused child/teenager may self-destruct; either outwardly with razor blades or inwardly by psychological traumas or eating disorders. Sadly there are many such young people in our society at present, who cannot come to a healthy place of care of their own bodies, because of anxieties and traumas in early childhood.

Tidiness is an area which often causes parents concern as their children grow older. Training is of the utmost help here. This can be done from early childhood without obsession, anger, nagging or emotional blackmail! Taking the time to clear up toys and clothes each evening with your young children, making it into a game before bedtime, will instil good habits. Telling them constantly that they are naughty to make a mess will have the opposite effect!

Allowing your school child to choose special new paint and furniture for their bedroom will give them a sense of respect towards their environment and also that their newly painted room is their own space to be cherished. Providing enough storage space, in the form of colourful boxes, drawers and easily reached wardrobes with hangers, is important as a messy child needs encouragement to become more orderly.

Children vary greatly in how tidy or untidy they innately are. A very untidy child may have real difficulties experiencing their bodies in the space around them and may need some therapeutic help, such as massage or dance movements, to 'grow into' their bodies more harmoniously. Others will benefit from extra time spent one-to-one each evening settling them down, folding their clothes for the next day, sorting out their school bags, putting their books and toys to bed carefully.

Many young people nowadays suffer from disharmony of left and right brain orientation, which not only gives them problems in reading and writing but also in spatial awareness. There are special therapeutic exercises which can be done to help this.

When you have teenagers, physical elements of care should already be well established into the daily habits of your offspring. If not, you can do very little now to help the progress except by gentle encouragement and huge praise if you see them making an extra effort.

It is not easy living in total chaos as a teenager; having to find enough socks to wear, trying to sort out a school uniform etc., looking for that vital slip of paper with a phone number on it. Teenagers may even feel stressed by their own mess, although they will never let on! As the parent, providing a large rubbish bin (which they empty themselves) and a wash basket (which they also empty into the washing machine, and have instruction about sorting colours and fabrics, so they COULD do it themselves!) and insisting the floor is cleared, so that they do their own hovering once a week, may establish the boundaries of the 'tip'! Going in and doing it for them may seem like an invasion of their privacy and may cause resentment. It is 'their space' after all!

As a family with young teenagers, we established a weekly time for a clean-up. I did certain areas of the house, and then left the Hoover outside the teenager's door. Some hours later the house was more or less cleaned! Keeping a regular time to do it was the key to success. I haven't heard how my children responded, in hind-site!

Other areas of the house can be equally kept tidy to a greater or lesser degree by establishing a few house rules early on in the child's life. They observe you, both parents, practicing these and it becomes the 'norm'; shoes off at the door, putting dirty plates/cups into the sink or dishwasher, hanging up coats, having a place for school bags. These are then the norms, the house rules.

Another rule we instigated early on in the children's life was to say where we were going and what time we would be back. If there was going to be lateness for any reason, we phoned. This was before the days of mobile phones! It was a courtesy to the cook, as the meal would be on the table at a certain time.

Chapter 28
Nutrition of teenagers

This leads me on to the question of food and teenagers. Our way of growing, developing, changing, and utilising energy for work and life is to take Energy from all around us in the form of food, light and fresh air (Ether) and transform it into our own bodily needs. If this process is not supported adequately in all aspects then the body rapidly becomes sick and cannot sustain life any more.

Unfortunately this very basic process is totally misunderstood in our current society and the government, health organisations and individuals are doing all they can to redress this in our very sick society, before we have a generation of invalids! Obesity has got to epidemic proportions in Britain and America. Jamie Oliver is passionate about school meals, which is the main daily nourishment of most teenagers. Magazines from stores such as Sainsbury's and Tesco's constantly are encouraging and educating us with 'healthy slimming recipes'!

Because of advertising, lack of parental care and nourishment (love) on a huge scale, and the food industry, which takes basic ingredients and transforms them into all manner of appetising, tasty, chemically filled 'rubbish food', we have now bred a generation of young people who prefer a burger, chips and Coke to a wholesome meat or fish and three vegies, which the war-time generation thrived on. Our current long-livers where those who ate well as children (between the two World Wars,) eating natural food which was grown without chemicals or additives.

It has been proven in recent research that certain foods can cause extreme behaviour patterns in young people, for example certain colourings and additives can exacerbate schizophrenias; even violent behaviour patterns have been found to improve dramatically with healthy food. Sugar often can cause outbursts of anger or aggression, and alcohol is known to cause very disruptive behaviour patterns.

Soft drugs are also the trigger of much aggression, lack of will power and personality changes in our young people, and are becoming a huge problem of our society at present. Recent research has found evidence that children who regularly smoke dope are less intelligent and suffer more psychological problems than those who don't. Parents can either help or hinder their children in resisting this readily available substance, by education and example.

Smoking tobacco is also something which is 'cool' amongst teenagers, and can then become a habit which is hard to break. Schools and parents working together can help the spread of this habit which is often forced upon children by peer group pressure. Helping a child to quit once a habit has formed can be much more difficult than prevention in the first instance.

Lack of Vitamins, particularly Vitamin D, and also Omega oils, notably Omega 3 can have profound effects long-term, not only on behaviour and learning patterns of teenagers, but also on fertility and conception of the next generation. Our diets are very poor in nutrients because of the fertilisers and over use of the soil for intensive food production, meaning that many teenagers on an average diet are in fact lacking these vital nutrients. Added to this is the reaction of the brain to excess sugars, especially in fizzy drinks with added fructose, and we have a strong case to understand the deteriorating behaviour of teenagers in our schools and colleges.

As parents the best thing you can do to care for your growing children is to provide healthy nutrition, in the form of regular, fresh organic meals, served and eaten together as a family at regular intervals throughout every day. I mention eating together as the shared meal also provides an essential social environment for sharing the ups and downs of the day, bonding as a family group and enjoying the quiet which such a mealtime induces. To eat with a tray in front of the TV or 'on the hoof' is neither good for the digestion nor the family unit as a whole. Mealtimes can become fun. It is not the time to debate in an aggressive way, or start to criticise the teenager for their behaviour!

If your young teenager suddenly starts to resist eating breakfast you can insist that they have at least a Smoothie before going off to school. This can be made by the parent and include an apple, or pear, some varied berries according to season, some almonds, ground up pumpkin, sunflower or flax seeds (which can be bought ready ground up). For extra vitamins you could add some powdered wheat grass (fairly tasteless) or some alkalising 'green powder'. Multivitamin powder can be added and even some Udo's Choice mixed oils, high in Omegas, or some vegetable protein powder. This will provide a complete meal for the morning and send them off with all the protein, carbs, fats, vitamins and minerals which their growing bodies require. It can be drunk in a sleepy state between their bed and the front door!

Healthy breakfasts can include eggs, or fish in various forms; and whole-grains, as in porridge, muesli, or healthy 'bars', and fruit are also good. A child who does not eat breakfast cannot spend a profitable morning in school and maintain concentration. Even pancakes and waffles are better than no breakfast! The young person should definitely not drink tea or coffee, or be encouraged to take a chocolate bar or a can of coke to drink on their way to school, which I observe almost every day as local children go to school, from my kitchen window! Bowls of cereal and white toast are highly processed foods, with added vitamins and cannot give the Energy which a young body is requiring for fast growth.

Lunchtime meals vary according to the school. It is safer therefore to provide a packed lunch, which the teenager can learn to make themselves. Peer pressure is huge in schools, but eating a healthy pasta or rice salad with chopped raw vegies, or making homemade brown bread sandwiches with chicken, sardines and mixed salad could become the vogue if eaten with enough confidence. Your teenager can actually become a trend setter if so inclined! How you get this to happen is your skill as a parent, built up over years of education and love. A child who has confidence and self-esteem will not mind eating healthy food in front of others!

When the teenager comes home from school always have something ready to eat and drink. "Mum, I'm starving! What's for tea?" is the real cry of a hungry growing body which has not had enough calories during the day. Rather than tucking into bought cakes, toast and jam, and more Coke (all sugary foods), try if possible to provide a really good sustaining snack, again with nuts or seeds in some form, whole grains and some protein, and perhaps a piece of fruit too. This might be at 4p.m and supper, a proper cooked meal, can be at 6.30-7p.m. They might even need something before bedtime too, especially if they have been active and outside all evening.

At weekends it is better if possible to eat the main meal at midday as the body digests better at this time rather than having a late meal. Drinking water with food is not good as it dilutes the digestive enzymes, but plenty of plain water should be drunk between meals. Again this is training from a very young age. Squash and fruit juices are full of sugar, very fattening and not nutritious. The only exception is pure fruit juice drunk fresh instead of a piece of fruit, which should be limited to a glass a day. In the USA sugar is even added to this! Always read the labels!

Fads and diets are part of becoming a teenager. We are bombarded with images of skinny females acting as models and very few normal healthy individuals can look like this! If your teenager is putting on weight then looking at their calorie intake and suggesting some changes, such as a simple GI diet for a while will not only improve their health but slim down the extra inches.

No way should a child be allowed to starve or do extreme dieting as this only suppresses the metabolic rate and causes more problems later on. Parents can help their teenagers best by educating themselves in dieting. Patrick Holford has some very sound advice and can be recommended highly. You can provide the ingredients that are healthy, as you do most of the shopping, and encourage your teenager to make educated choices.

They will also perhaps like to take a turn at cooking for the family sometimes, and this can be encouraged. Being creative in this way is very fulfilling for some youngsters, especially if they have a captive appreciative audience! A parent who denies the teenager a chance to learn cooking skills does them no favours at all, as we all have to learn to fend for ourselves at some stage. Learning it in the first term of college, away from home for the first time, can be traumatic! This applies to both boys and girls.

Anorexia needs to be mentioned as a serious and on-going problem of teenage nutrition. Because so many teenagers have a compromised diet and an unhealthy relationship to food, slimming may tip them into this serious illness. The mind/body connection is now recognised in this condition by doctors and psychiatrists. Children taken into hospital with this condition may receive counselling, as well as force feeding. But what is really going on? The child has started to reject their very life existence on earth, and is rejecting their 'temple'. Treatment should therefore be centred on LOVE and enabling the child to cope better with their life as it is unfolding. Peer pressure is also an element in this condition and friends may go on diets together and end up anorexic.

Helping them to connect to the earth, by being out in the fresh air, being around animals, planting seeds, taking in the sun and light is important. Obviously they are physically frail, but should not be kept indoors, as a friend's sister was told by her doctors recently. Gradually a love of the earth and their own existence on it will return, given the right therapy.

Obesity is the other extreme which is becoming much more common as a severe illness. This leads to Diabetes and is also an eating disorder. Instead of limiting just food, youngsters can be taught about quality of food, and healthy choices, and be encouraged to use their obese bodies in a more active way, so they are more integrated, and start to enjoy exercise more. Poor infant feeding can contribute to obesity in the teenage years.

Laying the basic patterns for a healthy lifestyle occurs in early childhood. What happens into the teens and how the young person takes up what has been taught earlier and adopts it as their own life habits depend greatly on the respect the teenager has for their parents. Respect is an innate ability to perceive the good in another person, without criticism. Hopefully the adult's own behaviour will earn them the respect that is due.

Eating habits are able to be changed by motivated adults and these changes can be reflected positively in their growing children, out of respect.

Chapter 29

Exercise in the teens

Teenagers can lose the ability to move their bodies in a healthy way, whereas others find pure joy in learning a sport or bodily skill. At around 12, especially in girls, their bodies may become loose and awkward, as their limbs grow fast. They bump into things and often feel tired and lethargic. 'Growing pains' are a phenomenon where the muscles and ligaments are overstretched as the long bones grow rapidly. Too much or too little weight will also affect this.

Most schools provide a structure of games and gym in the curriculum and these times can be important at enabling the teenager to use their body in a harmonious way. Running, jumping, balancing, using the apparatus in various ways, ropes and swings, as well as slow warm up exercises and stretches are all important for young bodies. Keeping the body toned up and fit is probably the most important thing in keeping well during these growth years.

Many schools also spend much time and effort on team games. These may include football, rugby, hockey, cricket, basketball, netball, rounders, tennis or cross country running, and swimming or other more unusual ones like lacrosse, baseball, fencing, or martial arts. Each different sport appeals to a different type of youngster, so choice and variety are important.

Sporting facilities vary according to school income and some of the most varied sports can be found in public and independent schools. A child who starts to excel in a sport will gain huge self-esteem and feel good in their fit body. Encouragement may be needed for the less sporty children to find a suitable outlet which is not so tough or aggressive, for example dance routines or swimming.

Every single child will feel better and more physically 'integrated' if they can do some form of sport. If your child is rejecting this outright see if there is another avenue which appeals to them, even if it is some out-of-school activity like sailing, canoeing, snorkelling, archery, horse-riding, rock-climbing, yoga or tai chi. To be good at something physical is important even if it takes a bit of time to find the right thing. It is about feeling right in your own body. Young children, unless physically impaired, have this naturally, but with teenagers it is important not to lose it.

Working as a team is often appealing, but your youngster may prefer something more individual, where they are pitting themselves against themselves, or the elements.

Walking is the very simplest and most natural of exercise, but one which is becoming increasingly rare in our culture of cars. Huge numbers of children never walk to school even. To take a walk regularly out in nature, combining this perhaps with some fun, a picnic, a treasure hunt, or some climbing, will do the whole family a lot of good. It is sad to see teenagers sitting at home at weekends, doing stuff on the internet while their parents are out walking the dog! It will also provide a time for conversation, which seems to flow more easily when you are on the move together.

Exercise is not just a matter of finances. Simple fun and exercise is possible without any monetary outlay. Being a little imaginative as parents when the children are younger will encourage imaginative outdoor play as they get older and more independent. Enabling teenagers to go out and play, because you live in a suitable environment is important. They are gaining a healthy relationship with the earth on which they live. If they are taught to respect the earth and enjoy the many gifts which it brings, they will be able to care for our planet much better as they grow older and wiser.

They can learn to read the changing weather patterns from the clouds and wind, they can follow streams and orientate in landscapes, they can feel danger intuitively, as an animal learns to sense danger with a '6th Sense'.

Suitable activities might include climbing trees, making camps and shelters in the forest, tracking games done in groups, caving, making safe camp fires and cooking meals for themselves, night-time experiences watching nocturnal animals, helping on a local farm, walking to a picnic spot, hill walking from youth hostel to youth hostel, or riding their bikes out into nature, adventuring ever further with a map and compass. They will need help and supervision at first, but once trust and knowledge are there they can be left ever freer to explore the local environs.

But what about danger, I hear you say! Nowadays we are bombarded with sad stories of children who are molested or murdered. How do you train a growing child to sense danger and act in a responsible manner to any person who is not fully healthy in their mind? Teach them the golden rules of observation, not going with a stranger, taking the precautions of having a mobile phone, some money, of telling someone where they are.

Fear attracts! That is a Law of Energy. If you fear a dog it will come and bite you! If you are frightened of being molested you are much more likely to attract this into your Energy field. Trust is a great thing. Whatever you sense this protecting Energy to be, if you open yourself to it as an adult you will become aware of its power. A child can develop a close relationship with this guiding protective Energy and will feel safe. Help your child to feel safe rather than fearful. We often pass on our own fear to children in an unhealthy way.

Chapter 30

Emotional care of the teenager

There are many areas which we need to consider in the emotional nourishment and care of our growing children. Families differ very much in this and it is often this aspect of childrearing which is most fiercely disputed. We tend to follow in the footsteps of our own parents and also the 'norms' of the society in which we live.

Teenagers will often compare their parents with other friends' parents, and healthy debate may arise from differences in upbringing. "It's so UNFAIR" can often be heard in arguments.

An area which is often fraught in the teenage years is the subject of pocket money. We give our youngsters their own money because we want them to become aware of the value of this form of Energy and to use it wisely as they grow up. We give it to them in love as we give them so much else. It does sometimes however become a bargaining tool. If the teenager has a sense of responsibility then money can be given in a lump sum perhaps once a month to be spent on certain items which are then chosen by themselves, such as clothes, shoes or presents.

If the teenager does not yet have that maturity then it is pointless for them to have substantial pocket money. They need first to learn the value of things, and what they *need* rather than *want*. Each individual is different in how soon this maturity is reached. Giving in to the child's every wish when they are younger will build an attitude of 'I can have whatever I want from my parents'. Children need to understand that money has to be earned and is a form of Energy exchange.

Some parents will allow their children to earn money by doing a job. I feel strongly that children can learn to help their parents anyway because they are a part of the family, and work is seen as something worthwhile, without always needing payment. If children are given chores from an early age onwards, such as laying the table, wiping the dishes etc. they become a part of the family work ethic. Extra jobs like perhaps cleaning the car, or mowing the grass could be used as paid work if the young person wants to earn some money for a special item. They can be helped to save up pocket money each week for something special. It then has more meaning.

Taking money away because the teenager has broken rules is a strong tool which is often used by desperate parents, but is it educationally sound? A loaded question!

Punishment is something which may be justified in certain situations, if the teenager has pushed their boundaries too far, but what is the most appropriate punishment for each misdeed? To give an imaginative punishment which will teach the teenager how their actions have affected the other person or thing is sometimes a challenge, but much more beneficial. To rant and rave in anger does nothing. To find out the motives behind their actions and try to understand what was happening emotionally is the first step. To talk about it calmly after they have thought about it will help. They do not enjoy doing wrong! Trust that your teenager does have a conscience! How you have dealt with your 2-3 year old will reflect now how you treat your teenager; except that now the teenager can communicate and has logical thought!

Corporal punishment has become illegal, even with your own children. In schools no physical touch is allowed. Sadly it still happens though, that children are shaken to death and one not infrequently observes children being smacked. Were you smacked as a child? What do you think of a short sharp tap to create a boundary for behaviour? Observe a lioness with her cubs. They will cuff them gently, but we as humans should be able to communicate with speech. At what level do you communicate with your own children?

Arguing endlessly and point scoring has little value, especially if the teenager learns that eventually you will give in and they can have their way. Pushing boundaries in this way is common and hard work if your teenager is particularly single-minded. Try to think through calmly want you will and won't accept beforehand, and then _don't_ give in. If you do it will be more difficult the next time you argue. Again it is very like a toddler having a tantrum. You can feel emotionally battered but don't give them their way, or else they will soon learn how to manipulate you.

With teenagers always try to be reasonable, and understand what pressure they are facing from peer groups. This is perhaps the most difficult aspect of this stage as you have little control on what they are encountering in the playground or after school. If your teenager is emotionally secure and feels totally loved and respected by you, they will have less need of conforming to their group, and may even become trend setters themselves. These strong individuals can be a very positive influence in a group of young people.

One of the biggest traumas or excitements your teenager will go through, and one which may perhaps undermine their confidence, is the first love experiences and then perhaps the sadness of being 'dumped'. Falling in love is a magical moment that most people will remember for the rest of their lives. It may be a love from a distance, a platonic or friendship love, or may become sexual.

Preparing your teenager thoroughly for the physical implications of making love, or having full intercourse for the first time, ensuring they know all about contraception and the dangers of pregnancy and infections may seem to some like the remit for their teachers. But nowadays it is often helpful to reinforce this information from home as it keeps communication open and you know that they have all the facts correct.

Making love always includes the possibility of a third person, a baby! Society's trend that teenagers have this experience younger and younger, makes this ever more of a reality. It used to be unusual to have sex before marriage. Now it is the norm. Teenage pregnancies, terminated by abortion, can leave a lasting trauma on the young person, both emotionally and physically. Much better that they do not need to go through it!

The moral aspects of becoming a parent with a young family, and the realities of a stable relationship between a boy and girl, are sometimes brushed over, both by the school and parents. True love is not the emotional feelings which we get; the excitement and heart flutters which we hear about in all the songs. It is a much deeper experience which comes from maturing, and it also has an ideal image which teenagers aspire to.

Sex is often blown out of proportion by hearsay and young men particularly can spend a lot of time thinking about it. Conversations about the sexual feelings they are having, in relationship to their emotions, may be helpful.

Open discussions on these feelings and hearing about adult's journeys into love and life experiences may help to balance the strong emotions of youth. Reading biographies may be helpful too.

One of the very biggest influences on modern culture and morals is television and the film industry. It has become the very fabric of our society, with trends and fads emanating from the various programmes that youngsters watch every day.

I have mentioned the very detrimental influence that these programmes and images have on our children, both in terms of content and also more seriously on their concentration span, imagination, and communication skills, not to mention eyesight and hearing.

With young children it is possible and commendable to strictly limit or avoid watching television. As a teenager in our society today it is hard if there is no television at all in the home, but parents can ensure that it is not on all the time, that there is control as to which programmes they watch, and that they do not have one in their bedrooms. Doing homework with it on as background noise and distraction should be avoided and watching a programme should only be allowed after homework has been completed. Late evening watching gets more and more unsuitable for teenagers, and sleep deprivation is a problem, as pupils are tired for school in the mornings.

Perhaps having a TV programme magazine and marking the things which each family member wants to watch at the beginning of each week might create an amusing debate! One or two programmes per day should suffice. At weekends perhaps a video could be chosen for all the family to watch together. Many of the popular teenage TV programmes are based on illusory scenarios of matchmaking, such as 'Neighbours' and 'Friends'.

I-pads, mobile phones and computer games are equally disruptive to family life. At school nowadays children are expected to work from computers. Teenagers rapidly learn these skills and can do their homework on the computer if necessary, but again the amount of time spent at the keyboard should be limited.

One very disruptive and negative influence on teenagers is the 'reality world' in Nintendo games which can be totally absorbing and very addictive. Better not to buy them in the first place!

A recent trend is listening to music with ear phones. It is now trendy to wear them all the time like an airline pilot. What effect is this having on their fine inner ear physiology, and also on their connection with the world around?

How, as a parent with a modern child, can one balance and control the use of these new communication methods? Developing alternative hobbies and interests diffuses the need to spend hours just chatting idly to friends in the evening on mobile phones, or watching hours of TV.

What things could be suggested and how do you get a sullen teenager to take them up?

Starting these hobbies at a younger age is the easiest way of enlivening your child's social and creative skills as a teenager. Introduce a new musical instrument when they are about 9-10. Establish regular times for practising it.

Encourage them to join brownies, guides or woodland folk, or take up a sporting activity after school. Having extra art lessons at about 11-13 with a small group of friends can be fun, or joining a youth theatre or dance troupe. Maybe learning a language or going on a foreign exchange for a few weeks, will give them confidence. Giving them a piece of your allotment and prizes for the best grown vegetables can be fun and productive.

Keeping pets, large and small, can be good as a regular commitment to caring for something. Dogs need walking every day, guinea pigs/ rabbits need feeding and cleaning, cats need feeding and stroking. A pony can be a real friend and a social outlet too, if you can afford one! If your child learns to do these things regularly they are also learning self-discipline and work habits.

All children are different and as a parent the skill is to provide and encourage the suitable hobby that suits your child's needs. Are they quiet and self-sufficient, or gregarious and physical? Do they enjoy reading and creative writing and how can that be channelled in the teenage years? Who are their best friends and what hobbies can be shared with them?

Changing schools at 11 can be disruptive for most children and often parents will blame the school for some of the behaviour patterns which follow this school move. In fact it just comes at the age where continuity is helpful for the child; so friends become doubly important.

Most parents with teenagers complain that they become a taxi service! This may be hard work and time consuming, but at least your teenager is enjoying a full social creative life and learning boundaries of behaviour and trust in the wider world, doing these various activities. Perhaps you can car-share with friends, or encourage your teenager to use public transport or a bicycle to get about? This also teaches them your attitudes to ecological issues and how to save vital resources. As they get older helping them to learn to drive is a good way to ensure they become independent and mobile, which to my mind is preferable to a motor bike!

Being available for your teenager, making time for evening discussions, helping with homework, talking about the ups and downs of the day are all ways in which you can help your teenager; being alert to their moods, keeping communication flowing, but not imposing or expecting them to be interested in your life either.

Teenagers are by definition 'selfish'. They are fully involved in their world and cannot yet see that you are anything but very embarrassing, old-fashioned, annoying and bossy! But they do still love you deep down!

Going to the cinema together, having a shopping spree, even attempting a family holiday together will cement relationships in a healthy way.

Emotional care does not mean imposing your will on the emerging adult. It means carefully observing and supporting where necessary. Encouraging and praising anything that is praiseworthy. It means being there when they suddenly crumble into children again over some small issue and want a cuddle and comfort.

Growing independence can be encouraged in the RIGHT MEASURE at the RIGHT TIME. This is individual for each youngster and can only be judged by you, their parent. You know if it is safe for your child to go to London with friends, or to a late party. You know how much you can trust them to keep in touch. These things have been gradually instigated over years of training from the cradle upwards and a healthy relationship with a teenager relies on healthy upbringing from young childhood.

Overcoming your own fears and hang-ups is very much a part of this process. If our parents were always fussing over us and telling us to 'Take care!' we have learned from their fear not to trust the Universe ourselves, and this attitude can easily be passed on to our teenagers. There is a big difference between being careful and responsible and being neurotic; between being free-and-easy and being fool-hardy. Observe how you are day-to-day with your children. Self-judge if you are at one extreme of this measure of trust, or at the other extreme.

'Letting go' of your children, physically and emotionally, involves LOVE which at its best perceives the growing individuality of the person and supports this maturation process. It is not about control or training; it is not about protection from danger or instilling fear; it is about ENABLING them to become themselves.

If you are having big problems with communication during the teenage years, do not give up. Never give up on a teenager; they are loveable and sensitive and wanting to do right, just as you are. One way forward may be to involve other friends, mature adults whom you trust to become 'surrogate parents' for a while. Having space away from you may enable them to become more able to express their angers and fears in a reasonable way.

Foster parents and social workers are society's answer to this dilemma, but take the young person out of the family where they are learning about themselves, and it may create more tensions. If possible, however difficult the situation becomes, keeping in touch with them is the most healing thing you can do. They are rejecting you, but you don't need to reject them. If the law needs to step in, family counselling is better than prison. A child becomes hardened and shut down by these experiences and may go on to become a criminal in adulthood.

Mental and physical problems can be healed before it comes to this. Ensuring a good diet, treating young children with love and firm boundaries, establishing rhythms of family life, integrating families into everyday activities and local groups, praising and enabling their uniqueness; all these things help to create a harmonious family life.

Chapter 31

Education for life

What happens during school times deeply affects our children. Therefore changes in education policies, teacher's habits and training are central to a healthy future generation. The government's spending is also central to the quality of education that children receive.

In recent years there has been a move towards more and more paperwork for teachers, a more structured curriculum and pressures for teachers to get their students through exams. One hears again and again from frustrated teachers who have given up their careers due to these changes. Teachers no longer have the time to teach!

Instead of training teachers to love and respect their pupils and see them as unique individuals who are in their care while they explore life and become adults ready to give back and change and help in our modern problems, teachers are given a remit to produce an educated product. How good a school is, is reflected directly in their exam results (and the OFSTED report). This is today's measure of success, irrespective of how integrated the pupils are as young people ready for a work life.

Not only is it a question of '*How* do we teach the teenagers?' but also '*What* do we teach them?'

Currently all pupils have to study English and Maths to a certain standard. Using English correctly is not just an historic journey backwards through literature, but also a living spoken language that we communicate with. How many children nowadays learn to articulate and love the sounds of the English language? Our 'speak' is now punctuated by popular slang such as 'OMG' and 'like', as well as many foul expletives! It is considered uncool and old fashioned to talk clearly and enjoy the use of a wide vocabulary. It is also a class distinction, no better than that of Henry Higgins fame! Our language has a rich heritage from several sources, Latin/French as well as Anglo-Saxon, with many nuances which can be enjoyed.

Teenage language is minimal, often copied from television or computer language which has now become common parlance. Having conversations with your offspring will help them to broaden their language use. Providing good books for each age as they learn to read is often left to teachers, but parents can encourage good reading also by visits to the library and books around the home.

Maths is often a subject which is disliked and feared by the less able. Finding a means whereby the mind can understand basic numerical concepts is the key to easy learning. Numbers are magic! And fun! They are in everything, the planetary movements, geometric forms, in the growth of plants and shoots, in physics at many levels. Teaching maths needs to be inspiring, and give one a concept of the vastness of the universe. Where is Infinity and how do you get there and come back again in numbers? This was fascinating to me when I was a teenager!

What about all the other vast subjects there are to learn about? Giving a young person the basic tools for survival in the world is often neglected, as the exam syllabus becomes more and more dominant in everything they study.

Some ideas for futuristic, practical education could include:-

- Nutrition and growing your own food; and then preparing good quality meals and the reasons for it.
- Relationships, family values, childcare, social interaction and problems, sex and love?
- Practical things in the home; how to mend a burst pipe, unblock a sink, change a plug, make a cupboard or bookshelf.
- Use of raw materials to create beautiful and useful objects, like pots, wooden things, woven and knitted things.
- Dealing with first aid situations and sicknesses without calling a doctor.
- Getting a mortgage or leasing a house. How do we buy and sell a property? If needed, can you build your own dwelling?
- How do we complete tax returns or applications for loans or benefits?
- What happens when you marry, get divorced, or need to be buried?

All these things could be called 'The School of Life'. They are all basic skills which we accrue through our own experience and which we would do a lot better if we had been taught! Sometimes friends and parents are not there to guide you through it.

The work ethic, or the will to work, is developed from a very young age, through activity and discipline. Our current attitude in most situations is that we have to work to earn money for things we want; a car, a house, clothes, I-pads, holidays etc. etc. There is little in our current society which shows us the VALUE of work in itself, for helping others and improving our environment.

The world of work is a complex one nowadays. There are infinite possibilities for jobs of various kinds, many of which are centred round sitting in an office in front of a computer. Most young people expect to go on to some form of higher education after school, College or University, which specialises them yet further to do a specific job. But what happens when there is a recession and the job market is tight? Many young people then take 'any' job which pays money for rent and food and beer and they may end up after 3-5 years hating it and feeling angry and stuck because they are not fully integrated with their real interests and skills.

Then a girlfriend turns into a wife, children come along, and mortgages demand that the job is stuck at, or else the job vanishes and the young person has to retrain and apply for further jobs.

But what about the REAL person, in all of this expectation? Where are their real talents; what is their true life purpose? Work is not always the obvious way to grow and express oneself. It may be through creativity, through social lessons learnt in diverse ways or through practical application.

In Germany, in some schools, teenagers do 'work experience' for 3 weeks each year from year 9-11 (15-17 year olds). They must choose and then apply for a post on a farm, in a social setting (hospital, nursery or institution), or a business environment, and write up their experiences afterwards. This not only gives them a glimpse into the world of work, but enables them to mature in many ways, becoming more resilient and self-reliant in a new situation, broadening their horizons before they go to University and specialise.

In England many pupils may take a 'gap' year after school which again helps them to mature and realise what their own potential is in life, beyond the shelter of the family home. Going out to a developing country and working with hunger and poverty can open their eyes to just how much material wealth we have in this country, and how we can appreciate it more and work with it better.

School trips abroad, apart from being socially enjoyable, do not have such an impact on the teenagers' development as going somewhere alone, where they are impelled to cope for themselves and learn further who they are.

Parents who have not had this experience themselves when young, may feel nervous at allowing their teenager to travel alone and go out into a strange and dangerous world. Even if the youngster is a bit lonely or stressed at times, the new experience can act as a stimulus for maturing and can be very helpful, enabling the teenager to appreciate their own home and parents if nothing else!

Everyone is different and there are no golden rules for one sort of education, but by giving support and encouragement in the right measure parents can help to ease over the problems which may occur at any stage of the child's school life. It is sad one hears that so many of our young people hate their school days and feel they were a total waste of time.

Creating a system of exams which recognises the various talents and diversity of pupils is the task of the education ministers. I heard only today that Britain wants to develop a 'Tech' exam which will encourage more practical students to achieve a qualification on leaving school. Hopefully it will be taught in an equally practical way.

Apprenticeships are a means of introducing more practical pupils into the world of work into vital industries such as engineering, plumbing and electricians. Without these skills we cannot function.

But other skills and training are falling behind sadly. Farming and horticulture, growing our food locally in a healthy way, is in crisis in this country because it is so undervalued. The care of our land is vital for the future health of the planet. Farmers struggle with government financial policies in agriculture, rather than the health of the soil being considered. Grants are given for growing commercial crops rather than asking what is appropriate for that particular piece of the earth. Sustainability will need to improve for future generations to survive.

Care of the elderly and frail is also very much undervalued and is the lowest paid work in this country, being done mainly by foreign workers. If it were given more respect and young people were encouraged, not to go into an academic nursing training done in universities, but to train in excellent hands-on care, we would have much less of a crisis on our hands in terms of caring for our Elders in a compassionate way.

These issues need to be tackled at government and local level, and introduced into secondary education, so that the next generation have the attitudes and skills needed to care not only for our growing numbers of older and sick citizens, but also for our sick earth, plants and animals, will is the future of all mankind.

Chapter 32

Going out into the world

The big step out into the stream of life usually happens at around 18 years, with young people choosing their study subject and what they want to do as a job. Education is seen very much as the stepping stone to employment and youngsters take their A level subjects with a future career and job in mind.

Is this the healthiest way of coming into a new working life? With all their talents and innate personal gifts and traits, how can they explore more fully who they are and realise their potential?

Parents can have a vital role in this. Exploring different avenues and keeping an open mind as to how the young person will fulfil their destiny will help them to link with their real personality and gifts, rather than taking up what is expected of them in terms of a 'proper job'. When I left school it was suggested that we either become teachers, nurses or secretaries (as girls,) or we might attempt University. Nowadays there are endless and confusingly large choices for employment and it is wise to have some advice from 'careers advice' before deciding. There are even tests to see what you might be good at.

Some young people go into the Forces as it is seen as an adventurous life with secure pension prospects; others go into the family profession or business as this is 'expected' of them. Many young people nowadays have a considerable period of unemployment after leaving school as the jobs do not fit their skills or wishes.

A maturing time from 18-21 is often helpful in deciding what is most appropriate. This could be spent doing some voluntary work, for example, with psychiatric patients, the elderly, working on the land, and charity work with children or disadvantaged young people. The chance to meet and work alongside dedicated adults is the most important thing, learning about the world of work and how it functions, but in a compassionate environment.

Often these years are spent either on the dole, still living at home and feeling disappointed in life and perhaps taking drugs or alcohol to excess, or at University or College, where academic studies are the priority, often only in one very selected direction of study. Bad habits and attitudes are formed in terms of work ethic.

Apprenticeships are gradually becoming more popular and the government has started to realise that this may be a way forward for less academic youngsters.

The Prices Trust does much good work in helping and encouraging young people to take up their passions and develop them further.

Nowadays many jobs in Britain are filled by foreign workers as they are more conscientious and thorough than British youngsters! We have literally bred a generation of lazy workers with high expectations of jobs in the city that pay well and have big pensions. Not everyone can aspire to £150,000 or so a year!

The recent crises in the banks at managerial level have highlighted some of these problems of 'illusion'.

So we can ask the questions

- What does our society need to heal itself?
- What skills do our young people need to create a better future for mankind?
- How can we all become more loving towards each other?

Without addressing these basic questions, we are quite likely to descend into further chaos, unemployment, recession, pollution and ill health. Only when things become extreme will we start to learn from our mistakes.

Already we have the answers to many of our errors and problems. We have invented new things to create a better world, but man himself is not yet changing to work with these inventions.

The old attitudes, that we still have to manufacture and produce goods in order to remain a healthy economy, are prevalent at Government level. Instead of looking at the health of the nation, our earth as a living organism, our plants, animals and children, we continue to look at the 'gross annual product' to measure our success as a country.

We need to wake up to the suffering of individuals, to the anger we see in our young people when their needs and ideals are not being met. They are the future.

Let us listen to them honestly and take heed, and enable them to grow to their full potential.

Chapter 33

Parent care

Letting go of our children at the right moment is the most important part of parenting. We can literally cripple them emotionally by our own need of them, if we hang on to them too long.

What right do we have as a human being to hang on to someone to the detriment of their freedom? Growing up is taking on freedom. If we have done a good job in parenting we can rejoice that our children no longer need us as they prepare themselves to step out into life.

It can be hard for parents to feel the loss of their 'babies' and some parents may try to compensate for this in various ways. Subtle depression may creep up if you have teenagers who are doing well and leaving home as confident young people. You may feel rejected or tired or at a loss in the evenings and resort to comfort eating, or watching large amounts of TV, or reading soppy novels, or even looking for a new partnership.

'Mid-life crisis' is the term sometimes given to this phase of parenting and may be very real for some. Depending on whom you are, and your maturity, you need to re-find or redefine your life.

Now it is your time again! If you are working full-time in a job already then this transition may not feel so huge, but for a dedicated full-on parent it may be right to start to look for some form of work or activity, to look at what you enjoy doing and the skills you have accrued. These may be very different from the ones you developed as a student before the children came along. I have met many mothers who take up totally new careers after their children leave home.

Depending on the age at which you had your children, this stage may even coincide with the menopause, which in itself is a huge shift of Energy and a massive transition.

Many parents nowadays are deciding to have their children later on in life, sometimes as much as ten years later than the traditional time of aged 20-30. If you have a teenager when you are in your 50's it can be demanding work both emotionally and physically.

Added to this you may also be dealing with aging parents who may need your attention and care, even if this is only from a distance.

Being a parent of a teenager is demanding and stressful, even if they are relatively 'easy' teenagers. You will be challenged in your beliefs, tested in your patience, drained of your financial resources, have your wardrobe raided, spend many evenings driving around in the car collecting them, and have to listen to their taste in music and be nice to their friends when they drop by for large meals on the spur of the moment!

Despite all this seeming negativity we all miss them terribly when they are not around. When the bags are packed for College or University, or their 'gap year' the house will seem strangely empty. When you go into their rooms the house will suddenly feel very big and unused. All this is quite normal, but be kind to yourself and know that the journey has been so worthwhile.

From becoming pregnant to the moment of leaving home you have been a parent dedicated to bringing up your offspring in the best possible way. You have taught them all you know and more. You have provided them with food, physical care, wisdom, laughter and the essence of who you are. They take that out into life with them and utilise it for their own lives.

'Parent care' is often negated but I strongly believe that a 'pat on the back' and some personal TLC will help you through this transition. Spend a bit of time finding out what you enjoy doing, where your strengths lie, and experiment with some new hobbies. Travel may open up your horizons yet further. Don't feel you have to rush into full time employment if you can't decide what your line of work should be. You may want to join a women's/men's group or take a short course in something.

Sadly our society has many financial and housing problems at present and many young people cannot afford to make the natural move away from home at the optimal time, as they have no resources to support themselves, no work and no chance of getting a mortgage.

Providing housing for your young adults provides a further challenge on the journey of creating a fresh relationship with your children. It is important to create this new relationship out of freedom. They are now adults with equal responsibility for themselves in life as you have. Treat them as adults and a new rich friendship can develop. Treat them as teenagers still and there will be resentments and problems sharing a living space. It is healthy and right that they grow away from you emotionally before they can come back as your friends.

As an adult reading this book you may have agreed or disagreed with some of the things written here or felt that they were a bit 'pie in the sky' and idealistic!

If you have your own teenagers you will have read this book hoping for some answers. The answers lie with you as parents.

How mature are you to help your teenagers to come fully into life? How do you react and behave as an adult in this crazy modern world? What do you eat, watch, smoke, drink, say or do, to give an example to your offspring?

Parenting is about becoming conscious too. It is the greatest learning tool we are given to become more whole ourselves. Observe yourself through their eyes and be grateful to them for pointing out your weaknesses. They are so honest!

Love them for who they are, not for what you want them to be or become. They are themselves, and have chosen your physical bodies as the tools for their further existence. The miracle of reproduction is not just about cloning. They will also have children who will have their own ideas and destinies.

Perhaps as they become adult parents themselves they will start to understand what you felt and did for them when they were children and teenagers. They will come to appreciate how much you offered them each day they were with you.

Sit back and feel happy and proud that you have done the most creative thing on this planet. You have enabled another human being to come into existence!

Chapter 34

Finding the link from Teens into Adulthood

A growing sense of the world around and a consciousness of morality and sense of 'self' is usually achieved by the time the young person is ready to leave school. They are now old enough to leave home, have a job, drive a car, and even be married. However it will be still several years until they gain life wisdom, or have a deeper sense of Life Purpose. They are still very vulnerable to outside influences and trends, may become easily led astray into bad behaviour patterns, time wasting or drink and alcohol.

This is the time when traditionally young people go to university or college. It is a maturing time, spent often in a strong peer group, when ideas start to be formulated. It is not surprising that some strong new impulses for society often come from students. They are at their peak of learning, absorbing and often also very idealistic. Society can do well to listen to young people, as truth often lies hidden in the angry outbursts or violence that we see in them.

On the TV we see images of young Muslims with guns, students demonstrating, football hooligans, young Germans taking down the Berlin wall, or city kids fighting the police and setting fire to buildings, stirring us to wakefulness of the problems which they perceive and we have grown accustomed to. They are the next generation and we would do well to heed their cries, even if they feel powerless to change what they see or feel is wrong in our society.

Because these young souls are searching for Truth, it is really important that they can be 'met' and understood by wise spiritual leaders to whom they look for guidance. So often they see only materialistic stuck selfish older people, who have joined the 'power gaining' behaviour which tries to overcome basic fears and puts up barriers to real human communication.

If they copy this behaviour, and try to make quick money or climb the power ladders, they become stressed too. How many 'Yuppies' these days suddenly wake up in their 30's and want to leave the city and try the 'Good Life'? Something in them subconsciously is unhappy with the status quo and wants to find a deeper meaning in life, but has lost the key to how to do this, often because the education they have received as they grew up has been so cramping of any life of the soul, concentrating as it does almost entirely on academic achievements.

The current World recession, society's poverty and social problems are reflecting this search for Truth. It is an outer manifestation of an inner soul condition, but is not recognised as such.

We see turmoil in many countries where young people are struggling to find new ways forward, as for example in Syria, Libya, Greece and many other parts of the world. Anger and chaos are often the status quo, with normal moral values being pushed aside for extreme behaviour, violence and a sense of desperation.

Currently house prices in this country have soared and youngsters are being *forced* into situations where they are living in community dwellings, sharing their space with others. It is seen as less than ideal to do this, as most parents would like their children to get onto the housing ladder and the security of a mortgage, but weirdly this is benefitting both the young people and the wider community generally.

If we live in shared housing we are reducing our energy consumption, and learning to Love each other, giving and taking in a sharing way. There may be opportunity of shared meals, car sharing and other supportive actions. Living alone, as many older people do in this country, especially after divorce, has meant a need of many more houses being built, which has many knock on effects on the natural environment and also on economics and energy consumption.

Cultural differences are interesting to see in this situation. Many people from overseas are content to live in big family groups, as used to be the case in poorer communities in cities here in Britain, before housing became provided by the State. Slum clearances, although they seemingly helped hygiene and sanitation at the time, dissipated communities and family groups with sometimes terrible consequences, which we are still feeling the knock-on effect of today. Families were literally torn apart by rehousing policies. The old work-house system was also a perpetrator of this.

As a young person growing up in Britain at present there are several very real problems. Jobs are scarce and State Benefits are being severely cut. New government policies are trying to force youngsters off the 'Nanny State' benefits system, but there are higher University fees, few apprentice places, and often a young person leaving school can be out of work for months if not years.

Quite often they may take up any job they can get because it is well paid and they feel they are achieving life status, but some years down the track they wake up to the fact that they hate their job and it has no relationship to what their gifts or passions are. By this time they may be paying a large mortgage or supporting a young family and they can't see a way out.

To avoid these scenarios it would be good if we in Britain recognised as a society the 'Maturation Years' up to about age 28, as they tend to do in Germany. There, the students study for longer, they may do military service, or even better civil service, where they work in an institution for a year or two, helping with children, disabled people, or the elderly, or in hospitals. Youngsters could also do land work on community organic farms, growing vegetables, picking fruit, caring for animals, or woodland work.

This would also hugely benefit society, which currently is desperate for more caring jobs, especially for the elderly and demented; and also on the land, which in many areas is lying fallow, or has been given over to factory farming or 'horsey-culture' which destroys the health of the land.

Carers are lowly paid and the tasks involved are seen as demeaning. If young people learned to do this in a loving way, supervised by wise and thoughtful mature workers who could show them how to respect their Elders, then our society would be much richer and more loving. Young offenders could be some of the first doing these tasks and then school leavers could join them. It could become a matter of pride to give these years of service to society. Payment need not be high. Budgeting is also part of growing up and help could be given to young people in these work schemes.

If young people were helped to live communally for a while and work in this way, they would mature with a broader consciousness of society's needs and be <u>less selfish and fearful</u> of economic failure. They could find their feet in the world and try out relationships in a broader context, without the pressure of 'getting a job, getting married and settling down'.

Some of the more privileged young people do this anyway, by travelling. All over the world youngsters can be found taking a 'gap year' which goes some way to recognising this need for maturation time, when they also can find meaningful work, sometimes in the poorest of world countries, but more importantly finding out who THEY ARE.

These very far-reaching changes would need to come from government legislation, but as we see, things can change from the root level up, when poverty and necessity *force* these changes gradually into our changing society.

Currently there is only one concept of education. It is seen in terms of academic achievement, and success is measured in terms of a good salary and job. Until this fundamentally changes, to encompass *the real education* of young people into loving mature adults, these attitudes will continue to be passed down through the generations of our sick society. We need to find ways to introduce young people to the School of Life.

Health and Dis-ease in Adults

Chapter 35

Working with the Planet Gaia

Many of the fundamental changes which we need to make in society in order to survive, have their roots in young people's training. This cannot happen however without an army of workers dedicated to saving Gaia, our living planet, which, just like our own bodies, is a living organism, made up of about 70% water, which through our selfish actions has become extremely sick.

Many places on this planet are now laid waste by man's activities. Huge areas of the oceans are polluted, with acres of plastic bags floating around, as well as with petrochemicals and nuclear waste, which all affect the creatures living in the watery depths.

On land we have seen the extinction of many thousands of species, because we have destroyed their natural habitat, cutting down rainforests, building dams, roads and cities, as well as raping the earth of her natural resources such as oil, minerals, pure water, and soil.

We have in this country cut down hedges, to create large agricultural areas, easy for machines to work, destroying the habitat of birds; we have sprayed large amounts of herbicides and agrochemicals on the land, creating dust bowls in some areas. We no longer have a balance in nature, so that cows get sick from eating meat products, wild animals are culled; cruelty and lack of thought, except profit, are ruling our farming 'industry'.

We are now seeing the results of our actions over the last century, where this destruction of our planet has escalated a thousand fold. There are terrible fires, earthquakes, floods, storms, droughts and weather changes which we could not have predicted. Some people are still denying global warming; others are predicting even bigger disasters! Weather patterns are certainly changing and air and sea currents too.

We see suffering on a huge scale with these 'natural disasters'; people in refugee camps, homeless and frightened; people killed and drowned and getting sick. Others dying of starvation from failed harvests. We see these things in our sitting rooms daily brought to us on the TV, and what can WE do?

Some people raise money for these afflicted, so that aid can be sent to them; governments also promise large sums of money, which sometimes reach the people but more often are swallowed up by corrupt governments who want to live as we do in the West. Aid agencies try their best to help and charity has now become a normal part of our lives.

Pictures of starving children, thirsty or sick, are everywhere. Churches send out helpers, money is raised. We are all conscious of the 'Third world' problems, but WHAT DO WE NEED TO DO here, today?

Each single individual on this planet is learning the same lessons. How do we each individually, at each moment, become more loving?

In the West we live comfortably. We are very greedy and rape the Earth on a daily basis, when we buy more and more material goods, imported from across the world using raw materials from vast mining areas, causing pollution and using cheap labour, often in terrible working conditions.

Firstly we can become more conscious and more grateful! We have everything we could possibly want and MORE. New gadgets appear daily on the TV adverts. Do we NEED to buy more? Can we manage to live more simply; and also more consciously? If there is less demand there will be less manufacturing. We are only seen to be successful if our manufacturing output is rising. Changes are beginning to happen with the recession. People are beginning to look for new ways forward.

Our governments measure success in terms of 'gross national output of goods manufactured and exported,' instead of looking at the sort of society we are living in, how we relate to each other and how those less able than ourselves are treated.

Can we share our car with others? Can we do fewer journeys? Can we reduce our material needs so that we do not buy the latest and best of every gadget; a new washing machine, or mobile phone, or fashion garment, a new laptop, or whatever we fancy? We talk about retail THERAPY! How much of what we no longer need or use can we recycle? Are we aware of where our landfill goes and the effect it has locally and globally on the earth?

Do we care for our local land and people? Is our own patch of garden loved, fed with organic natural recycled matter, used for food production, and healed? Do we care about our neighbours? Do we know their names and know their problems and frailties? We do not need to try and live their lives for them, but just be there in a supportive way if they need us.

Do we care for our local environment, picking up our litter, not allowing our dogs to foul in inappropriate places, not polluting the environment by keeping our cars revving, or using loud thumping music as we drive along, or in our houses? Do we leave doors and windows open with the heating on? Do we utilise water as if it were a precious commodity, even in the rainy season?

Are we aware of things happening in our wider community? Do we take an interest in the development of our town or village? The new Localism Act gives ordinary people the opportunity to become more involved in local decisions; about planning, development, and social housing. This legislation is also open to huge corruption at local level and reduces safeguards on our countryside being overdeveloped.

What about our food! Have we found a source of local organic farm vegetables which can be delivered jointly to a group of neighbours and friends, saving transport costs? There are more and more 'veggie box' schemes around the country now. Do we shop at huge supermarkets and throw away the packaging on many items each week? Has our food been flown in from abroad at great cost ecologically? How much waste food do WE produce each week, when we buy more than we need?

Simple daily changes, if taken on by enough people, would create vast changes in the way our economy works. Because manufacturing would become less of a driving force, people out of work would be encouraged to start looking locally for solutions.

Local trading and exchange schemes (LETS) are happening around the country. These could become a necessity of life rather than an idealistic game! Credit Unions are now more common, where local money supports local initiatives.

People skills can change. The strong active ones could work on the land and with the animals, and building and repairing eco houses; the weaker ones could tend the children, the elders and gardens. Work could become more local with less commuting and pollution.

Currently the poorest paid jobs are the ones which are most needed to heal our society; caring for children, the disabled, and the elderly and working with animals and the land. All these areas have become 'big businesses' with plenty of middle men soaking up the profits. A carer is typically paid at £7 an hour, working hard looking after a client. The client pays the Care Company £18 an hour! Who is getting the profits and what do they do with it?

Milk payments to farmers are so low that the farmers can no longer sustain their cows. Government subsidies are now running agricultural policy rather than what the land needs for its health.

Land in cities could be used for food production, utilizing the city farm approach and roof gardens and allotments. This is already happening in some parts of Britain. In larger rural areas, land management needs to be less government driven and more local needs driven, with small mixed farms, reducing cattle, pig, sheep and meat production and growing more vegetables and fruit, varied according to local needs and climate. This is work intensive, but our bodies were made for work and activity! Machines have taken over in many situations.

Huge factory farms do nothing for the land, produce highly polluted milk and meat, and are cruel in the extreme to the animals. They are not based on LOVING the animals. It is small wonder that cows are developing TB. They are sick because of the way they are treated, NOT because of the badgers!

Local communities need to find LOCAL SOLUTIONS to sustainability. In Africa, China or India, worldwide in fact, there will be different solutions from Europe, dependent on local traditions, diet and climate. Each community is responsible for its own children, elders, disabled weak and sick and its animals and land. Some areas of the world have already become 'uninhabitable' because of changing weather patterns. What local solutions might there be in this scenario?

How does this differ from the 'good old days'? Are we not just going backwards to a less developed world? On the contrary! We have learned consciously what works and does not work. We no longer have serfdom and powerful Lords of the Manor. We no longer have intertribal warfare (at least, most places have heard of democracy!)

We have communication with computers and phones. We can even have shared washing machines, run by locally produced power and using less water. We can honour and conserve water, and purify it naturally through a local reed bed. We can travel short distances using electric cars, produced in small numbers at local level, and powered by solar panels, or on electric trains to other parts of the country, but we should not NEED to do so because our life and work remains local.

We can build new houses which are carbon neutral or even feed electricity back into the local grid. Our own community can become self-sustaining, and we can link with other communities locally and further afield mainly for support, education, interaction and harmony. Our decisions and laws can also be made locally. Our finances are local and our economy is local. SMALL IS BEAUTIFUL!

Life could slow down; arts and crafts could become more central to our cultural life again, and we could take a pride in our life and work.

Health care could be provided by local Healers and Energy Workers. The NHS and the drug companies could be obsolete! People can take responsibility for their own health and stress levels, reducing sickness, with no need for surgery or major interference. People will learn again that the plant kingdom has healing in it.

All these basic changes are possible and are already being practised and refined in small pockets by futuristic individuals around the world. It only takes a consciousness and will to change what we are doing. We are all capable of co-creating this 'Ideal World'.

But that change will most probably be forced upon us by crisis, fear and painful disasters. There may be a breakdown in the national transport of goods around the country created by the rise in fuel prices; there may be extensive flooding, cutting power lines, blocking roads and disrupting services. There may be pockets of extreme poverty amongst some individuals of working age, who are unable to get jobs or housing, and therefore need to learn to live harmoniously in groups for support, growing their food to prevent starvation.

Multinational banks and financial institutions may go bust leaving rich individuals suddenly with nothing except their material goods, as money is only an illusion anyway and Mercurial in the way it can appear and disappear without warning.

Some individuals predict a 3rd World War. We now have huge Superpowers who vie with each other; China, who own vast tracts of the world and natural resources; the Muslim world which is seemingly so against the traditional capitalist 'Christian society' in America and Britain; the drug lords who are also involved in the arms trade, all underground and seemingly evil. All these are fearful of each other and wanting a materialistic existence, guarded by missiles and ammunitions.

We are indeed capable of destroying ourselves and the planet on which we live, and every human being should become aware of this fact and make a decision whether this is what they want, or if they want to work for the GOOD.

If the world is to become a better more peaceful place we need to learn to trust each other and do away completely with the production and distribution of arms.

"Man will always make wars" I hear you say!

The Mars-like quality of aggression is a real force in our make-up but it can be successfully countered and balanced by the peaceful and loving Venus qualities of listening to each other in LOVE. It can also be channelled into other areas, such as martial arts, sheer physical activity such as digging, the arts (speech and drama particularly), sports, gong work, which heals on a vibrational level, and relationship counselling on every level, from families and individuals, to nations.

Again what can we do? I have read that the negative suppressed Energy of anger in our 'nice' society can build up into a cloud of aggressive Energy and help create wars. If we therefore deal with our own anger issues first, not by suppression and putting them under the carpet, but with understanding and channelling into the positive energy of Mars, we may help to create world peace.

Something needs to be said here about our society in terms of health and safety, litigation, and insurance claims. We are living in times of HUGE FEAR, where the individual can no longer take responsibility for himself, but is told continuously what he must and mustn't do. Children cannot be taken out by group leaders, for fear of an accident; we are fined if we do not wear our seat belts. In every part of society now there are rules and regulations which stop us from being creative, community minded and expansive. Most people have more and more insurance policies of different kinds.

There is a natural 'law' in Energetic terms which says that FEAR ATTRACTS! This means that if one is fearful, then an accident is more likely to happen to us. If we are frightened of a dog, the dog will sense that and come up and bark or maybe even bite us! Children are being instilled with fear from an early age. No job can be done without umpteen insurances and CRB checks. Everyone insures themselves against every life eventuality. If something negative is going to happen to you (i.e. you are attracting it into your energy field perhaps as a learning lesson,) life will find a way for this to happen! No amount of insurance will stop you having an accident that you 'need'. Fear of it happening only makes it more likely.

What is the opposite of this fear? It is LOVE! If we can truly fill our hearts with love and compassion in every situation and remain alert and conscious in every minute, then nothing can befall us. This requires TRUST.

This chapter has laid out the basis for a new and loving society. A complete Utopia, I hear you say; unrealistic when we have to pay the bills? No! It is achievable and the SHIFT which is already starting will show just how achievable this is. It is entirely dependent on the 'Critical Mass' or enough people in the world needing and wanting change.

I am an optimist and already see all the seeds for Positive Change. There are many in the world right now who are thinking and talking about this shift of consciousness. Some special Souls are here to help us specifically to make this shift, and there is much potential LOVE being given to us right now.

Let us therefore stay awake and link with others in meditation and renewed practices of simple harmonious living, remaining conscious of the footprint we are leaving on Gaia. Are we helping to heal our planet by the way we live, or are we raping her? Can we honestly say at the end of each day that we have helped the earth, society and ourselves to be healthier? Are we getting the balance of our lives right, at this very moment in time? Only each individual knows the answer to this question.

Chapter 36

On Nutrition

Food needs to be enjoyed first and foremost, as it is our way of connecting ourselves to planet earth. Our bodily substance is made up of what we eat. Cooking a meal, shopping and planning menus can become a real chore and a struggle when you are feeling unwell, so it is important to keep it simple. But it is the most important thing that we can change ourselves, on our path to healing and if we get this right we can start to feel in charge of our own lives again.

With many illnesses having their origins in toxicity, it is of the utmost importance to try and cleanse your body as much as you can. One can also try and rid the body of some of its excess acidity.

These dietary suggestions are for your new life, not just to try for a few weeks. A complete change of eating habits may take a little while to get used to, so introduce new foods gradually and experiment with different things that may be new to you. Try not to get obsessive or anxious about it all, as that can create acid thoughts too, which in turn creates more toxins. Don't become afraid of food! If you do a radical detox you may get headaches for a couple of days as the cells cleanse and all the toxins circulate around your body. Drink extra water to 'flush them out' and allow your body to rest an extra amount, as it otherwise will add stress. Ideally do not do anything radical!

There are many excellent websites and books on dietary changes. You may become interested in this vast subject, but initially do not get overwhelmed by everyone's research and knowledge. Keep it simple.

Foods to avoid

In order to detoxify your body try to **avoid** these substances from day one.
Always read the labels!

- **Monosodium Glutamate** [found in many highly flavoured foods, instant soups, sauces, crisps, Chinese meals.] This has been found to be highly poisonous to some individuals, and may cause muscle spasms as well as headaches or tummy upsets.

- **Aspartame,** found in artificial sweeteners, many low calorie drinks, and sugar free chewing gum. This substance can also accumulate in the body tissues and in America where low sugar fizzy drinks [e.g. diet coke] are consumed in large quantities young people have been showing symptoms similar to Multiple Sclerosis.

- **Caffeine,** found in tea, coffee, coke, chocolate and some high energy drinks. This over stimulates the nervous system, causing sleep disturbances, muscle spasms and palpitations or hot flushes and is a complete poison to anyone with a hypersensitivity to caffeine. Decaffeinated coffee and tea are not good substitutes as most of the decaffeinating process involves the use of toxic chemicals as well.

- **Sugar, especially sucrose.** The use of sweets and added sugar as well as cakes and preserves is undoubtedly connected with an increase in Type 2 Diabetes in our society and also fungal growth in our bodies. Often in Fibromyalgia, when the whole body has been stressed and the adrenals, insulin production and thyroid are out of balance, excess sugar can lead to the condition of Candida throughout the body, which causes leaky gut and toxins in the muscles, lungs and brain, giving symptoms of Fibromyalgia. It is better therefore to assume that there is Candida around when detoxing and cut out most sugars. A little honey, dates, or natural sugars from fruit can be used sometimes, especially if you have sweet cravings, which will gradually change as you start to rebalance your tastes. You could try agave and rice syrup too, or liquid fructose. It is better though to rely on the natural sweetness in vegetables to satisfy our need for this taste.

- **Alcohol.** Giving up this may seem radical for some, but alcohol is extremely toxic to a sick body, especially the additives put into wine making. Once you are cleansed you may want to perhaps try an occasional glass of organic wine. Alcohol is an accepted part of society, but it is also a foreign fermenting substance, which can upset the fine balance in our systems. You only have to observe the behaviour of youngsters under its influence to realise what a potentially harmful toxin it is.

- **Colourings and flavourings and other additives.** These are added to very many foodstuffs nowadays and become cumulative in the body. ALWAYS READ THE LABELS and try if possible to cook meals only made from fresh organic ingredients that will contain nothing but the odd slug or greenfly!

- **Mind altering drugs of any kind, including prescribed medicines.** It may take some time before you are ready to come off prescribed painkillers or antidepressants if you are taking them, but make this your final aim, as long-term use of these create toxins also and can suppress your brain activity. Recent research indicates that they may also contribute to the development of Alzheimer's disease. Many people go to their GPs for help and are prescribed large amounts of allopathic drugs. We have become a society of pill poppers. It can be frightening to walk your path alone with a chronic illness, which is why it is so important to get the support of friends, family and good therapists who can walk along beside you on your path of Healing. Keep communications open with your doctor though as you never know when you will need their help and guidance. Reducing your medication is the first step, but do this with medical guidance, especially steroids and antidepressants

- **Giving up smoking is a vital part of your healing, but may need professional support, hypnotherapy etc.** Take it a step at a time once you are feeling a bit better. Nicotine, like other artificial substances, acts as a strong toxin in the body. It also effects the peripheral circulation and has a similar effect to an adrenaline rush, which your body may crave if it is exhausted, but does NOTHING to help you to heal.

General help for the metabolic system

Gradually introduce more and more fibre into your diet and use the foods listed as **Alkaline** in the Appendix. The acid/alkaline balance must be considerably changed to reduce symptoms of disease.

If you do this too quickly you may find you are windy or get loose stools. Don't fear, just ease off a little and persevere. Your body WILL adapt and gradually the minute Villae in your small intestines, damaged by poor food quality and stress, will heal. This can take months, depending on the severity of your condition.

Try to buy **Organic** fruit and vegetables whenever possible. This may be a little more expensive but it is money well worth spending, as chemical sprays that accumulate in soil [and also deplete the soil of other trace elements that are vital to healthy bodily functions] are extremely poisonous to sensitive bodies. If you cannot buy organic food at local shops, try getting food from a local farmer's market or order a weekly box online from a company such as Riverford's, who will deliver lovely fresh local grown produce.

A good rule of thumb is to try and eat at least 2/3rd of a plate of vegetables at each main meal [lunch and supper]. This can be as salads, or lightly steamed, stir-fried or oven roasted vegetables [using slow cooking so as not to burn the olive oil.]

Eating a variety of different colours of food means that you have variety of minerals and vitamins, so pick a rainbow selection and eat a little of many kinds of vegetables grown locally and as seasonal as possible. Try to leave them in the fridge for a minimal time, as each day they sit there they 'die' and lose some energy. By doing this you are taking in the greatest number of Vitamins and Trace Mineral elements as possible, and also linking your body's energy to local Earth energy which is healing in itself.

Of course the very best food is that dug straight out of your garden. Maybe you can look forward to a time when this will become possible, even if now it doesn't seem likely. Raised beds and no dig methods means that once set up they take very little physical energy to cultivate. Herbs, which are particularly rich in minerals and vitamins, are a good place to start. Keep a few handy on the kitchen windowsill.

An interesting and 'Holistic' way of planning a meal is to think of eating all the different parts of the plant in one meal. This could include a root vegetable [e.g. carrot], a stem [e.g. celery], a leaf [some green salad or fresh herbs], a flower [e.g. broccoli, borage, marigold], some seeds or nuts [pumpkin, sunflower, almonds, walnuts, pine nuts], and some fruit. The qualities of all these parts are different and in Macrobiotic terms contain a good balance of Yin and Yang Energy [expansion and contraction of energetic substance.] Some contain high protein, and stored energy; some have more sugars and give you instant energy.

We have been led to believe that a 'good diet' contains carbohydrates, proteins and fats [and that we should not eat too many of the latter!], minerals and vitamins. I will look at each of these elements separately.

Interestingly all these substances can be found in a purely vegan diet, in the different parts of the plant!

Carbohydrates

These are starchy foods, and give us long lasting energy. They are broken down less quickly than true sugars, and therefore act as 'coke on a slow burning furnace.' It is important that we eat a certain amount of these, but many people nowadays are becoming intolerant of gluten, found in wheat most especially. It can cause irritable bowel syndrome, wind and inflammation in the small intestine. Often if we leave wheat out for a while and concentrate on healing the gut with organic cooked vegetables and rice or quinoa then we can reintroduce organic cereals gradually after a while with no ill affect. It is primarily the chemical sprays on the cereals that we become allergic to.

In Britain the staple food is bread, often using highly refined white flour with many additives, flour improvers and very little food value. The sprays used in wheat production go into the grain head more easily than most other grains, so could it be the fertilizers, which are causing the sudden increase of 'gluten intolerance'?

Try replacing wheat bread with rice cakes, oat cakes, sour dough rye bread, yeast free 'Village Bakery' rye bread, pumpernickel from Germany [some varieties have wheat in them], delicious but expensive 'sprouted grain bread' available in whole food shops, or try making your own soda bread with a variety of non-wheat organic flours and wheat free soda. Spelt bread is made from an ancient form of wheat and may be better tolerated. The slow-rising, double knead method of bread making is more easily digested. Alternatively replace the 'sandwich meal' with a mixed vegetable salad and add some cooked brown rice or buckwheat/ rice pasta, seasoned with herbs - delicious!

Try to start each day with a Carbohydrate meal. This gives you plenty of fuel after the fast of the night and will sustain you until lunch, except for fluid. This could be muesli, made from organic mixed grains, avoiding wheat, and added organic seeds, sweetened with some fresh fruit pieces such as berries. It is best to soak the grain for 15 minutes or so to release toxins found in raw oats. This also makes it easier to digest. Or you could make some porridge if it is a cold day, which warms the digestive tract.

Proteins

It is a matter of preference whether one is a meat eater, fish eater, eggs and dairy eater, but these all contain first class proteins, and as such are known as 'essential' to a healthy diet. If you choose to reduce the amounts of these proteins in the diet, you can be equally healthy as a vegan, either strict or partial.

However it is very important then to consume enough vegetable protein, as protein is converted into amino acids, the building blocks for new cell growth. Vegetarian proteins should include <u>combinations</u> of pulses with seeds or nuts, grains with pulses, or grains with nuts/seeds. These are known as second-class proteins. There are many vegetarian recipe books on this subject available.

If you do decide to stay as a meat eater, try to reduce the amount you eat by at least half, as meat [and all first class proteins] is <u>very</u> acidic and therefore do not help achy muscles and joints. It is important also to source organic meat, which can be very expensive.

Fish is also not without its problems. Heavy metals, such as mercury, are found in high doses in some deep-sea fish, and these can be toxic to a sensitive body. Small oily fish such as sardines, mackerel and sprats are best to eat regularly. Try to eat these at least twice a week.

The debate of WHAT one eats is complex and comes down to life-style, constitution and family habits. To change radically overnight could throw the body into shock, so make any long-term changes gradually. Just keep in mind the acid levels and the toxins in inorganic meat, fish, and milk and egg production.

Becoming a vegetarian certainly makes one feel 'lighter' and more energised. For some though it can be an ungrounding experience, so you feel floaty and unreal. Try it for yourself.

Dairy Foods

Many people nowadays become allergic to dairy products. It can create excess mucous and also irritate the lining of the gut. Again, this is largely due to the foodstuffs that the cows are fed on including hormones and antibiotics. Try replacing milk with organic soya, rice or almond milk. Yoghourt, which helps stabilize the gut flora, is important too. It is available as goat or Soya Yoghurt. Organic goat's cheeses, feta and cottage cheeses are available too. Some allergic people can tolerate organic goats milk and yoghourt, and even organic cottage cheese, others don't. All these products are now widely available in supermarkets. You may find you can occasionally tolerate a little organic cow's milk or yoghourt at a later stage.

Fats

These are vital for our health. Much is written these days about 'bad fats' and cholesterol rising, causing heart disease and strokes. Cholesterol is not a DIRECT result of eating fat, but a much more complex process, often as a result of too much stress. Dehydration of the cells causes the cells to wrap themselves up in a coarse oily coating to prevent themselves being destroyed. This is measured as Bad Cholesterol.

If you cut out fats altogether, as some Slimming clubs would have us do, the cell walls have no building blocks and one can become very ill. Instead ensure you have enough GOOD FATS.

These include olive oils, hemp, sunflower, walnut, sesame, etc., in fact a large variety of organic vegetable oils. It is interesting to note that the Omegas, which we read so much about now, differ according to where the plant grows. In our colder climate we need mainly Omega 3. Flax and fish oils; as we move south towards the Mediterranean the oils have more Omega 6, olive oil and seeds; in hot climates they have Omega 9.

One can therefore adjust the type of Omega according to season and temperature, adding oily fish in the winter, and eating lighter oils in the summer.

Vitamins and Minerals

These substances are vital in small amounts for healthy cell function. For example Magnesium gives the cells the 'light' quality to refresh and cleanse. Nowadays factory farming does much harm to the soils and erosion from wind and rain, coupled with the use of inorganic fertilizers, means that the plants themselves do not contain the vital nutrients that our bodies need for health.

Therefore you may need to take some supplements, at least initially. Some books have confusingly long lists of high dose supplements, which are maybe not necessary.

Using Supplements has become common practice and until recent EU directives on the certification of all medicines, [which has meant some companies have gone out of business because of the high cost of legalising a product,] these were readily available over the counter in both pharmacies and supermarkets. The people in Whole food shops are generally knowledgeable and can often advise on their use and dosage, but it is probably best to search out a recommended nutritionist to get this highly complicated subject sorted out.

The body normally excretes any excess supplements, but in a state of toxicity, which already exists, high doses may make the matter worse.

Generally Vitamin A, C, E and B complex [especially B6 and 12] and Magnesium are supplements that the body requires, but there may be other vital ones missing, such as Zinc, so try to get help on this vast science.

Many excellent books have been published where you can go in depth and learn about different supplements and their actions.

There are several different ways you can be tested to see if you need Vitamin and Mineral supplements. Check this on a website about mineral and vitamin testing, to read about live and dried blood analysis, and mineral kits which rely on tasting methods to test levels.

What can I eat and drink?

With such a long list of 'No no's' you may well be wondering what is left to eat!
Fruit and vegetables, avoiding too many potatoes, as mentioned before, make up the bulk of your new diet, but many other things can be added for a good mixed diet.

Beverages

Herbal teas are now widely available and are becoming more normal in cafes and homes. Always carry a few spare ones with you in case you get caught out.

The fruit mixtures are generally not good because they contain artificial flavourings. Tea from fresh leaves is best, made in a china pot, and allowed to infuse for 5-7 minutes before sipping slowly.

A recently published list of the best alkalising teas included: -

- Rooibosch [red bush tea from South Africa], which can become a good substitute to your English cup of tea, made fairly strong, with Soya or rice milk added. If you are used to sweet tea, try the Soya milk with apple juice until you are more used to it. It can also be drunk black.

- Peppermint tea is good after a meal to help digestion. There are various mixtures available, or use fresh leaves.

- Detox mixtures are helpful, including ones using fennel and other herbs.

- Ginger and lemon cleanses and stimulates the digestion.

- A calming 'sleepy time' mixture can be good to sip at bedtime.

- Try growing a few yourselves, including sage, good for bad throats and winter colds; thyme, another warming tea; marjoram, cleansing; chamomile, for tummy upsets and lemon balm, refreshing if allowed to cool for a hot day. Rosemary is warming to the system and enlivens the circulation; lemon verbena is also very refreshing, but susceptible to winter frosts.

An herb garden outside the back door can be a wonderful place to quietly go and watch the bees buzzing and smell the different aromas. Planting lavender nearby is also helpful for a stressed body and mind.

Coffee substitutes

Many people miss their morning cup of coffee. The thicker substance of this milky drink can be sustaining and comforting, whereas herb teas are thinner and more thirst quenching.

In the health food shops you find a variety of coffee substitutes, including Yanno, Barley Cup, No Caf and Dandelion coffee mixtures. Instant powders are easiest to use, but dandelion root ground up and brewed for 7-10 minutes makes a dark bitter coffee mixture that is strained and milk added, and is an excellent liver cleanser.

Coffee gives the mind a clarity which you may crave and gives the 'kick-start' energy for the day, but don't be tempted to take a short-term fix which will further weaken your system, and delay your healing.

Water and juices

If you are unable to afford an Ioniser, which gives you alkaline water, try to drink spring water but only out of glass bottles. Plastics used for bottled water give off toxins, especially if kept in a warm place in the sun. Drink as much as you can, as the pure water flushes out toxins and often dehydration is a basic cause for ill health.

Each person's body is different in its need for daily water. It depends on the climate, central heating, activity, renal function, amount of fat in the body, the state of the cells and fluids themselves and amount of salt consumed.

The salt/water ratio is controlled in the kidneys and as long term dehydration and too much salt have often stressed these, it is important to LISTEN to your own body. Are you thirsty? When? Is your urine pale and clear [healthy] or dark and strong smelling? If you pick up the skin on the back of your hand is it lose or firm? Does it rebound?

Some books recommend x amount of water to be drunk daily. Do not take this too literally if you have any kind of congestion in your circulation as you may make it worse. Reduce your salt intake gradually, using first rock salt, then 'low salt' if you need a little in cooking. As you get healthier your natural salt /water balance will improve and you will have a better sense of how much water you need to drink. Ideally you should aim at needing no salt addition at all.

Water should not be drunk with meals as it dilutes the digestive juices and saliva acts as an important first place where digestion starts as it mixes with the food. Instead have a glass near you and sip it throughout the day. Ideally don't drink anything half an hour before and 2 ½ hours after eating a main meal.

Drink extra water in hot weather, if you are going on a journey, especially flying, or if life gets a bit more stressful

Fruit juices can be healthy if pure and organic. Avoid the cheap cartons of 'juice drink' as they contain large amounts of sugar and juice made from concentrate has little value as well. Only drink fruit juice instead of eating a fruit, best taken between meals, as the acid is less well digested as part of the main meal. Don't replace your water with fruit juices. One is vital to life; the other is a liquid food.

Many people are allergic to the sprays used in orchards and especially on oranges and grapefruits, and grapes. These fruits are best avoided at first unless organic.

Lemons are very alkalizing for most people surprisingly as they seem very acid. A very healthy way to start the day is to drink the juice of half an organic lemon, mixed with some warm water, at least half an hour before breakfast. You can also use them liberally in salad dressings and just drizzled over vegetables. They lose Vitamin C quickly so fresh squeeze them and do not heat them unnecessarily. Cut a slice into your drinking water too. You may be someone who cannot metabolise these fruit acids into alkaline; trial and error is the best way to find out, with urine testing for pH.

Second class proteins

As mentioned before proteins create essential building blocks for the cells, but unless you are consciously combining them together they do not create full amino acids and cannot be utilised fully by the body.

Nuts and seeds.

These can easily be freshly ground up in small quantities just prior to use in a small coffee grinder if you have any dental problems. They must otherwise be very well chewed, or else they can irritate an already sensitive small intestine.

Freshness is important. Check the sell-by date and only buy organic ones. Store nuts in screw top jars in a cool place, as they easily grow toxic moulds, which can be poisonous, so use them quickly.

Nuts and seeds can be eaten with grains to create 1st class protein, as on muesli, or added to vegetable meals and salads, where there are also pulses or grains. Good varieties are pumpkin, sunflower, linseed [which is especially good for healing the small intestines, soaked for a few hours] pine nuts, almonds [the most alkaline], walnuts and cashews and also chestnut purée and coconut milk or cream.

Pulses

Some people can find these hard to digest so soak them thoroughly for several hours, and then rinse them well can get rid of the unwanted toxins, which create windiness.

Eat them occasionally in stews and soups, especially in winter, or cook some ready to create a mixed salad and keep in the fridge. Add a few lentils if cooking rice to go with curry, or have a simple meal of baked beans [organic low sugar variety] on wholemeal toast if you don't feel like cooking. Always be aware of combining them with a grain or nuts/seeds.

Soya is a form of protein, and can be taken as milk, yoghourt, tofu curd or beans. Ensure you eat organic non GM varieties only. They may be helpful for balancing oestrogen in the menopause, but some people are allergic to them.

Grains

There are many grains that have been cultivated over centuries from wild grasses, and each has a different quality. As with the Omega oils, some are more suitable for hot climates, some for cold. They must all be well cooked and masticated to help digestion, as the carbohydrates need to be well mixed with saliva to start the breakdown of substances in the gut.

Try some of these: -

- **Barley**, especially good as a winter stew, or as flour mixed with other grains in bread. It is warming to the digestion and especially good in winter.

- **Oats**; porridge, muesli, flapjacks, crumble toppings, both sweet and savoury, contains toxins if eaten raw without some soaking. It is also warming to the system.

- **Wheat**; bread, pancakes, cakes etc. Whole-wheat grains can be soaked and well cooked, seasoned with herbs and tamari as an accompaniment with vegetables. Wheat is our staple in the west, but causes problems for some as it holds artificial fertilisers in the kernels and has high gluten levels. Always use organic wholemeal flour to get the goodness. Cous cous and cracked wheat are varieties of wheat and useful alternatives to rice eaten with a main meal, providing you are not wheat intolerant.

- **Buckwheat**; as above, a nutty taste, and the flour makes super pancakes. Also very good for the circulation as it contains rutin, which strengthens vein walls.

- **Maize/corn**; can be eaten straight off the cob as a vegetable, or as a flour, for thickening etc. Corn bread as made in America makes a nice variety if you are wheat free. Try making popcorn in a large saucepan for some fun.

- **Millet**; this grows in long tendrils and is best known as budgerigar food, but is an extremely healthy grain from southern Europe and Africa. It contains silica and is a natural diuretic and cleanser. It needs fairly long, slow cooking and can be added to soups or served as a base for mixed vegetables. It is bland in taste so needs seasoning with fresh herbs. It can also be made into a milk pudding if cooked slowly in the oven.

- **Quinoa** [pronounced keen-wa] or amaranth; this is a north American Indian grain which is becoming better known as is extremely healthy. It can be slow cooked as porridge, as an accompaniment for vegetables or as flour makes good nutty tasting cakes and scones, best blended with rice and Soya flour.

- **Rice**; well known in Indian cooking, but brown rice is much more nutritious if well cooked. The husks which are removed in white rice contain B Vitamins. Rice flour is useful for baking and blends well with other flours. Brown rice is an excellent staple food if you are fasting and cleansing for a few days. Black wild rice is also a nice alternative.

With all grains long slow cooking is important and they can therefore become a bit of a chore to cook if you are not well. A hay-box or slow cooker may be a way around this. However try different ones and keep some in the fridge for instant high-energy food if you are very tired. Rice puddings are easy to prepare and very comforting if you haven't much appetite. You can try a spoonful of sugar free jam on them for an extra treat!

Sprouted pulses, grains and seeds are very healthy and full of vitamins and minerals. Try growing some on your windowsill, in a special sprouter, and rinsing twice a day. Once they show green tips and long white roots they can be lightly stir-fried or added to salads, but be careful to rinse them off very thoroughly beforehand in running water, as they can contain toxins if not. You can also buy them fresh from the supermarket or whole-food shop, and again they will need thorough rinsing before use.

Treats
We all like to treat ourselves to something tasty from time to time as a comfort if we are stressed or depressed and it is very easy to resort back to old habits of a bar of chocolate, a cream cake, a glass of wine, a packet of biscuits or a steak. Try to have a little store of healthy snacks to nibble on if you feel like this, so a small 'sin' is better than setting yourself back health wise and chastising yourself afterwards as you suffer all your old symptoms.

Some foods like this might include a mint carob sugar free bar [like chocolate, available in good health food shops]; sugar free fruit chewy bars, 85% or 70% organic chocolate [just a small piece!], date bars, a really nice ripe mango or peach, some homemade fruit sorbet, a banana smoothy, some low salt organic crisps, some well washed organic dried fruit, a handful of cashew nuts. None of these are 'good' for you [except the fruit and nuts] but may stop you climbing the wall and feeling miserable and in small quantities should be all right.

This chapter has gone into a lot of detail about food, the reason being that food and drink is the biggest single thing we have control over on our path to recovery. If you can concentrate on this chapter first you have a high chance of making some real changes in your health over time. Have patience and persevere. We are literally what we eat.

Chapter 37

Diabetes, Arthritis, Cancer, Hypertension and Heart Disease

Seen in the light of this whole book, one can start to ask oneself why the body creates certain illnesses. Each individual has strengths and weaknesses or constitutional traits. This can be observed well if you look at the astrological birth chart in terms of the elements of fire, earth air and water. Where the planets were at the time of our birth seems to affect our innate state of balance.

We may also carry within us weak genetic make-up from our ancestors. This is interesting to trace back, if you know the family history of illness. Weaknesses may not necessarily show up as the same disease but can develop into something else at a deeper level. This is referred to as miasma in Homeopathy and is something of great interest to these practitioners.

None of us are perfectly balanced. We are all unique! If the body goes beyond its own natural ideal state of balance, because of stress, dehydration, abuse or trauma, then the body goes into a state of crisis and starts to create symptoms of disturbance or illness. This shows up in different areas of the body, depending on our constitution and inbuilt weaknesses.

If someone creates a brain tumour, for example, one can begin to look at the things which may have caused this. It could be due to environmental or electromagnetic toxins, long-term stress, or dietary abuse. The person may have had emotional stress, marriage break-up or loss of a job. Because stress affects the adrenal response it will create an environment of acidity in the WHOLE body which shows up as disease in the brain. Why there? Because the person has a constitutional weakness or vulnerability in that area!

Dehydration and acidity at cellular level is the cause of ALL disease, which then shows itself as different illness pictures. It may be that the person has a constitutional weakness in the autoimmune system, inherited from the parents, and then the acidity may show up as arthritis. Or they may have a weakness in the digestion which then develops into ulcers, or colitis.

Diabetes is an inactivity of the pancreas in youth (type 1 Diabetes) which may be an inherited weakness, often accompanied by emotional immaturity, or it can be because of over-indulgence and increased acidity as we get older (type 2 Diabetes).The cure for Type 2 is to completely change the diet and detoxify the whole body. This can be achieved even if tablets or insulin are being taken.

However it is important to work closely with the doctor in this case, as the body must become used to a different diet and lifestyle if you reduce medication.

Fat is also a way that the body stores acid. If the person is obese it is a sign that the acidity levels are rising, and a warning that any sort of illness is eminent. Our body tries to protect us from illness by storing fat. Similarly if fat starts to build up inside the arteries it is a sign of stress and acidity. Raised cholesterol is also a sign that something is not right with the hydration of the cell. In order to protect itself from further dehydration the cell creates a fatty protective layer around itself. Statins are not the answer!

Raised blood pressure is linked intimately with the emotions. If the person's emotions are linking too strongly into the physical matter of the body, the heart and adrenals are affected and this in turn raises the person's blood pressure. Fear, stress and long-term unhappiness, with an overproduction of cortisone and acidity can bring on raised blood pressure. It can be also an inherited weakness from a parent for the body to respond in this way. Obesity and lack of exercise are definitely contributing factors and changing these can help reduce blood pressure naturally.

In heart disease and circulatory disorders this picture goes one step further. Heart disease is often inherited and it seems as though the blood pressure 'picture' has gone yet deeper to affect our most stable organ, the heart. This may also create abnormalities which lead to aortic aneurisms or strokes of different kinds. Known as the 'Managers disease' one can understand why this is so prevalent in people with stressful jobs.

Many cancers show themselves only gradually as time goes by. The body has in fact been in a 'pre-cancerous' state for many years beforehand and has been stressed and acidic. It is this toxicity which breaks down the finely balanced mechanisms within the cells, so that rogue cells start to develop and grow. Dr Young has proved that cancerous cells put into an alkaline environment revert back to their normal structure.

Again one can ask what one is doing that creates acidity and dehydration in life; smoking, drinking, imbibing large amounts of sugar, coffee, alcohol or environmental pollutants. Or is it because of long-term stress from a bad relationship, poor self-esteem, not finding the right life path, bankruptcy, an accident, or other life crisis? Often it is hard to find the link with the cause which may have started the process some years back.

If the cancer is treated traditionally with radiotherapy, chemotherapy or surgery the effect is to block out the tumour in its location but the body <u>still has cancer</u>! In fact it may become more sick and acidic as a result of the stress of the illness and fear, and the side effects of the drugs and treatments given.

When people say they have been given the 'all clear' it is rare that they do not go on to develop further tumours in another place a few years on. There is no cure for cancer except by a complete change of diet, lifestyle and mental/emotional realignment. Medicines alone will not change the course of the dis-ease which is systemic in the broadest sense.

One treatment for cancer which may be of interest and worth mentioning is the use of Mistletoe used homoeopathically. Seen from the holistic perspective mistletoe resembles the cancer in its growth on the tree. The mistletoe also contains alkaloids, and creates a mild fever which induces a state of healing as cancer is a 'cold' illness. 'Like curing like' is often used in homeopathy. There is a clinic in Switzerland where this Iscador treatment has been used for some 60 years

In arthritis there may be a cure if a total change of life is possible. But often the emotional changes required are beyond the person's ability in this lifetime. Chronic conditions are often the greatest teachers of patience and other life lessons. Sadly many of the anti-inflammatory and steroid drugs which are prescribed are making the condition worse in the long-term as the toxins from the drugs increase the acid levels.

Pain is experienced in a high degree in these chronic conditions and one can ask the question, *'What is pain?'*

Supporting the whole organism in a holistic way is the only positive way forward. This will include herbal and complementary treatments (baths and massage,) detoxification, change in diet and possibly counselling and psychotherapy. Cure may not be fully achieved. (In Germany these sorts of treatments are common practice.)

However, on a more positive note the general energy of a person can be hugely improved simply by healthy living practices, including reducing stress, improving diet and increasing fresh air and exercise.

A subtle sign of impinging ill health on any level is sleeping problems. Nowadays many people suffer from insomnia. Keeping healthy routines of bedtime and ensuring a deep un-drugged sleep will help the body to maintain and improve its health. At a cellular level the chemical exchanges that occur during deep sleep ensure the repair and maintenance of the body, particularly with the exchange of calcium and magnesium.

On a mental level we are able to 'digest' our experiences when we sleep well. It is no chance happening that we spend about a third of our lives in sleep! On a soul level we are able to recall our actions throughout the previous day and how we have affected others by our words, thoughts and deeds.

We are constantly creating patterns of energy between people, and this can be negative or positive. We may have felt angry, sad, fearful or jealous. These negative feelings will create patterns in our aura which need to be understood and healed as we sleep.

Sometimes you can feel this heavy negative energy around someone who is becoming sick. As human beings we can learn to protect ourselves from this or we may become affected by someone else's negativity. Cancer has a very particular negativity, as does MS, and rheumatoid arthritis. It is hard for those nursing these conditions long-term to remain positive.

When thinking about ANY illness it is important to have an intuitive imaginative approach to understanding the illness picture, and then glimpses of the truth may start to appear. The scientific explanation may be accurate but may only be part of the whole picture. Lateral thinking with the heart may bring answers to deep questions of this sort.

'Destiny illnesses' are hard to understand at times. These may include things such as Motor neurone Disease, MS or Parkinson's. As practitioners there may be no glib answers to be found for an emerging condition, but often the patient themselves, through suffering, will come to new insights about their condition and the life that has led them to this point where they have to stop and take stock and concentrate on caring for their physical body.

Compassion which comes from those standing around their sick loved ones is a very real positive healing energy. It is often these people who may have the strongest transformational experiences as they will need to become selfless, patient and compassionate whilst caring for their loved ones. During my career as a district nurse I was amazed on many occasions to see the strength which some carers were able to sustain, sometimes over years.

Our society has little time for these 'Saints' who are often working unrecognised behind closed doors, but are making a very real contribution to the 'health of the earth' as a whole, through their devotion and care.

Chapter 38

Fibromyalgia, chronic fatigue, candida and ME

A group of illnesses which is becoming ever more prevalent in our society, but is little understood by the medical world is the phenomenon of lack of Energy and pain, which is found in the above conditions. These illnesses which can create havoc in an individual's life and leave them bedbound at worst and unable to work fully or sustain social contacts are on the sharp increase.

Symptoms vary from general malaise and lack of motivation, to severe collapse or post-viral debilitation. It is generally thought that the immune system is affected, and also the hormones, digestion, nervous system and sleep patterns.

Pain can be so severe that the treatment prescribed is Morphine and patients will literally become drug addicts with years of suffering and depression and a very poor prognosis. Many different drugs may be tried over the years of chronic malaise.

Most often when the usual tests are done on the patient, blood tests, urine analysis, x-rays etc. no abnormalities are found, which makes these conditions hard to diagnose and treat.

These patients are often perceived as 'problems' by the GPs and they may go from Doctor to Doctor looking for someone who understands their condition and can give them some hope and help.

Many of these people will become the clients of complementary practitioners because some short-term relief can be found in a treatment, but cost is often prohibitive.

They are also often the ones who may be counted as 'scroungers' in the benefits system but who may suffer even more through poverty and homelessness.

Having personally suffered from Fibromyalgia I have done some research on the acidity levels, as tested by the pH of urine and saliva at different times of the day and after certain activities. It is through the work of Dr Young that I started to understand the holistic implications of cellular health, acidity and alkalinity. It is the key to improvement.

If these patients in particular were able to completely change their lifestyle and diet, increasing exercise gradually and cleansing their whole system, and improving their mental outlook which also affects their health and immune system, then cures might be seen more often. One hears of cases of ME when the patient decides they are going to get better and they do so, which is why it is sometimes bracketed along with hypochondria and depression. However, speak to any patient and they will tell you how real their symptoms are!

Anyone with these conditions needs patience, reassurance and lots of support. One's body becomes like a barometer of healthy living. If you slip back into old habits of behaviour or eating, then symptoms can return, as in the classic 'Fibroflare'. As the brain also suffers from inflammatory changes, muzzy thinking and headaches/ migraines can also be a problem. Everyone is different but I challenge anyone, without causing offence, who has been unwell like this to have a go at changing their lives for the better!

I do hope that the reading of this book will help you and others to come back to a state of renewed health and life purpose.

The Age of Wisdom

Chapter 39

Elders

There is a wonderful poem by Jenny Joseph, written in 1963. The title of the poem is 'Warning' and the first line is 'When I am an old woman I shall wear purple' and I suggest you look it up and enjoy reading it! The old woman in the poem gives herself permission to live outrageously and do all the things that society forbids, all the things she has always wanted to do.

Purple is also the colour associated with wisdom and spirituality. Wearing purple could denote therefore that we have reached maturity.

As we grow older it is as though the shackles of our upbringing and the 'norms' of society loosen a little and we can begin to play around with an image of whom we feel *we really are.*

Have we yet discovered our Truth or have we been so busy living life actively 'out there' in the world that there has been little time or inclination to look inside and learn the Wisdom of Silence? Do we recognise the real thread or 'Leitmotiv' that has run through our lifetime and know for sure that it was not all wasted but was leading ultimately to the knowledge of our Self and the understanding of our limitless Light and Power which we hold within us.

Pondering on how we have acted towards others, be it in a helpful or hurtful way, in our brief life here on earth, or what have we learned from the pain which we have suffered both physically and emotionally, or by traumas which have been wilfully or unconsciously inflicted on us by others, gives us the oportunity to ponder on our lives in a meaningful, conscious way.

This life that we have led thus far, if we are to give it any Purpose, other than gratification and selfishness, needs to be understood by us as we mature. This is often referred to as Wisdom and we can learn to be <u>very</u> wise as we grow old! Only when we have learned sufficient do we then pack up our bags and go!

Old age need not be a time of suffering, loss, loneliness, poverty or disempowerment. Our society in Britain at present is very bad at recognising what Elders themselves can continue to usefully contribute to the whole of society. We have become a society of productivity; our success is measured in terms of material output.

What is our retirement bank balance? Can we afford a comfortable retirement full of treats, such as cruises, or other exotic holidays, clubs, retirement flats in good locations and probably someone to do our cleaning or gardening as well?

Or are we doomed to become the problem 'Pensioners' who demand ever higher amounts of investment from the government, needing home care, health care, hospitals and nursing homes?

'Service providers and receivers', and Old Age Care have now become big business for those in the private sector, who build and run Sheltered Housing Schemes, Retirement Flats or Residential Homes.

The Government is currently panicking about the expenditure of caring for an increasingly aging population, and withdrawing much of the support structure that it instigated with the National Health Service since the 1940's. Private insurance for future healthcare is now becoming the norm.

The name 'Elder', which is the term I use for those of us who are maturing gracefully, is used by indigenous peoples such as African Tribes, (e.g. the Bushman of the Kalahari,) the North American Indians, and the Aborigines. It is a term of deep respect.

When you finally become an Elder or a Wise Woman/Man in one of these tribes, you can help the whole village community link to their Ancestors or 'History', and find the answers to many of the community's problems by deep meditative consultation with ancient Energy. Elders are linking to the departed souls who have gone before them.

As I have been very fortunate to travel widely in the last 20 years, visiting many of these cultures, I have observed how peaceful and fulfilling old age can be; women sit quietly in mud huts, their physical needs met by the younger women, while they may help tend the young children, or read the runes; or, as in some other European cultures, the elderly men sit in the sunshine outside the family houses or in a local café chatting or playing cards and 'putting the world to rights'.

Often there is a special chair near the fireplace where Grandmother spends her days, rocking gently and muttering to herself. When she becomes too frail to sit, her bed may be brought down into the living area. She is accepted and at peace within the family circle.

Families in Britain with modern lifestyles, commuting, and jobs which take them all over the world become geographically dissipated and the Elders no longer are the natural matriarchs or patriarchs of the community.

Instead they become the 'Problem Parents' who are visited occasionally at Christmas, who one feels slightly guilty about all the time, and who eventually have to be 'put into a home'; or dealt with by a care package being set up in some other appropriate way! It then becomes a stress as to whether the right care is being provided and whether it is affordable.

Active Grandparents in modern Britain are seen as a very useful resource for working parents, to care for the grandchildren during times of emergency, or maybe on a regular basis, or when there is another new baby born, or the parents want a break during the school holidays. Then the children are sent off to Granny for a few days. Having little day-to-day contact with them, the children may play them up and totally exhaust the grandparents or get a thorough spoiling and then leave Granny feeling bereft until next time. Living in a retirement seaside resort, I observe this scenario daily, especially on the beach, and amongst my many friends who are grandparents!

(I personally have not yet become a grandmother, and as my children often remind me, I am impatient to reach this precious time. Instead I care for other people's babies and children, often when they are in desperate need of help and in some crisis situation. It is very revealing and has enabled me to ponder much on childcare in our modern world.)

From the point of view of the maturing person themselves, once they become an Elder, there is always a feeling of wanting to remain independent and unique, especially in a civilisation where individuality is encouraged at all costs. There is no longer any expectation that people will be cared for by the family.

What is the difference between Independence, Neediness and Co-dependence? How do we each find the right balance in the uncaring society in which we live at present?

Only by learning respect and love for each other, and understanding each other's needs fully, can we come to a right balance in our communities. Each one of us has _unique_ needs and wishes, and there is _no one answer_ to everyone's needs.

There are millions of Elders in our country who are living in isolation, becoming cut off from their communities. They may only see a carer once or twice a day for a few minutes, and then the door shuts again and they are left only with their televisions or a small pet as company.

In my life's work, I have experienced many different set-ups of care for the elderly by;

- Working as a nurse in geriatric wards in Hospitals, in Residential Care, Abbeyfield Homes and Nursing Homes of different types and standards.
- Doing live-in jobs as a temporary carer for the better-off, who still choose to live in their own homes.
- Working in Community Care with various agencies and as a District Nurse, visiting people who live as independently as they can, but who often suffer huge loneliness.
- Having friends who still have their parents living next door or in a room in the same house and doing some respite care for them from time to time.

- Working with the Alzheimer Disease Society as a respite worker, giving spouses a vital break from their demented partner for a few hours.
- Having been a Hospice at Home nurse, sitting with dying people in the dignity of their own bedrooms, until they find the right moment to pass peacefully into a new dimension.
- Living and working in Spiritual Communities where Elders are supported and respected. Here, because of Faith that there is a positive existence beyond death, their passing becomes a celebration and is given a space of dignity and respect. The whole community may be involved, not only in sharing their care, but also in a meditative way to be with the departed soul on their further journey.
- Having many friends who are older than me, who feel vulnerable because they are not sure how their lives will end.
- Attempting over several years to set up a community for Elders, based on active living and co-dependence, of which more in a later chapter.

With all these diverse experiences, I still do not believe there is only one answer to the 'problem of aging'. It is much more about the Elder feeling loved and supported in whatever set-up THEY choose, and that they also are able to continue their personal growth and loving, right to their last breath.

We cannot look into the crystal ball and see what lies ahead for us, but I believe that preparing consciously for our Final Journey and learning to LET GO of fear, material possessions and control is the ultimate goal for a peaceful Old Age.

We can gain in Spiritual Insights and Wisdom, knowing that what we have lived out here on earth is only a mere shadow of Reality in the broadest sense.

Physical and emotional care is only one aspect of becoming older. The Spiritual dimension becomes ever more real and important as we approach the moment of transition to another dimension. Our death can be a fearful trauma, or a peaceful journey.

This book is not intended to be a dogmatic thesis on my beliefs. It is hoped that by reading it you may be able to stop your busy lives and ponder for a while the Truths of Life and Death in a deep meaningful way.

Death has become a totally taboo subject in our society, although like birth, which is such a joyous event usually, it affects us all eventually.

Medical science has come to a point where often life can be maintained almost indefinitely, (as seems to be the case currently with Nelson Mandela,) but how appropriate is it to use this knowledge and power for each individual?

Do we, like the North American Indians (who wander out into the grasslands alone and wait for death to come), know when the moment of death is right? By sustaining life artificially with drugs, machines and operations are we in fact meddling with a natural event? Are our bodies ready to give up Life Energy, and disintegrate into earth substance? How can we as human beings know what is right when we now have Godlike power?

To quote the Bible;

To everything there is a season and a time to every purpose under the heaven. A time to be born and a time to die...

(Ecclesiastes Chapter 3, v.1 and 2)

These are questions which I have mused on often, as I have seen the suffering or peace which comes, as Elders grow ready for The Last Journey. Each individual is different; each passing is a unique happening.

But preparing for this momentous event of death is vitally important if we are to make this our own Journey, in Consciousness, without stress, pain or fear. Instead of ignoring the inevitable, or feeling apprehension whenever we think about it, or trying to prolong our life artificially, we can come to a place of Peace with the reality of it, to muse upon what WE believe, what we would like to happen around this time, and prepare our loved ones also for this moment.

Becoming an Elder joyously is just part of the preparation for this final event.

It is also about living positively during the last chapters of our story, of taking stock and enabling others to learn from our experiences, of giving our many gifts back to the earth and to our companions who have travelled with us thus far.

It is about remaining interested in life and the changes which are occurring ever more rapidly on this planet. It is about living fully in each moment, in a life which becomes ever more precious the shorter it becomes.

Chapter 40

Aging bodies

Our bodies, as physicists have only relatively recently discovered, are made up of tiny particles of gyrating Energy. When we touch ourselves it is only an illusion that we are solid! Each single cell contains mainly fluid and is constantly replacing itself, guided by thousands of different chemical and electrical processes and the thing we know as DNA, or 'cell intelligence.' It is hugely complex and so fascinating, but most of us take it for granted and do not care, so long as the 'machine' works for us.

The single most complex part of our mobile bodily structure is the brain and many people believe that our brain is our ultimate intelligence and that without it we are nothing. It is the complexity and uniqueness of it which gives us the possibility to be fully human; in our communication, creativity, mistakes, learning and actions.

But beyond this dimension there is also the 'Master Mind' which enables everything to remain alive, changing and replenishing itself constantly.

How do our cells know when and how to renew themselves? Why does our hand remain hand-shaped even when it grows from a baby to an adult and replenishes each cell every 7 years? These mysteries have always fascinated me.

If we think of the movement of the fluids and chemicals within each cell, and compare that to the movement of the stars and planets in our own comparatively tiny solar system, we begin to have an inkling of the enormity of everything, and we can feel the very presence of a Creative Energy which masterminds the growth and destruction of all things.

Some people will call this super intelligence God, others Allah, Chi, Prana or whatever the human mind has invented to conceptualise this enormity. I chose to call it Universal Creative Energy as we can understand it better using this term.

Alongside the concept that we are all created from One Energy is also the reality of our Uniqueness. The fact that human beings can think and feel separately from others and say 'I' is a sign that we are not just a blob of Energy, but that we each have an Individual Core.

I personally, along with millions of others alive at present, believe that this core has Intelligence which remains even after our physical structure has dissolved. It is not dependent on the working of our cellular brain but is greater and freer, and will come many times in new forms to this earth. In this we are different from all the animals on this planet. Human beings have self-consciousness, morality, and can choose our own Destiny.

So, understanding this concept, we can recognise that our Energy as we age in the physical sense begins to diminish. Even our brains may do so, stopping us from thinking clearly, but our unique 'I' is still there till the very last beat of the heart, and the last breath, when it starts to gradually withdraw from the cells, and dissipates into the great Whole or Universe.

This is described in many ways by different religious beliefs but is essentially the same. Religions with their different terminologies tend to separate people and even cause wars, but if we can learn to speak a 'Universal Language' we could start to understand and accept each other better. It is fear which separates us from our fellow human beings. Dogma and Faith have no place in Universal Truth.

When we are conceived, Universal Energy links with the reproductive cells and rushes in. From this moment it is forming our bodies within our mothers, according to the blueprint it receives from our parents, but from the moment of birth and the first breath, we become separate and unique.

From birth on, Energy not only replenishes and replaces the millions of cells in our bodies but we also start to die! Death is a process of dehydration, as each cell has to die if it is no longer sustained by fluid and energy.

As we age, our bodies become more and more dehydrated. This shows as skin looseness, wrinkles, dryness, sagging breasts, dying hairs, which turn us white or bald, deteriorating hearing and sight and other senses, stiff dry joints, brittle bones, lax muscles and a weaker digestive system.

Our brains may also dry out and cause forgetfulness, slowing down of thoughts and eventually dementia. Once the life energy has expired and the heart and circulation of fluids has stopped, and we have died, the physical body rapidly disintegrates and dries up further, only leaving the bones, which are more mineralised, to remind us that we were once here.

The Energy, which once enabled us to run around and play, work and reproduce, dissipates back into the earth and the air, enabling it to be recycled and used again by others. Our core however, as intelligence, (referred to by many as the Soul or Spirit) continues in other forms. We are now said to be in 'Heaven' or wherever our Faith supposes it to be.

Some people believe that without our brains we cease to exist at all. Death is therefore a terrible blank end.

Many older people fear the natural processes of aging and will do anything they can to prevent their bodies showing these signs. Nowadays we can go to extreme lengths to try to remain young and beautiful. We can inject fluid chemicals into the skin as Botox to stop the wrinkles; we can paint creams and powders on our skin to cover blemishes; we can put chemicals on our hair to keep its colour. We can have corrective surgery to stop us sagging.

We can chop our bodies open and insert new metal or plastic joints, we can insert other body parts and organs from dead people to sustain us, we can have machines to breath for us, change our blood to work as kidneys; we can have a machine inserted to keep our heart beating regularly.

We have learned to sustain life almost indefinitely. Modern medicine claims to heal and care, but its main aim is to keep us alive by whatever means, so we do not have to sink into an abyss of the unknown after death.

Recently I gave a talk on Health to a group of more than 30 ladies from the WI. I asked how many of them were taking some form of medication. I was shocked to discover that it was 100%! Our Doctors do their best to treat and support life and reduce suffering. Their skills at diagnosing what has gone wrong with the 'machine' are second to none.

However they do not comprehend the fact that Life Energy is sustained by good nutrition, positive thinking, exercise, light and life, and however many tablets are taken, this will not compensate for a Healthy Lifestyle, and self-caring. All allopathic medicine is dead matter and has unwanted chemical reactions in the body, known as side effects. There are more deaths from over-medication in this country, than from any other cause! Is it necessary to take all these tablets, or do we need to learn something else about Health to help us live actively as we mature?

We have also been brainwashed by years of modern medicine to believe that if we go to the doctor and get some tablets we will be made 'better'. All we are doing is changing some of the chemical composition of our bodies, usually with severe side effects.

Tablets may reduce the pain or inflammation temporarily, but *why has it occurred in the first place*? What have we done, eaten, or thought which has contributed to this imbalance of our innately healthy systems?

It is not necessary to be ill if you are old! It is not necessary to go regularly to the doctor, take tablets, or have operations, physiotherapy, tests, x-rays or other expensive treatments. Given the right food and enough fluid, light, rest, love, fresh air, good thinking and time YOUR BODY WILL HEAL ITSELF and REMAIN HEALTHY!

This is not to say that there won't be some natural changes as we grow older. We are not meant to live in our physical state for eternity, and just as an old oak tree gets thicker bark, less leaves, and 'wrinkles' and eventually falls over and rots, so do we also deteriorate and eventually die.

Healing Energy, which can re-enliven a sick body, can be accessed from the Universe, as is done by Healers. They channel the Energy from all around into the client's body and it is used in whatever way and measure the body needs it. Beyond this treatment is also the client's mind and thoughts which can help or hinder this process. I have trained as a healer and realise that everyone has this same potential. It is only a matter of remaining open and loving to vibrational Energy.

Whether you believe this or not, there is plenty of anecdotal evidence to support what I am writing about. I leave you with this thought to research it further.

There are some practical ways in which you can, as Elders, support a natural flow of Energy, and enjoy good health despite increasing age. By looking at your diet, lifestyle and the way you think about things you can live fully and positively up until the time when you need to move on from this life.

None of us were intended to be immortal! In the Bible it mentions 'Three score years and ten' (i.e. 70) as being the optimal length of life. Nowadays men and women are living on average much longer than that.

Perhaps we can see any time after 70 as being given to us as a Grace, when we can in fact give back our own Energy to the earth; when we have fulfilled our life purpose and we are now helping to heal some of the sickness of the planet.

Chapter 41

The Problem

Sometimes you will meet a really old person who seems to shine with an Inner Light. They radiate Peace and Joy, and look almost transparent. They are wise and gentle, and one can feel safe with them. Their eyes have a faraway look that seems to understand the world. These are the Elders who may be respected and who can help us.

How different this is from the person who is in physical pain, who may be sick and overweight, burdened by a body that has become too tied down to earthly matter. They may complain constantly about their condition, act selfishly and seem to be very fearful and demanding. They take a whole concoction of tablets, rarely sleep peacefully, eat little wholesome food, and spend many hours watching television. They have little real quality of life and seem to be waiting to die, even asking frequently why they are still here.

Sadly this latter type of person is seen only too frequently amongst Elders, in homes and hospitals, away from their family and friends. It is this fact that has driven me to write this book;

- To help a few more people to understand what they can do *themselves* to come to a place of health and peace before they are ready to die;
- To enable relatives and carers to approach aging with more respect and reverence;
- To understand what they could do which might help their clients/relatives to feel at peace again.

Caring for Elders need not be draining or depressing, as it so often appears to be. Elders have lived full, interesting lives and are now able to reflect some of that goodness back to the world, given a listening ear, time and opportunity.

They have wonderful stories to tell of their adventures and want to be heard. That part of their lives, their memories, can be more real to them than where they are now. They reflect another generation, with different values and experiences.

They are not just 'Mrs Jones, in Room 3', who doesn't like her egg overcooked, and often pees on the floor and screams at night; they are a young woman who has perhaps fulfilled a vital role in the French Resistance movement, or been the first woman who studied at Oxford for a degree, or been a nationally known singer.

I have been very privileged during my career as a carer/nurse to meet many interesting souls who have then sunk into oblivion due to a system which no longer recognises them as whole people, but lumps them together as the senile, full of problems and grief.

How would you feel if you were suddenly transported out of life at short notice and separated from all your familiar treasures which meant something to you? If you were labelled with a wrist band, bossed about, even shouted at if you were slow, pulled and pushed roughly, and given umpteen tablets to take? If you could no longer linger over your morning tea in bed with the paper, hug the cat, potter in your garden, chose what you fancy for lunch, or phone a friend to go out for tea?

If you are uprooted into a care situation you may feel angry, resentful, confused, bereft, or depressed. Life is not worth living any longer! You feel totally DISEMPOWERED.

This is the final plight of many, many elderly people in this country. Because of the difficulty of keeping the family unit together in our modern society, older people very often end up living in houses too large for their needs, without a partner and finding they no longer can cope with the day-to-day tasks of running the house. They dig their heels in and say that they do not want to move. It is their home and all their memories are there.

Then one day they may become unwell, often with a urinary tract infection or 'flu and they cannot eat and drink enough. Their blood chemicals rapidly become unbalanced and they get confused, maybe wandering out in their nightgown to find help, and a caring neighbour will contact a relative or the doctor. The decision is made that they need to go into hospital or a care home and from then on things rapidly deteriorate.

Taken from their familiar surroundings the Elder no longer has the points of reference which they need to feel safe and individual. They rapidly become institutionalised, fretful, depressed, and the most common question to visitors is "When can I go home?"

This can become very distressing for all concerned. Guilt is not a happy emotion at the best of times, and when it is your own mother or father who is sad and no longer 'compos mentis' it can be very stressful indeed.

However good the care home and the carers are, it is still a place to go to die and not your own environment with all your familiar objects around.

Another scenario, if the relatives have been sensitive to this former trauma, is to bring in live-in carers; a very costly alternative. Suddenly the elder has to share their house with a middle-aged bossy lady who cooks food you don't like, sits around making mobile phone calls, may not even speak English very well, and you don't trust her not to take some of your precious jewellery either!

There may be a succession of these ladies and you never know who is going to do what, which ones are good or which lazy and you become frightened, demanding and cantankerous even if you were usually fairly happy. Eventually your money runs out and the house has to be sold to pay for your care and so you are dragged off to a local care home after all. Neither of these scenarios is happy at all!

Another more positive way might be that you have downsized at an appropriate moment to a small bungalow or flat with an on-call button and although you live alone, you have friends and neighbours who are aware of your frailty and pop in regularly or take you out.

They can help to organise some community care for you, perhaps some weekly meals on wheels (a fast disappearing commodity in England!), and shopping for fresh vegetables or someone to change your bed-linen and hoover through. A young lad from the local college comes to do the garden sometimes and you enjoy chatting to him about his future hopes and dreams. You may have given up your garden altogether but have a beautiful communal one to enjoy.

You read a lot of interesting books and have learnt to meditate so that you are peaceful and self-sufficient and can ponder on who you are and your past life activities and what they meant in terms of life lessons.

You watch little or no television and may have a small pet to care for and keep you company. Your home is pretty, full of family photos and memories of your rich life.

Regularly your family, who live locally, appear and take you out, so that you can enjoy your grandchildren without stress and see them grow and develop. They love hearing your stories about your past adventures! You get fresh air and sunshine, and even if you can't go out, you sit in your little garden watching the bees and butterflies.

You paint sometimes or do some sketching, listen to music and sometimes go out to a concert or good film, taken by your family or friends. You may like to go to church or a community group or activity, to meet other people.

As you become frailer you may need various aids and these can be provided by the local district nurses and carers, so that you can still enjoy your daily bath, your nails and hair are kept nice and any other physical deterioration is monitored and cared about.

You may go to lunch regularly with your family and sit and enjoy the busy feel of a young household, glad at the end of the day that you can return to your quiet private space.

Once in a while you telephone your elderly friends. As time goes on more and more of them have passed on, so every evening before you sleep you talk to those who have gone and remember the lovely times you had together. You pray that you will meet them again in Spirit when your time comes.

One day you may feel rather tired and go to bed earlier than usual. During the night you peacefully die in your sleep and you are found the next morning by the neighbour who has a key and has noticed that your curtains are still drawn.

This is a very peaceful way to go, and could be the way you chose it to be. It is so much more dignified and natural than being cared for in an institution.

There are many variations between these two examples, and hopefully you can prepare sufficiently to know that when the time comes, your wishes will be taken into account and you can have the care and death which you have wanted.

We all have to die at some point. Most people currently do this in hospital or a care home. Increasingly there is a trend for people to want to die in their own home environment, and given love and support this should be possible. I will make some more suggestions in a later chapter as to how you might organise this.

Old age is NOT a problem. It is only perceived as such because we have lost touch with the truth that it is a journey for the individual, which needs supporting and enabling, rather than controlling.

Government policies need to change in line with new trends, to support financially and legally peoples' diverse wishes. The problem is that this has not yet happened!

Chapter 42

Right living for Elders; Nutrition

Our bodies are what we have made them over many years of habits; habits of eating, sleeping, working, exercising, being creative, loving, and thinking. We are intimately linked together in all these things and how we behave affects us in every way.

We are also formed by our early years; our first nutrition, nurturing, and care from our parents which builds up our bodies in a healthy way. If this has been lacking we may well suffer ill health as we get older and frailer.

Our education will also have affected us; whether we were encouraged to be creative, physically active, and whether we were enthusiastic about learning. Many children suffer greatly because of an inappropriate education, in the years of crucial development, if they are unhappy or bored, or academically forced.

Our genetic inheritance is also a factor. We may inherit weaknesses or illnesses which our parents have as a result of generations of poor living. Diet, poverty, and upbringing are all factors.

Another aspect which is more subtle but may nevertheless be very significant is what is termed Karma. This is a 'package of lessons' which some believe we bring with us at birth on a soul level, to work through this lifetime, and to enable us to learn about how we behaved in a past lifetime.

There are also those who read Astrology. The birth chart which maps out the influences of the whole cosmos at the moment of our birth can give clues as to the life, health, strengths and weaknesses of an individual, which will colour their entire life journey and also their health.

There is also most obviously that which we may just call 'Life happens!' We all have many diverse experiences and traumas throughout our long lives. Some people sail through life virtually unscathed, while others suffer huge stress and angst from what happens to them.

Baring all these factors in mind there are still many things we can do NOW which will benefit our physical bodies in terms of nutrition and stop our bodies from premature aging and ill health.

The present and how we live and feel today creates our future. It is never too late to start living in a new healthy regime!

Food has increasingly become poorer in quality since the introduction of agrochemicals after the last war. Prior to this people's diets were generally better than now, in terms of fresh vegetables, pure water, fruit and plain cooking. The food industry does much to con us to the contrary!

Additives, preservatives, pesticides, colourings, flavourings are all added, and our bodies have to cope with them. We also get into bad habits of snacking on sugary foods, drinking caffeine and alcohol, eating easy to prepare ready-meals, where the ingredients have been processed, frozen and bear little resemblance to a growing plant.

Going back to the concept of Energy in everything, the plant starts to lose some of its Energy as soon as it is picked. The fresher and the less processed we can eat it, the more of this Energy is available for us to enjoy.

It will go to each cell and the micronutrients will help to heal and restore all of our cells, keeping us healthy, younger looking, and more energised.

We will become more hydrated and may even loose some of the wrinkles which are beginning to make us look old!

So as a rule of thumb try to eat fresh ORGANIC vegetables, raw or lightly steamed, and reduce any foods which are processed, overcooked, frozen, GMO or otherwise tampered with.

At the same time cut out sugar, refined flour, caffeine, and reduce alcohol, and red meat.

Your diet may need to change considerably to start detoxifying. Take it gently at first and drink plenty of fresh filtered water to get rid of the toxins being released.

A very helpful book is Patrick Holford's Optimum Nutrition Bible, as well as other books by this very knowledgeable nutritionist. He also suggests taking supplements, as the body's basic needs can no longer be met in our unhealthy lifestyle. The soil has also become sick, so that the crops grown on impoverished soils do not have the trace elements (minerals and vitamins) which we all require.

Recent propaganda from the Press indicates that these supplements may harm you rather than heal. It is a backlash from the pharmaceutical companies who are becoming increasingly alarmed that the 'health food lobby' is getting more and more popular. They have billions invested in allopathic medicaments and government monies are also tied up in these drug companies, so of course the public are conned.

Getting some good supplements is vital to increasing your energy levels. You will need a multivitamin and mineral supplement, with high dosages, as well as omega oils 3, 6, and 9. Your brain needs care too, so as you age you could take some special nutrients for it, as suggested in Holford's 'Alzheimer's Prevention Plan'. Other supplements might also be beneficial for particular health conditions.

The numbers of people suffering from dementia is increasing at an alarming rate. Although the government is addressing this to some extent with care facilities, few have asked the common sense question 'Why?'

We are <u>overusing</u> our brains by driving cars, watching TV, computers and fast moving sensory experiences. Our brains have to work much harder than they used to, in our cerebral world of technology. Compare life now to how it was in 1948 (at the start of the NHS). We are asking so much more of our physical and emotional bodies. Therefore they need extra support to prevent early deterioration.

We have created a world of convenience foods, machines to do our work, fast time schedules, and stress. Modern young people seem to be born with a capacity to absorb more of this stress than the older population. We, the Elders, therefore have to take heed of this fact and act accordingly, supplementing our inadequate diets to compensate.

Locally grown food is always best. Support your local grower who works very hard for a meagre wage because they believe in what they are doing. Veggie-box schemes are starting up all over the country. The more the customer demands, the more the government will consider supporting these ventures in their agricultural policies.

Buying all your veggies at the supermarket encourages road transport and pollution, air transport and more pollution and we are running out of oil! Reduce your food miles, eat seasonal vegetables, and you will be absorbing local Energy.

Most 'Organic' vegetables found on the shelves are imported from Spain, have been picked when under-ripe, and may also have been irradiated, but this does not appear on the label. There are also up to 26 'EU allowable' sprays used in organic commercial growing!

Best of all you could look at your garden patch, however small it is, and see if you can produce some of your own food. Raised beds, filled with good quality compost are easy to manage, without a lot of stooping or digging. You could put some onto the lawn, and thus reduce mowing time! It is nicest to grow fast salads, greens and roots, all of which are easy and do not need a lot of aftercare, except some water. Don't bother with potatoes or tomatoes (unless you have a green-house), both from the deadly nightshade family and both prone to blight.

Herbs of various kinds are bursting with goodies and can be added to colourful salads throughout the summer. Pick fresh every day. These will also encourage bees into your garden to fertilise some soft fruit, which is lovely in a breakfast Smoothie on a summer's day.

Without becoming obsessive, make food a priority in your life. Always eat a healthy breakfast, with fruit, and sprinkled ground-up seeds and nuts. Porridge is a good option for winter mornings, with sprinkles on the top! Enjoy raw food in season, warming soups and stews on cold winter days.

Eat your main meal at lunchtime to give it time to digest and reduce what you eat in the evening, preferably with nothing but a warm drink after 6p.m as the night-time shouldn't be spent digesting.

As one ages, so the need for calories is less, so you need to reduce the amount you eat gradually. A light but tasty meal is much more enjoyable and will keep you fitter.

Protein and good fats from fish oils, nuts, seeds and pulses all should be included as well as eggs. Forget what the Doctor tells you about cholesterol. Statins are not the answer! A healthy mixed diet, reducing margarines, red meat and cream is much easier and healthier. It will also reduce blood pressure, improve diabetes, get rid of excess weight and muzzy-headedness.

Taking plenty of fluids is vital to good health. Unless your circulation is compromised with a heart condition, aim to drink at least 5 glasses of filtered or spring water a day, however much you are rushing around. This should be increased in hot weather or if you are exercising. There is little need for teas and coffees, but if you do fancy a warm drink then try Rooibosch tea, which is caffeine free or Green tea, high in antioxidants, or grain coffee powders, available from health shops. There are also lots of tasty herb teas around now, all worth a try. Do not add sugar to drinks, but add just a little honey or agave syrup if you really need to.

Milk is for babies, (baby calves only!) and so if you want a creamy texture to your tea and coffee substitutes, add a drop of almond, oat, soya or coconut milk to it. These are becoming available in most supermarkets now.

When you do your shopping take a good pair of reading glasses and always read the labels. Avoid all additives, preservatives, salt, hidden sugars, corn-starch and syrup, hydrogenated fats and any 'E' numbers. You will be amazed at how little you will want to buy off the shelves!

Instead go to the fish shop, the butcher (for chicken, rabbit, local lamb or turkey), the greengrocer and even the baker, although bread needs to be limited to one slice a day. Try putting a couple of slices in bags in the freezer, so you can enjoy fresh bread if you fancy some, but again try to buy wholemeal organic bread, preferably sourdough which has a natural rising method.

By now you may be saying "But I can't digest all these things". It is true that if you are elderly the digestion may be less efficient, but try therefore to gradually introduce more roughage in the form of cooked/puréed vegetables and a bit of salad. Soak all the pulses very well and only eat them at lunch time occasionally. Introduce brown rice, Quinoa and oatmeal into your diet, all high in Vitamins B, essential for good brain power.

You may find that your bowel movements change somewhat. How many elderly people are chronically constipated and need to take daily aperients?

The lining of the small intestine, where digestion takes place, is covered in tiny waving Villae which get damaged over time with a bad diet. These will take time to heal but will increase your absorption of nutrients and make you feel much more energised. Stick with the new regime and you will be amazed!

Green Powder, containing many finely ground vegetables, is a huge help in healing the gut and also making you more alkaline if you tend to acidity conditions like arthritis, fibromyalgia and cancer. You can add a tablespoonful to water or a Smoothie to help your energy. A good website including many recipes is www.energiseforlife.com. Amazon sells 'Amazing Grass' super-food which is tasty and provides all the nutrients you need.

If you live on your own it is often difficult to manage the shopping and cooking of healthy meals. Often portions in supermarkets are too big for one. Instead of resorting to a small ready-meal, which has been frozen or highly processed, have you thought about linking with a friend or two to share your main mealtimes together? Then you would only need to cook once or twice a week and could have the enjoyment of someone else's cooking and a trip out. Ask your friends if they are interested in this idea!

Luncheon clubs, although they provide a vital link to others socially, may not be as geared up to healthy eating as you would like to be. Try educating them to buy local organic veggies and reduce their red meat cooking; reducing fattening puddings too, replacing them with fruit or natural yoghourt. Spotted Dick, bread pudding etc. are always favourites with the elderly, but other things can take their place.

Your tea or evening meal can become very light, just some salad, a boiled egg, some sugar-free baked beans (Whole Earth), or a sandwich with chicken/seed butter and salad. Oat cakes and rice cakes make a nice alternative to bread.

As you become older your chewing capacity and teeth may become less good. You may have false teeth and not manage raw veggies any more. A food mixer then becomes an essential piece of equipment. You can lightly steam-cook your veggies then puree them briefly. Keep the juice from cooking for your next soup or bouillon drink. Don't just resort to tins or processed foods. Remember that the first part of digestion takes place in your mouth, so mixing with saliva, eating slowly and chewing well helps your digestion.

Reading or watching TV while you are eating takes Energy from the stomach, where it is needed, to the brain and reduces your capacity to digest. Try and avoid this completely.

Winter soups, homemade, can include lots of different veggies and also pulses, or grains. Try soaking pearl barley or spelt, cooking it long and slow, to make a sustaining meal base.

Instead of having morning coffee and biscuits and afternoon tea and cake, try out alternative snacks, including a natural fruit bar, some sliced fresh fruit, a few raisins with cashew nuts, and a drink of herb tea. Healthy choices are endless!

Very good luck with your new diet and remember that everything you put into your body gives you Energy. The fresher and less tampered with it is, the more Energy it will give you and the better you will feel.

Lifelong habits are hard to change or break, but your incentive can be the knowledge that you will feel better, have more energy and be able to have more fun and do more if you eat healthily, not just for a few days, but from now on. A NEW YOU will start to immerge. People will start to comment how well you look too!

Chapter 43

Right-living for Elders; Exercise of body and mind

"If you don't use it, you lose it!" is a common expression which you may hear when referring to exercise and the Elderly. How true it is!

Muscles start to deteriorate after a mere 6 hours of not being used, so constant exercise, regularly done as part of life, is much better than going to the gym once a week!

How old you are and how frail depends very much on what type of exercise you can start to do.

The gift of becoming older is that you no longer have set work hours, so you have freedom and TIME to exercise!

Natural walking out in the fresh air is the first one to concentrate on, as it moves the body in many gentle ways, helps the circulation, the heart, bowel movements, a feeling of wellbeing, and also gives you Light. Each single cell receives more oxygen as you walk briskly, thus energising every part of your body.

We absorb much of our Energy through Light and fresh air. There are people who can live on Light alone; who do not need to eat any food at all! This is an esoteric path and not to be tried out by anyone, but there is good scientific evidence that it is possible, given the right preparation. It proves however that when we go for a walk outside we are benefitting our bodies.

How often and how much you walk depends on your current fitness, but try to start gradually and work up, doing a bit every day.

If for any reason you have a sedentary day then go straight back to a walk next day and build it up again. Two shorter walks are probably better than one longer one that tires you out. Listen to your own body and when you feel tired stop! Try to gradually go up a few hills too, so that your heart begins to pump a bit harder. If you have any discomfort, breathlessness or pain, take it gradually.

Chose a pleasant route and look at things as you go. About 20-30 minutes brisk walk will benefit you. Being in touch with nature is very important for our mental wellbeing. The constantly changing seasons, the flowers by the path, the birds or animals and children you may spot, even in an urban environment, will bring renewed interest in life. If you live on a busy main road, try not to walk where traffic fumes are worst, as we breathe in loads of poisons from them. Go down the side streets where it is quieter.

Having a dog may help you to go for walks, as some people feel vulnerable or lonely walking on their own; or joining a 'Walking for Fitness' group may be the answer. Here you can chat to others, and the walks are graded according to fitness levels.

Chose a time of day when you are feeling at your best to take your walk. This may be first thing in the morning, or later afternoon after a rest, but try not to walk on a full stomach if you can.

Once you are feeling much fitter generally you can start to think about other exercise regimes which you enjoy.

Swimming not only stretches and relaxes you; it also builds up your stamina. Chlorine in the pools can be problematic for some. Be sure to shower well afterwards. There is usually some fitness or aerobic classes at some point during the week if you need motivation and like group activities. Often pools will have a special session for the over 50's. If you have sore joints or are overweight there is nothing more soothing than the weightlessness of water. Don't get cold and resist having coffee straight afterwards, as it will undo most of the benefit! Drink some warm, not iced, water or herb tea instead. Try to swim at least once a week if you can. You will find gradually you can swim further each time, if you have been a swimmer in the past.

Yoga and Pilates are both done in classes and often you can find a class especially for older people. Stretching your muscles and toning them will help them to stay healthy. An added benefit is the deep breathing which oxygenates the cells, and the sense of mental calm and wellbeing which can be achieved with the help of a good teacher. Your balance and stamina will improve too. Practicing for a few minutes every day at home is the best way to get into a healthy routine. Having some inspirational music, enough floor space and a non-slip surface are all you need to get started.

If you are already fairly stiff or disabled with arthritis, injuries or other problems, you can also exercise on a chair. Moving what you CAN move is of benefit to the whole body. You are never too stiff to exercise a bit. Rotating your shoulders, moving your arms, ankles and knees will keep them supple.

If you have nerve problems and cannot move, such as in Motor Neurone Disease, Parkinson's, MS or after a stroke then PASSIVE movements, done by someone else on a very regular basis, every few hours, does a lot to reduce your toxicity and increase your feeling of wellbeing by bringing oxygen to the cells. Your skin will be better able to cope with constant lying or sitting, your bowels will stay regular.

Massage is the next stage after passive movements and is hugely beneficial to <u>all</u> Elders, whether they are sick or not. The Lymphatic drainage system, which takes care of immunity and toxins in the body, the toxins in the muscles and joints are all moved by regular deep massage. Digestion will be improved, and a sense of wellbeing and relaxation can be felt for days afterwards, improving sleep quality. Gentle massage is now available in many beauty salons, but you may find more benefit if you find a therapeutic masseuse, who is highly qualified in different physical problems and may take a more holistic approach to your health.

Reflexology is a gentle non-invasive treatment on the feet or hands. Because it is addressing the whole person through the periphery it is deep acting and very relaxing and you don't need to get undressed except your stockings. Mobile therapists can come to your home and treat you on a couch, bed or reclining chair.

Good therapists take time for YOU, and what you are paying for is an hour or so of one-to-one care and attention, advice and listening which you will not find at any GP surgery. Many therapists think broadly about health and may be able to give you some extra advice on diet or lifestyle, or just listen to your problems which cause you fear and stress. About 20% of the population now use complementary therapies.

Acupuncture, using the ancient Chinese knowledge of the Energy meridians, can be extremely beneficial too. Using tiny needles which are inserted around the body, blockages of the Energy flow are addressed. How long the treatment will benefit you depends on what other issues are going on in your life and how quickly the body returns to its 'blocked' state. Pain and congestion are very common as we age, rather like a stream which gets blocked up with silt. By clearing the blockages, the body detoxifies more easily. This can also be helped hugely by diet as stressed in the last chapter.

Acid from an unsuitable diet accumulates around joints as arthritis. Taking pain killers and steroids does nothing to help this situation except create more acid in the tissues. Detoxification and cleansing is the only thing which will help any kind of inflammation which is going on. This is especially true if one eats a lot of sugar, tea, coffee, wheat and alcohol.

Diabetes, a huge problem in the western world is caused by over-eating the wrong foods. Keeping strictly to the suggested diet, you may rapidly be able to come off tablets and feel much better overall.

Our minds, if not used sufficiently as we age, can also become slower, even to the extent of losing track of space and time. This is old age forgetfulness and different from clinical dementia which I will describe later. Going out and about and relating to others with similar interests will help. It is said that doing Sudoku and crossword puzzles helps to exercise the brain!

There are many sociable sporting activities which are available and suitable for Elders, depending on your interests, finances and fitness levels. I live in a retirement town by the sea and we have the choice of croquet, bowls (indoor and outdoor), petanque, walking groups, folk and old-time dancing, line-dancing, tap dancing and others. Joining such a group can bring hours of fun, new friends and physical exercise.

Exercise needs first and foremost to be fun. When you relate to your body in a positive way you are giving it the message that it is still useful and you are still integrated with it. The body is our tool with which we relate to the world.

On a mental level it is important to exercise too! In the town where I live we have scrabble groups, bridge clubs, interest groups on many subjects, talks, societies, churches and support groups of many kinds. There are also poetry and book clubs for those who enjoy reading. When my mother was in her 90's she was visited regularly by a volunteer from the local library, who became her friend and chose several books for her each month.

If we neglect the body and mind, we very soon become distant from the world and all it gives us and we are already on the way to passing over into a world where we no longer need a body and a brain; i.e. we are dying! Many older people give up using their bodies to their full capacity and sit for hours in a chair, looking at the television.

Keeping interested in everything around, nature, people, places and local happenings is very different from sitting watching the news 3 or 4 times a day, which I have observed some old folk doing. Negative news drains energy, and unfortunately there seems to be little positive news given out on the BBC!

It is 'real life' with all its different aspects, which keeps us happy and healthy as we journey towards the end of our lives. We need to feel part of life and that we can contribute something, however frail we become.

Chapter 44

St John Communities

Having a family is certainly a great help in keeping a healthy connectedness to passing time. Grandchildren, great-grandchildren, nieces and nephews can send photos; keep in touch via Skype and telephone. Family gatherings where the Elder is surrounded by different generations can bring a sense of continuity and belonging. They are the matriarch or patriarch of the group. I have observed Elders, whom I have cared for, being much more content and focused if they do belong to a large family. They chat happily about their children for hours.

If one feels alone and unwanted, old age can be much more difficult. Fear of dying alone and destitute can be very real.

If you do live alone and have no family or close friends, then getting in touch with the voluntary sector may become a life-line. There are people who can visit you, and possibly arrange to take you out to a local club or meeting. There are luncheon clubs, whist drives, bingo, day care facilities, organised trips out in a minibus and several other things depending on where you live.

Isolation is a very soul destroying state of mind. We are naturally social creatures and being alone for many hours on end can bring on depression or dementia.

Old people who live alone often lose touch with time, may get up in the small hours and think the day has begun, or never go to bed at all. They may stop eating properly and just snack on a jam sandwich and a cup of tea. Before long the body starts to degenerate as well as the mind. Hygiene is neglected and it does not take long before the physical body becomes sick.

Hospitalisation then is necessary and aftercare has to be arranged on discharge, usually to a costly residential or nursing home. This is distressing for everyone concerned and may take weeks to organise. There are literally hundreds of hospital beds at any one time in England taken up unnecessarily with this scenario.

Our current care system is struggling to cope with thousands of Elders in this predicament. Another answer of the current government and care sector is to provide 'sheltered housing', where a flat with a warden and a common room is provided. This does not really address loneliness, unless the resident is motivated to go out and meet their neighbours. A gradual decline may still occur and the resident who has moved from their old neighbourhood may not settle and often feels very isolated.

Residential homes, if well run, can provide more company, but it is essential then that there are activities, outings and stimulation. Again cost is a huge issue as to whether this excellence of care and individual approach is there.

The Abbeyfield Homes have got a good mix of socializing at mealtimes and privacy, where the two main meals are shared, but each resident has their own small flatlet or bedsit. Sadly the small family units that were found in most towns in England are being 'upgraded' to become bigger, more impersonal and modern and have lost much of their personal touch that comes of belonging to a small family with a 'housekeeper'. More health and hygiene rules mean that residents can no longer just wander into the kitchen and help with meal preparation if they feel like doing a little something domestic. Instead there is an ever greater divide between staff and residents, the carers and the cared for.

Several years ago I had the oportunity of working in a community based on the ideals of the Austrian philosopher Rudolf Steiner. It was a Camphill community in Yorkshire, a village set up for adults with learning disabilities. Each household consisted of a housemother and father, who often had their own children, and several disabled 'villagers' who mainly worked in craft workshops or on the land, according to their capacity.

One household in this village was set aside for Elders who were now of retirement age and becoming frailer. During the day other younger villagers came in to do housework and help care for them. There were no 'staff' or 'clients', but each day saw about 20 folk sitting down to lunch together. There were young volunteers from oversees who lived there too. Some afternoons there was a concert or slide show, at other times the Elders were invited out to other community houses for lunch. Sometimes there was an outing to the local village or some beauty spot nearby.

One lady of 99, whose daughter had Down's syndrome and also lived in the village, was cared for physically by a part-time nurse. She sat quietly in the lounge and observed the children coming and going, heard the concerts and saw everyone at their work. Everyone loved to talk to her.

Being such a varied and mixed aged household had the advantage that some were more able bodied than others, and youth was also there. It was a calm and happy place.

I then later went to The Findhorn Foundation in Scotland, a Spiritual Community based on love, and saw how the Elders in that community were encouraged to remain active, were cared for voluntarily by other younger members, and given the oportunity to give advice and counselling to others.

It was after these experiences that I decided to try and create a Community for Elders in Devon. I advertised and made contact with a group who were thinking along the same lines, and we even found a property which would have been ideal; a former residential home which was closing down. The name "St John Community" had come to me in deep meditation and I was inspired by my vision.

The basic concept was a 'family set-up' of single or married people of varying ages, independent and with few care needs. Everyone would have their own bedsit and bathroom, but eat main meals together, as in the Abbeyfield homes and Camphill.

Because there were to be no paid carers, each person there could fulfil some role in helping the others. Some could take on part-time cooking, housekeeping roles; others might help with the financial set-up, others work in the garden part-time, or create cultural richness.

It is very much the same sort of community ideal one finds in a monastic or convent life, but these people would not be dedicating their lives to God or religion but would be a modern version of this, where Love of each other, respect of privacy and space but also communal sharing was the ideal.

Any Community is made up of each person's unique contribution, and each individual becomes reflected in the Whole.

Many 'Hippy-style communities' were founded between the 1970's and 2000's, some more successful than others, but few or none of them encompassed Elders, who are so much part of our society. They mainly were made up of families and working people.

In order for a St John Community to be founded, financially there was a need for a group of people who would have the courage to invest in shares to buy the buildings, redeemable on death or leaving. As this would be a totally new venture, despite several attempts, the right group and buildings never came together to make this vision a reality.

Many people were inspired to make contact however. A shared way of living is often very appealing particularly to those Elders who don't have any family, who want to have 'fulfilment of old age' as I have been describing in the previous chapters. There would need to be sufficient younger people as well, committed to these ideals, in order to sustain the practical side of living together, as well as perhaps children, though not necessarily.

Purpose-designed buildings suitable for such a venture or an older style building with land could be used, although many of the latter demand huge upkeep. Everyone would need to contribute financially to the running costs, but these costs would be far lower than residential care, and easily affordable by pensioners, if some of the payment were also in lieu of some work hours. Everyone would have a role, decisions would be made together and the good of the whole community would be held.

It could be run as a non-profit business or a charity, and because it becomes the residents' own home, with no staff or clients, and not an institution, there would be less stringent rules on health and safety.

The public spaces could also perhaps be used for educational workshops, meetings, cultural events and artistic ventures or any other input depending on all the individuals' personal talents and interests. Everyone would enjoy the freedom of creativity, which is the Essence of Life.

There have been one or two attempts at similar projects in various places around the world. Holland gets close to villages for Elders; America has some very good examples of independent community living, as do Denmark and Germany. In Britain there are a couple of Co-housing projects where Elders can buy a flatlet and become part of the community, but as far as I am aware if one becomes frail, there is a need to move on to a residential or nursing home.

The problem remains unresolved until the government realises that this might be a way forward and will support planning consents and financial aspects to a greater extent. It is not a business run by outside agencies, but a home for a group of people who decide they want to live together with mutual interdependence.

We also need to become less selfish and egocentric in our wishes in order for such a community to work harmoniously. There is a tendency anyway for people to become more fixed in their needs as they mature, and less able to adapt to the needs of others.

Perhaps having read this you may feel the ideal is completely unrealistic and 'pie in the sky'. However I believe that this model is still the best for those Elders who are not socially supported by a nuclear family, and my dearest hope is to see such a project grounded somewhere and eventually for there to be communities within each village and town.

Interestingly small shared households are springing up all over Britain, as rented house prices rise steeply and mortgages are ever more difficult to come by. Three or more working adults may live together, each having a bedsit, and they may choose to eat together on some occasions. This model has also been taken on by a few pensioners.

Until our attitudes within society change radically about Elders and their role, and there is a basic understanding that we are all on a Spiritual journey which can be supported by others, and that our life is not just about productivity or enjoyment, but about who we _are_ in essence and how we become the greatest possible creation of this, then we will no longer have a situation where Old Age Pensioners are rated as second class citizens and become more and more of a problem to the rest of society.

Chapter 45

Personal Power and Creativity

Only today I heard on the radio that an increasing number of people over 70 are still working full time or actively seeking work. It appears that this may be one way that Elders are now trying to assert their lost potential; by continuing to be employed for a wage and produce something, they can maintain their dignity for that bit longer. Then they still have a useful role in society, as perceived by the younger generation.

Conversely, retiring could be seen as a further oportunity for personal growth when <u>time</u> is now freed up to do all the many things which were not possible during a busy working life.

Many Elders long for the day when they can hang up their suits, white shirts and ties and put on their gardening clothes, or their artists smocks, or even their drama costumes!

Strangely this day is being deferred more and more as the pensionable age is put back. The assumption that the general population is keeping healthier, and therefore living longer, has led recent government policy to put back the retirement age. This is also for financial reasons!

There are so many potentially creative things which can be tried out when you start to 'Wear purple!' This is your time and space to discover your hidden talents.

Sadly some Elders when they finally retire miss the structure of the workplace so much, and find it so hard to be self-disciplined that they cannot initiate a new lifestyle and become bored, morose and eventually sick.

Music may have been a neglected part of someone's life. Learning a new instrument, or even trying to learn one at all for the first time can bring a huge sense of satisfaction. Listening to music, going to concerts, or opera can bring great joy.

Joining a choir and having fun with others singing in unison or harmony can bring new friendships and fun. Rhythm helps to establish a regular heartbeat, singing improves the oxygenation to the cells by deeper breathing, remembering the words helps memory, and harmony singing helps listening skills and hearing. Singing also lowers blood pressure and alkalises the system!

Art and crafts help the creative urge to blossom. In everyone there is a hidden artist of some kind. It is just a matter of finding it. Choosing colours, working with form, be it in oils, pencils, pastels, water colour or acrylics; all these things help to fine-tune the senses.

You could also try woodwork, tapestry, knitting, card-making or any other craft or skill. There are many groups and classes available and new friendships can be formed here too.

Taking up any new hobby, be it sailing, model making, fishing, learning computer skills, writing novels, learning a foreign language or reading interesting biographies can stimulate and empower you, stretching your imagination in new ways.

A phrase I love is "You learn something new every day!" If you can truthfully say every evening before you go to sleep that you have learnt and understood something new, perhaps challenged yourself in a creative way or conquered a new skill that day, you will still be alive and growing. You will be using your personal power.

When you fall into bed after a boring long day and are only conscious of your aches and pains and grumbles, and think the world is becoming a terrible place after listening to only bad news on the TV, then you will fast be deteriorating into a grumpy old woman or man, fit for neither God nor beast!

'When you are old you *can* wear Purple!' It is this power which can lead you towards a state a fulfilment and contentment. Strive for your very best, discipline yourself as though you were still in the workplace, and make each day memorable. I never feel sadder than when I meet an Elder who is waiting to die. They have lost this power completely; they have lost the will to live.

Chapter 46

Dementia, Alzheimer's, and Parkinson's

As the conditions of Dementia, Alzheimer's and Parkinson's are becoming more and more prevalent in our society nowadays they merit a separate chapter. In our small town of Sidmouth in Devon we have an exceptionally high number of people with Dementia and we aim to become a centre of excellence here in the coming years, with shops adapting to elders needs, and the community becoming more aware.

Sadly there are few families now who have not been touched in some way by these devastating conditions. There are now many, many 'silent carers', partners or children of the afflicted, whose lives are drastically changed by conditions which are only slowly becoming recognised and supported by the current health care regime.

But why is this so? Is it a fact that there are now many more cases or are they just more exactly diagnosed and treated than before? It is true to say that there are now an increasing number of younger people who are being diagnosed at an early stage of these diseases. I wonder if their brains are malnourished and over-stressed by modern living to the extent that the cells start to die off prematurely?

Inflammation can cause devastation at a cellular level in many parts of the body, (for example by creating arthritis, heart disease, fibromyalgia, diabetes and cancer) and this can also affect the brain. The main causes of inflammation are pesticides, heavy metals, Monosodium Glutamate, Aspartame and other toxins found in our food and environment. Not infrequently Alzheimer symptoms appear after long-term use of tranquilizers, antidepressant drugs and heavy painkillers. Only by protecting the body from all these things, by eating organic food, taking nutritional supplements (especially Omega 3 and glutamine), and avoiding toxins which create free radicals, can we remain healthy.

It is the cerebral cortex which is mainly affected in Dementia and shows up as holes or 'tangles' on brain scans. The result is an inability to store recent information which has come into the brain, creating short-term memory loss which gradually becomes more and more extreme. Some people cannot remember sequences of things; others find that their dexterity diminishes.

If one thinks of memory as an imprint of Energy which creates a pattern on the energetic field, then it can be better understood perhaps. As the Energy weakens, so the imprint will also become weaker. Past happenings have already imprinted themselves and are therefore accessible more easily, until gradually they too fade.

A wonderful book which explains this very well is 'Contented Dementia' by Oliver James, which describes how to treat people with this condition, so that they can remain in the reality of their past memories and not become panicky that they do not remember recent events.

People treated in this way can live calmly and peacefully as their emotions will be stable and their carers will go along with whatever past scenario they are repeating, to make sense of current events.

The golden rules are;

- Never ask a direct question especially about recent events
- Never contradict them
- Encourage them to relate to past memories, and learn from them

Memory cafes are fast becoming popular in many towns and cities in England where memorabilia are displayed to trigger memories. Old songs are sung and a good time is had by all. These times also provide vital support for carers who may feel desperate and isolated trying to care for someone they feel they have already 'lost'.

Much can be done to improve things by eating the right foods and avoiding toxins and the right nutritional supplements can stop the disease getting worse quickly. An excellent book is by Patrick Holford on 'Alzheimer's Prevention.' Modern drugs, although they may hold the progress for a short while, may make it worse eventually, as explained by Holford.

Emotionally, if you are caring for a relative with dementia, there is deep grief as the person whom you knew and loved gradually disappears. They may be physically fit and well and able to exercise and eat for quite some years, but mentally they are gone. As the illness progresses these things also fade until death approaches.

From a Spiritual perspective it is sometimes hard for someone approaching the end of their lives to 'let go' of their material controls, desires and habits, sufficiently to pass over into the other dimension. They may have become too earthbound. Dementia and Alzheimer's gives people just this oportunity to 'let go' gradually. One can no longer control the environment around, and at the end the body also is out of control. So it can be experienced as a blessed release when the end finally comes.

It is very hard for their carers, but they too have endless opportunities for growth in terms of patience, tolerance, understanding and reading another's heart rather than head. One cannot use the brain to communicate, but the heart forces remain steady and the emotions can be gentle and warm, particularly if there is no fear of 'losing oneself' using the method described in Contented Dementia.

It is vital for carers at home to have breaks and other creative activities to refresh themselves, as being stuck day after day with a partner with dementia can be soul destroying and very tiring. When I worked for the Alzheimer's disease Society as a relief 'sitter' in the late '90's, it was forbidden for us to spend more than 4 hours relieving any one carer. That is an indication of how stressful it can be!

If you have cared day by day for someone with a failing memory there will come the moment when it is right for them to go into a specialised care home. You may feel real guilt about this, as you have been doing a good job up until now. You may fear that people won't understand them and make them more distressed.

By giving the staff a full picture of who they USED to be and how they are now able still to relate to some of these memories, you have given them a context in which to relate to the Elder. Writing down their likes and dislikes, their little foibles and what they 'act out' may be very helpful during the transition period from home to full time care.

Physical care will become heavier and heavier as time goes on. Don't feel bad about handing this care over to trained nurses or carers. You have done your bit with all the love which you could muster. Give yourself a pat on the back for a job very well done. You can now grieve your loved one's passing in peace and start to take up the threads of life again.

Visits may or may not be beneficial at this stage. At least if you do go in to see them you can check that they are being well looked after, even if they no longer recognise you. However the sense of hearing is the last one to go, so you may be amazed at what is absorbed through this sense and there may be unexpected glimmers of recognition from time to time. Just giving them love and comfort is a gift in itself.

Given the right care and understanding they will be at peace to continue their journey until the moment comes for them to breathe their last. That is the ultimate 'letting go' which many people find so hard to do at the end.

Getting an accurate diagnosis in the early stages may be difficult for some neurological conditions. We all have forgetful moments as we age. We may forget where we have put our keys, or leave a kettle to boil dry, or forget someone's name!

These are common happenings and do not mean you are necessarily becoming demented. But you can still check your stress and tiredness levels (as stress, lack of sleep and brain overload often causes forgetfulness), and make a concerted effort to improve your diet and exercise regime. There are also specific memory exercises which can help if practiced. Our brains need to be cared for, just as much as the rest of our body does!

Asking for professional help, going online to check out symptoms and getting your friends to support you, are all important if you do think you may be 'losing your marbles.' It can be very frightening at the beginning as realisation dawns, but don't sit alone with it or try and bluff your way through. There are things which will help. Go out and find out what YOU can do.

A special word about Parkinson's is needed too. It is a condition where the emotional and soul life of the Elder becomes so confined and ridged that it starts to reflect on the physical. The brain is affected in its motor nerves, so that movements become ridged and blocked. Eventually every bodily system is affected. People who develop Parkinson's may have been very particular or controlling in their thought patterns.

The mind and body are so integrated that this is often the case in disease. Mobility becomes 'stuck' just as thinking and feeling is also 'stuck'. Gradually everything ceases to move.

Doing massage and passive movements can be helpful in the latter stages, and variety and mental stimulation will help too. The person becomes almost locked up inside their body, although their thinking may remain quite lucid.

Movement of any kind will help the Energy which is becoming torpid and sluggish.

It can be a most frustrating condition for carers and patients alike, and involve long-term care in residential settings. Compassion and great patience is needed in day-to-day care as the person gets ever more disabled and slower.

Again looking at the nutritional aspects early on and giving supplements may be helpful in slowing down the condition.

Chapter 47
On being a grandmother/father

Although I have not yet reached this honoured position myself, I would like to include some thoughts about being a Grandparent here, as it is a very special role to fulfil and somehow epitomises the role of the Elder in our society. I have observed many of my friends becoming grandparents for the first time and realise there are many hopes and expectations.

The acute pain you can feel when your offspring are going through some life crisis is very real, and one can feel very helpless, knowing that they are now adults and all you can do is BE there for them to listen and perhaps offer gentle advice. They are now adults and have their own life lessons to learn. Letting go of being a parent is part of this learning.

When one of your own children becomes a parent for the first time, there may be some strange conflicting emotions, which are perhaps not appropriate to express directly to the expectant couple, but may nevertheless colour your first excitement and involvement with the new arrival.

You may still feel like a parent to your own child and may agonise about their fitness to have children at that particular point. Are they in a stable relationship? Do they smoke, are they housed securely, do they have enough income to feed a new child, do they have the emotional stamina and maturity to care for such a helpless tiny being?

You may want them to do things 'the right way' as you learned to do from your mother. They may have very different ideas, especially if it is your son's child, and the daughter-in-law comes from a very different social or ethnic background. How much and when can you say anything, without seeming bossy or controlling or critical?

Each generation goes through this dilemma, as fads and fashions constantly change and what we did with our children is now completely 'old hat!'

Rather than going in with all guns blazing to try and convince them of how to do things, try a softly approach asking gentle questions, seeming interested and giving some hints if asked. Your real wisdom will shine through if you are a mature Elder, and the questions will start to arise naturally.

Modern life has moved on, so that many of the things we might consider wrong are now being done frequently with new babies. They are a part of modern life and are the next generation. However the main cause of all mistakes is that the parents are not in touch with their maternal/paternal instincts, and are living a life of material selfishness which is hard to observe if as an Elder you had to work hard to get what you had.

Example is the only way to teach. Love is acceptance, but also one can show how things might be done better by staying in a calm space oneself and just giving total love and attention to the child. The parents will absorb some of your teaching this way and not feel threatened by criticism.

You could also try questions, which may seem innocent enough but might get the mother thinking along new lines. However hard it is, don't jeopardise your relationships at this delicate moment. Babies are very resilient and have chosen to come to these parents and learn through their mistakes.

Enjoy the oportunity of a very special relationship with a grandchild and enjoy handing them back at the end of the day! There is a reason why it is so tiring looking after young children. They literally are absorbing our Energy like sponges in order to grow and thrive. There is good reason why biologically we do not have children beyond a certain age. We cannot give them enough of our own Energy to thrive.

The role of the Elder and Grandparent is to gently give guidance and show by example how Universal Energy flow works. Many parents deny their children this Energy fully as they are spending too much time rushing around or trying to earn a living and also giving their children to others to care for. Their very own Energy is the best for their children.

Grandparents can have a unique role in enabling the child to play. The 'old-fashioned' nursery rhymes, street games, finger and lap games, and fairy stories can enrich the child's imagination and playtime.

Practical household activities with young children can also help them explore the world of matter, which is fast becoming mechanised. We can help instil a sense of wonder and <u>reverence</u> in the young child. Doing washing by hand, digging the garden, caring for pets, washing up, baking, ironing and so on are all fast disappearing skills which the child loves to 'help' with, especially if they are given the right small tools, strong and sturdy, not plastic and breakable or gimmicky.

Imaginative play can have an important role, if the grandparent provides simple dressing up clothes or house-building materials, or bits and pieces to play shops, schools and so on. A big sandpit or a trip to the park will help get them moving and exploring outside.

The next generation is in your hands if you can remain conscious and loving. You can have an active role in balancing the more technological modern life of your offspring with healthy living routines and nutrition. Children can learn a lot from their Grandparents about healthy ways of being

Chapter 48

Living with a terminal illness and dying

Many people nowadays in later life are told that they have a terminal illness and that they only have 'x' amount of time to live. There are many life circumstances which might bring on an illness of this kind and the most common of these conditions is cancer, (followed closely by heart and vascular diseases, including strokes.)

Once you are in this situation, it is often as though your destiny has been taken from you and the Doctors are now running what is left of your life. There may be umpteen hospital visits, surgery, chemotherapy, radiotherapy and new drug regimes. Seeing an oncologist regularly they may tell you that the cancer is now spreading and that you have to prepare for 'the worst.'

Getting ill in later life can be a real shock to the emotions. Up until now you have worked and played hard and rarely if ever seen a doctor. You trust the 'machine' to work for you and you still have many plans for your retirement. It is now time to stop and take stock.

That is what any illness forces you to do. STOP! Have you been living as healthily as you might have done? What causes this illness to occur? Is it just fate or an angry God, or can you understand what has brought you to this place in your life?

There are no immediate answers for many people in this predicament, and you might spend some time feeling angry, shocked or depressed.

Time, though, is a most wonderful gift when you are ill. Lying quietly in bed or on the sofa you can think back through your life and all it has meant to you. You can remember your actions and how they might have affected others, your relationships and where they were less than good. You may get inklings of why your body has created illness, or what has gone wrong in the pattern of things, so that life has ground to a halt.

It is not about having guilt feelings, disbelief, anger or loss, although all these emotions may be present in grieving your own demise, but about learning lessons of life. We become wiser through an illness; it cannot but change us for the better. This may be hard to understand and swallow if you are in pain or feeling frustrated and frightened by what is happening.

Healing occurs when PEACE is attained, whatever the outcome on a physical level. You may heal physically, having had treatment with surgery etc. or you may have a recurrence of the symptoms which ultimately leads to death.

Cancer is perhaps unique in that it enables you to live, sometimes for years, with the reality of death. It is a 'death sentence' almost certainly, however you can heal much of what CAUSED the cancer to occur in the first place; be that stress, unhealthy living, deep bitterness and anger over a life happening or an emotional impasse.

My mother had severe breast cancer at the age of 50. She had radical surgery, and followed this by a spell of treatment in a Swiss Clinic where she had injections made from homeopathic mistletoe. She had counselling about her life and changed her diet. She learned to relax and let go more and from then on always went to bed every afternoon for at least an hour. She gave up tea and coffee and got much less angry. She lived until she was 97, when finally a fall, surgery on a broken hip and 2 weeks later a heart attack enabled her to pass over.

Another close friend of 47 also had cancer. She had the same injections, went to America to learn about the special Gersen diet, lived very frugally, and tried to heal herself. However emotionally she was guilt ridden, and felt a failure. She was also frightened of pain and death. After 5 years the cancer got the better of her and she eventually died very peacefully. She had come to a place of recognition and healing within herself.

What enables one person to heal and go on living and another to die? It is very complex and each individual has their own journey. It is NOT about how many lots of chemotherapy and radiotherapy you have, but more about whether you can make the life changes necessary to go on. This involves not only lifestyle and diet, but also emotional and spiritual factors. Being 'Healthy' is a truly holistic state of being.

I have taken cancer as one common example of sickness, but the above comments can be appropriate for any life threatening or chronic condition.

Sometimes an accident will have a similar effect of 'stopping you in your tracks', or may mean that you then go on to live a very different kind of life, and have to learn patience, tolerance and many other things as part of your journey. Others around you will also be affected by your disability and may have to have great courage and endurance to carry on life with all the stresses of becoming a carer.

The 'Meaning of Illness' may be a totally new concept to you. Reading this you may strongly disagree. I can only put it as a suggestion, from my observations of thousands of sick people whom I have met during my life as a nurse and therapist, who have either healed and changed their life patterns, or relied on allopathic treatments and then eventually died.

In the broadest sense Forgiveness is the real issue here. If we suffer things as a victim we often harbour bitterness and anger. If we LET IT GO in the fullest sense, we have forgiven ourselves and others the mistakes which occurred, and then we can move on.

"Forgive us our trespasses, as we forgive those who trespass against us" from the Lord's Prayer is well worth musing upon.

How we approach death is a very individual journey also. Many people do not like to think about it, or speak of it even. It is totally taboo. There may also be bad jokes made about dying.

There comes a time though when the person starts to realise that they may not be immortal and they know that sooner or later they will have to say goodbye to this physical world and to all their dear ones left behind.

They may be very frightened if they have no faith that there is a life beyond death, or they may be longing to 'Meet their Lord' and maybe go to Heaven and feel no more pain or struggle.

As one gets older the reality that life is getting shorter starts to dawn on most people in some ways. Death of a young person seems cruel. Death by accident, murder or sudden illness is also a tremendous shock for those left behind.

But a death at the end of a 'good life' when the person is getting old and frail seems a happier event and their lives can be celebrated if nothing else.

The moment of death it may come after a long struggle. There may be pain, breathlessness, discomfort and so when the final breath comes it is a huge relief. The last gurgling sound as the lungs give up the breath and the larynx relaxes may be frightening to some, but to others it may be a relief that the end has come. Death can be sometimes a little like labour pain, with a moment of bliss as the 'new birth' is achieved.

Often people chose to take this step on their own and may wait until the early hours before dawn when all is quiet, before slipping away when no one is there beside them. At other times it can seem a comfort to have all your family around you in love, holding your hand.

The Japanese have a wonderful tradition that when you have your 60th Birthday you are given a red silk waistcoat and you officially become an 'Elder'. From this time onwards you have fulfilled your earthly destiny and you are learning to LET GO.

Letting go of material possessions, or the need of them; letting go of past anger and quarrels; letting go of stuck beliefs, emotional patterns and hang ups; letting go of all neediness. The list is endless! As an Elder one can learn to live contentedly in the present, with no Egotistical wishes or demands. That is what is aspired to at the end of a good life in Japan. Perhaps in the West we can learn from that.

As aforementioned, this knowledge is also held by North American Indians, Maoris, Aborigines, Bushmen, Tibetan Monks, Hindus and many others. Surely they are not all wrong?

Western traditions do not honour death as a 'passing'. It is a frightening happening which we dread, that we do not talk about. We are out of control when it happens. Most people die in a hospital environment which is frightening in itself, where one feels totally out of control and sometimes a mere number.

Just look at the faces of the relatives who come in to be with the patients in their last hours. They are scared stiff, not knowing how to act or react. They cluster around the bed, often hoping against hope that the patient will not go just yet, that the doctors have got it wrong.

Afterwards they scuttle away, leaving the nurses and doctors to do their bit and feeling awkward and grief-stricken, hardly knowing what is happening at this momentous time.

There is very little reverence for the body after the person has left it in death. It is now simply a dead body for science or the mortuary to deal with as they see fit, until it goes through a final disposal. Sometimes bodies are in cold storage for months if a court case is pending or if the cause of death has not been fully established.

To give your body over to medical science literally means to have it 'pickled' and dissected by medical students, which of course is necessary for them to learn about anatomy and physiology, but one can ask oneself what happens to the finer Energies which are gradually separating from the physical matter?

Should science wait until this process has completed before diving in? What happens in the case of transplant organ donations where certain organs are removed as soon as possible after death, before the body has even started to stiffen up?

Altruistic donation is now threatened to become the 'norm' unless one carries a card to request otherwise. The government is pushing for this due to a shortage of organ donations. Medical science in its greed and wish to prolong life for everyone has lost track of the realities of Death.

This statement may offend some people who wish to donate their bodies. Does Grace and Love play a part here, when the ultimate sacrifice for another human being disturbs the Energy flow from the body back to the earth?

As a human being one cannot have answers to these many questions unless you are enlightened. It would be very interesting to hear the opinions of the wise men and gurus.

Perhaps we should rather be asking the question of WHY people become sick and need transplants in the first place. Is it genetic inheritance and therefore perhaps Karma, or is it from an unhealthy lifestyle which brings one to a state of sickness and inevitable death?

Over thousands of transplants and interfering with the death process, what will be the effect on the earth over time? An interesting question to muse upon!

Once the deceased body is released to the relatives they can go through the mourning process fully which brings the whole process to a peaceful acceptance and conclusion.

Mourning always has several stages, including disbelief and shock, anger, sadness and finally acceptance and peace. Each of these stages will be gone through in healthy mourning for a loved one and may take months or years.

If any of these stages is curtailed or negated then the griever may become stuck in the process and start to suffer unhealthy abnormal grief, such as hanging on, depression, insomnia, anxiety or other psychological disturbances.

It is important if working with bereaved relatives that these processes are recognised and allowed to flow and open up. If you have friends who have lost dear ones, recognising these stages and allowing the person to talk and talk will be most helpful.

Sometimes people feel awkward about approaching someone after they have lost a relative. They may even cross the road to avoid speaking to them. This can be very hurtful and will set the person back in dealing with their grief. Telling your own story or saying "I know what it feels like!" can also block a healthy outpouring. Everyone has their own journey with grief, and we DON'T know, as everyone is unique in what they experience. Just offering a space to talk when they want to is the most helpful thing you can do.

Chapter 49

Preparing for death

Once you have an inkling of your own mortality and can embrace it wholeheartedly in a positive frame of mind, you can start to think about what it means to let go of your earthly body completely, and you can the start to plan what you would like to happen to you around the time of this mighty transition of consciousness, your Final Journey.

If you can conceive of the Energy which created you and has been a part of you, ever changing, ever moving, since your conception, you can start to understand how this will now need to gradually disperse again into the Universe. Each single cell in your body contains Energy, and has been there to enable life to happen in all its many ways, both consciously and unconsciously.

For a moment close your eyes and feel the movement of this Energy at cellular level as a kind of gentle buzzing all through your body. Imagine you are made up of millions of dancing particles infused with Light, rather than solid matter.

The physical Energy is only the first layer. Beyond this are many finer and finer layers of coloured Energy which radiate outwards, known as the Aura, leading out to our highest purest Eternal Beingness, which touches into the physical but expands into Regions we cannot conceive of, except occasionally in meditation.

When we take our final earthly breath, the Energy starts to depart from the denser physical shell. This takes about three days, depending on the age and condition of the person. If you see a body after death you can perceive this happening in subtle ways.

During this important time it is good if the body is not moved too much, and certainly not chopped around by the coroner if at all possible. Often a post mortem needs to be done if the person has not seen a doctor in the last weeks of life, so that the cause of death can be confirmed. For this reason alone, try to keep in touch with your Doctor if you are frail or unwell.

In the hospital or at home, (if the death occurred there,) the Death Certificate will be issued once the cause of death has been established, and then the relatives can request the deceased to be dealt with in whatever they like.

Most people do not realise that they have choices in this. Undertakers usually take the body to their premises and embalm the body, dressing it in a white or pastel 'nightgown', putting make-up on the face, and making it look pretty, before the relatives say goodbye in the chapel of rest and the coffin is then closed prior to disposal by cremation or burial, which may be some days or weeks later.

Normally a costly coffin is provided, with wood and brass, which is then transported from the undertakers to the church or crematorium in a hearse for a final service before it is burned, or buried in a graveyard. There may be elaborate flowers, the relatives can also travel in a large black car to and from the service, and then everyone goes back to the house or a hotel for the 'wake', usually tea and cake and chat with all the relatives.

This whole business costs upwards of £3000 in Britain and is the 'norm'.

Other cultures have other traditions, some burning the body straight away, some burying it. Often the ashes are scattered or buried in a ceremony of some kind later on. Some people like to keep the ashes close to them in the house, in an urn or wooden box, as it represents the last of their dear ones actual body.

Whatever your faith, religion or beliefs you can start to craft your own Final Journey and write down your wishes, making your relatives aware of what you would like. In this way some of your own personality goes into your demise and you show others a bit about your personal attitudes, faith and hopes.

Your Will can include a page about your funeral wishes.

Prior to that you can make a 'Living Will' which describes the care you would like, leading up to your death. This may need to be signed by a solicitor to make it legal, as I discovered with my Mother's Living Will.

Some important questions to think about:-

- Do you want to have any treatments which can prolong your life, such as resuscitation, life support machines, or strong medications for pain relief?
- Do you want food to be stopped at any point, and drips to be taken out?
- What is your attitude to euthanasia; if this were legally possible in this country, or do you want to go to Switzerland?
- Do you want infections to be treated with antibiotics which may prolong life after pneumonia?
- Are you keen to donate your organs to be used by others?
- Do you want to die in hospital or at home? Nowadays there are no set rules about this.
- Whom do you want with you at this time if possible? (The only guaranteed person is you!)
- What environment would you like as you die? Candles, incense, music (live or recorded), open windows, readings, silence, cuddles, massage, or any other things you find helpful or soothing in a loving way? It can be a bit like giving birth, and making a birth plan in advance!

And then for afterwards;

- At death do you want to be laid out formally, or just allowed to lie comfortably in your bed? What clothes do you want to wear for the journey? Do you want someone particular to give you a wash and dress you for the final journey? Do you want any jewellery left on you?
- Where would you like to spend the days immediately after death, (providing you do not need the coroner)? It is possible to engage the services of the undertaker or have a 'do-it-yourself' situation, providing it is hygienic and no smell arises. I have sat with people in their own home for up to three days after death with the windows open, while people visited to say goodbye. They may sing, pray, talk to the deceased, read the Bible, light candles or weep. In Irish families it was traditional to have a party; that was the true 'wake'; i.e. remaining awake for the first three days with them, until the Energy has dispersed.
- What kind of coffin would you like? There is an increasing trend to have ecological coffins which are biodegradable, in cardboard, woven wicker or even wool or felt. Or you can choose a more traditional wooden one for yourself beforehand.
- Where and by whom would you like to be transported after the three days? You could choose your own family car and relatives to carry you, or a pony and trap, or wagon! Or the usual hearse.
- Is there going to be a ceremony and if so where will that be? In a church, or a more informal setting if you are not religious? By the graveside or in a hall?
- What form will the ceremony take? Some people enjoy writing their own memoirs to be read out, or chose poetry or particular music. The final farewell need not be sad and black. Many modern funerals are becoming celebrations of the person's life. Your wishes and those of your close relatives can make an unusual event. You could stipulate that everyone wears bright colours!

There <u>are</u> a few rules about being buried in registered or sanctified ground, as otherwise people might be buried in an unsuitable way or place, but one can apply for a licence to be buried on private ground such as your own garden, or in woodland burial grounds where no marker stones are used and trees are planted on the site for future generations to enjoy. You will need to contact the local council and get the services of a gravedigger. Sometimes a local undertaker will be willing to help with a 'home-made' funeral in these aspects alone.

Looking online at 'Green funerals' you may be surprised how far all these new ideas have developed. This information may give you some new ideas to follow up. Costs can be drastically reduced this way too.

Flowers are traditionally given at this time. They are a solace for the relatives and can show sympathy, but also serve a very important function of allowing the deceased's Energy to dissolve into the earth. As the flowers fade and lose their Energy, so does the body too, so to lay flowers near to the corpse is a help. Nowadays a huge amount of money is spent on flowers.

Having trained as a florist, I realise also how very un-ecological they can be! They are generally imported from overseas in planes, sometimes grown with large amounts of fertilizers and pesticides, and they are then cut into shapes with plastic, cellophane and metal being used, which is not biodegradable. It is much better to choose locally grown flowers supporting a local economy or pick some from the garden to lie on the coffin.

You might also like to help your relatives by making a list of people to invite to your funeral! The first few days after your death will be busy ones, and it would be sad if anyone were missed out, especially if your near family comes from far afield.

Whatever you decide you would like, talk about it beforehand with your family and friends so that they know your wishes. Nothing can be guaranteed but at least you have had your say in the matter.

It also helps to disperse some of the taboo, gloom and doom around death. Of course you will be missed and grieved but if people see you as being positive and non-fearful it will help them too.

You can actually help to educate and change attitudes which will enable others to benefit from new ideas.

Our death is an inevitable happening. But it can be seen as a journey to a more exciting and happier place.

Chapter 50
Afterwards

What about after a death has occurred? Many people describe a numbness initially or a feeling of having a very 'open heart' and wanting to connect on a deep level with others. It can be a Time of Grace even, when families come together in a new way in forgiveness and reconciliation.

There will be many practical aspects to deal with in the first few days. Having someone who has been through it before can be a huge support. Firstly, there will be the disposal of the person's possessions. If this is done quite soon after death in a positive vain, it will help the on-going soul to separate harmoniously from their material things.

Energy from the deceased is imbued in their possessions, particularly if they haven't 'let go' of them psychologically, which is why some people like to hang on to an item of clothing or a precious treasure of some kind which holds happy memories. In this way they feel they are connecting more strongly with the one who has passed over.

Giving the clothes away to charity may be a good neutral thing to do, and personal possessions can be divided amongst the family.

Quite often while this is going on you may feel the person very close to you in the room, and you may even see them dimly. This rather strange phenomenon is the Energy of the soul life still lingering.

The soul, or 'feeling' Life Energy, will be experiencing many strange and new things in the early days after death, particularly if the death has been sudden or violent. Some souls may not fully realise that they are dead and observe the grieving and funeral as if from above. Gradually it dawns on them that they have journeyed on and they are being supported, greeted and shown the way forward by departed friends and relatives. This can be a jubilant reunion indeed.

They are able to return to their loved ones on earth to comfort and support them in their grief, particularly if those left behind are able to strongly envisage their faces, voices, smells and memories of happy times.

Talking about the departed person's life in a positive and humorous way can benefit the one on the other side, as the process of understanding their life now begins. They will start to relive all their earthly experiences; but instead of just as a memory, it is as though they are looking on at what they did and can feel the emotions of those they affected either negatively or positively. They therefore understand deeply the effects of their actions whilst on this earth and what their life has meant in the broader perspective of things.

By now you may be reading this with total disbelief! My task here is not to convince you of anything but to open up questions which you may like to investigate further.

Spiritualists and psychics are to be found everywhere if you want to connect with the Energy of a loved one. However, a word of warning! Many less talented clairvoyants may be picking up your own Energy patterns that are around you, with your feelings and hopes, and can give quite inaccurate readings. You may be disappointed.

The most helpful thing you can do for your loved ones on the other side is to let go of your need of them; to send them love for their journey, as you might to someone who has gone abroad to live; and not to have any expectations that they will visit you with advice or consolation.

If you do not believe there is an afterlife in any form, you may be pleasantly surprised by feeling them come close to you from time to time in a loving helpful way. Great forgiveness can occur also with difficult relationships, as I have experienced personally. Sometimes the physical and emotional presence of someone on earth that you encounter may be antagonistic, but once they are dissolved you can perceive a much more benevolent side of their being and work with that in prayer and meditation.

Some Elders, who have worked a lot spiritually in the latter part of their lives and have resolved many of their mistakes, and connected again in a loving way with enemies before they pass on, are able to dissolve their feeling life quite quickly after death. They do not spend long reviewing their lives and pass on to more distant spaces, and rarely come close to the earth.

Others who may have suffered a traumatic death in youth and are still confused and angry at their passing, may wander for years in a grey zone of learning and will need help to pass on. There are people working actively in Northern France with the British soldiers from the First World War. They are tragic figures from this time of massacre and need specialist spiritual rescue. One can feel the pain of these souls as one drives through the area even today, if one is sensitive.

Some healers take this rescue work very seriously and work concertedly to help any lost souls who need guidance. Many who have had near death experiences have described a brilliant Light at the end of a tunnel and a feeling of complete Love which surrounds one. This is named the Christ Being, whom we shall all meet on the other side, irrespective of our faith or religion.

We cannot prove in any way what we are going to experience. We can only anticipate with excitement this New Journey which we all embark on eventually when we die.

Chapter 51

In conclusion

Because we are all individuals the journey of becoming an Elder is unique for each person. By reading this book in an open frame of mind you may find yourself thinking more deeply about the end of your life, and you may also begin to wonder what you have achieved and what happened to all the dreams of your youth.

Regret is not a happy emotion and remaining positive in the PRESENT will have the effect of keeping you focused and true to whom you are. We all make plenty of mistakes as we go along, and we may have come to dislike certain repeated mistakes which seem a weak part of our makeup.

That is where the clue lies. When you understand yourself and can see the repeated patterns, then you have self-knowledge and wisdom.

So what can you do to improve? Or do you simply want to be peaceful and enjoy life in your latter years. Self-flagellation does no-one any good! The Christian Ethic is to ask for <u>forgiveness of sins</u>.

'Letting go' is a form of Forgiveness. Holding onto bitterness, jealousy, anger, fear, remorse or other emotions from past relationships or happenings does nothing for us. True forgiveness is a total letting go. Perhaps only when we find this Inner Peace are we ready to journey onwards?

It is ironic that sometimes the hardest lessons have to be learned in the last few weeks of our lives; through pain, loss of self-respect and control in a hospital or nursing home environment, or even by becoming severely disabled, demented and needing total bodily care. We can learn to experience true <u>gratitude</u> through experiences such as these also.

I would not wish sickness onto anyone! However if sickness arises and is born with fortitude and patience, much can be learned.

Living happily in the NOW, you can respect your physical body by giving it healthy food, enough exercise and fresh air, and encourage the mind to still itself in prayer and meditation, so that the final journey is prepared for, just as one might prepare to go on holiday for a long time.

You can say farewell to friends, making sure that all past difficulties in relationships are resolved and honest, even if it is not possible for them to be completely healed. You can tidy your affairs, ensure your loved ones are going to be safe and happy, and make decisions about your funeral.

You can do the things you have always wanted to do, such as take a journey to a special place. Make a list of them while you think of it!

Fear is the greatest enemy we have when it comes to death. Becoming an Elder is about overcoming fear of death. We now have time to work daily on this, until we find a point of Peace.

Enjoy what is left of your life to the full. Live each day as if it were your last, so that when you go to sleep at night you can say "that was a good day, worthwhile in every way".

Enjoy the simple things of life; watching a sunset, smelling a flower, hearing a blackbird singing on the tree, seeing a child play. Say a big "Thank you!" to the Universe for all the beauty which exists around us.

Try to avoid getting into a negative way of critical thinking, which can be so destructive, not only for others, but also for ourselves.

Stay open in each moment as to what is being asked of you. It may be a kind word to someone in the bus queue. Or helping someone find some information to improve things, or giving a cheery smile to a complete stranger, or caring for an animal.

Whatever your gifts and strengths, use them fully in your last years and they will be a true gift to the earth and humanity.

I wish you well in your final years and enjoy your journeying.

Appendix

Notes;

This list of Alkaline and Acid foods was compiled from material found in Dr Robert Young's 'The pH Miracle' book and is not fully complete. All foods can be listed as either acid [-] or alkaline [+] depending on the effect they have on the body and the rate of metabolism.

As can be seen from the list, most first class proteins are highly acid as are also sugars and junk foods. It is therefore important to try and eat as many alkaline foods [vegetables] as possible and limit the amount of acid foods. Fruit is acid too, because it contains a lot of sugar.

A very helpful in depth book on acid/alkaline balance is by Christopher Vasey: The Acid-Alkaline diet for optimum Health. He describes in detail the chemistry of metabolism and shows also how some people cannot cope with 'weak acids', which includes acid or sweet fruits, yoghourt and acid cheeses, honey and vinegar. Check it out if the normal pH diet isn't working for you. He also gives in depth details on testing for acidity in the body.

PH testing sticks for urine and saliva are available on-line and are the only accurate way of testing whether you are acid or alkaline.

A useful rule of thumb for a maintenance diet would be 20% acid food and 80% alkaline, but this depends on the individual and their acid level at any one time.

Note; the unusual grasses listed are ingredients of the 'Supergreens' produced by the company 'Innerlight' [www.innerlightinc.com].This powder can be mixed with water and drunk throughout the day. It is available on-line. Several other companies now produce green powders made from wheat grass and other grasses and alkalising foods. It is worth doing your own research.

www.energiseforlife.com is a very useful English website with lots of aspects of this complex subject covered; diet, water, alkaline mineral drops, supplements and lots of support.

Note that rice becomes neutral if soaked for some hours before cooking. All sprouted foods become more alkaline. Olive oil is alkaline, whereas Sunflower oil and margarine are acid.

The pH of water is dependent on the source. Ionisers can be adjusted to create quite alkaline water [pH 10] and when a sufficient volume of this is drunk it helps the whole system.

Becoming more alkaline, you will loose weight, get more energy and boost your immune system.

Pathological Cells, such as cancer cells, HIV, Candida and bacteria/microbes in the blood revert back to healthy cells when bathed in an alkaline solution. This is important biochemical research which Dr Young has done.

Because of this important work one can assume that anyone suffering 'dis-ease' is in fact running acid. Dehydration is another huge cause of acidity.

Remember that everyone's body is unique and what works for one person may not be right for another!

The pH of some foods.

Vegetables

Peas +0.5
Asparagus +1.1
Artichokes +1.3
Comfrey +1.5
Green cabbage March +2.0
Potatoes +2.0
Lettuce +2.2
Onion +3.0
Cauliflower +3.1
White radish +3.1
Swede +3.1
White cabbage +3.3
Green cabbage December +4.0
Savoy +4.5
Lamb's lettuce +4.8
New peas +5.1
Kohlrabi +5.1
Courgette +5.7
Red cabbage +6.3
Rhubarb +6.3
Horseradish +6.8
Leeks +7.2
Watercress +7.7
Spinach March +8.0
Turnip +8.0
Lime +8.2
Chives +8.3
Carrot +9.5
Lemon +9.9
French beans +11.2
Fresh beetroot +11,3
Spinach not March +13.1

Garlic +13.2
Celery +13.3
Tomato +13.6
Cabbage lettuce +14.1
Endive +14.1
Sorrel +11.2
Avocado +15.6
Red radish +16.7
Cayenne +18.8
Straw grass +21.4
Horsetail +21.7
Dog Grass + 22.6
Dandelion +22.7
Barley Grass +28.7
Soy Sprouts +29.5
Sprouted radish +28.4
Alfalfa Grass +29.3
Cucumber +31.5
Wheat Grass +33.8
Black Radish +39.4

Organic grain and legumes
Brown rice -12.5
Wheat -10.1
Oats? acid?
Barley? Acid?
Brown rice soaked 24 hours neutral.
Quinoa ? +
Buckwheat -0.5
Millet-0.5
Lentils +0.6
Soy flour +2.5
Tofu +3.2
Lima beans +12
Cooked soy +12.8
Soy nuts +26.5
Soy lecithin +38.0
Sprouted = more alkaline.

Nuts and seeds
Pistachios-16.6
Peanuts-12.8
Cashews -9.3
Wheat germ -11.4
Walnuts -8.0
Pumpkin seeds -5.4
Sunflower seeds -5.4
Macadamia nuts -3.2
Hazel nuts -2.0
Flax seeds -1.3
Brazil nuts -0.5
Sesame seeds +0.5
Cumin seeds +1.1
Fennel seeds + 1.3
Caraway seeds +2.3
Almonds +3.6

Fats
Margarine -7.6
Sunflower oil -6.4
Butter -3.9
Ghee -1.6
Coconut milk -1.5
Olive oil +1.0
Borage oil +3.2
Flax seed oil +3.5
Evening primrose oil +4.1
Marine lipids +4.7

Fish and meat

Freshwater fish -11.8
Ocean fish -20.1
Oysters -5.0
Pork -38.0
Veal -35.0
Beef -34.5
Chicken -20.0
Eggs -20.0
Liver -3.0
Organ meats -3.0

Milk etc.
Hard cheese -18.1
Quark -17.3
Cream-3.9
Buttermilk +1.3

Bread
White bread -10.0
Biscuits -6.5
Wholemeal bread-6.5
Rye bread -2.5

Sweets

Sweeteners -26.5
White sugar -17.6
Beet sugar -15.1
Molasses -14.6
Fructose -9.5
Milk sugar -9.5
Barley malt syrup -9.3
Brown rice syrup -8.7
Honey -7.6

Condiments

Vinegar -39.4
Soy sauce -36.2
Mustard -19.2
Mayonnaise -12.5
Ketchup -12.4

Drinks

Spirits -28.6 _ -38.7
Sweetened fruit juice -33.4
Tea -27.1
Beer -26.8
Coffee -25.1
Wine -16.4
Fruit juice natural -8.7
Mineral-water –
acid, depending on brand
Tap water - acid
Alkalized water -+

Appendix 2

Section Heading Required

WATER IONIZATION - THE ULTIMATE WATER? YOU DECIDE!

Cellhealth

Cellhealth Ltd

Please visit our website for further information or contact Cellhealth Ltd for sources or further questions

Cellhealth Ltd
Tel: 01992 525800
Email: info@thewaterionizer.co.uk
Website: www.thewaterionizer.co.uk

The human body is between 50% and 70% water, mainly dependant on age, so hydration is the most important factor in keeping the mind and body healthy. A human body can survive without food for a few weeks, but the mind will become delirious within days without water. The brain has priority for water and if it's dehydrated people will feel tired, irritable and nauseous. In fact without adequate hydration the brain will take water from other parts of the body, especially cells, resulting in chronic cellular dehydration, also known as ageing and ill health!

Drinking the correct amount of water per day will help to curb appetite and increase the strength of the metabolism, prevent internal infections and lower high blood pressure, which in turn will reduce cardiovascular disease. Also, the risk of heart disease will be reduced. Water is even important to the mouth as it stops decay and infections. So, one can view water as the ultimate barrier from illness and the liquid that sustains good health. How much to drink? 8 glasses for all is clearly not the answer - The World Health Organisation state that it is based on your weight - take half your body weight, then allow one fluid ounce per one pound of body weight. 180 pounds means 90 fluid ounces - 4.5 pints.

Two of the main obstacles to drinking water are that it's not encouraging for anybody to drink tap water, knowing that there could be many contaminants still in the water, often coupled with the smell of chlorine, and bottled water is just so inconvenient, expensive and not necessarily less free from contaminants, (according to a recent Government survey) than tap water. The most common excuses people use for not drinking enough water are that if they drink too much water they have to go to the toilet too often or they don't like the taste! People forget that the major function of urination is to eliminate toxins from the body.

A great number of the population, choose to drink tea, coffee or beer and younger people like to drink sugary, carbonated acidic drinks, all producing a diuretic effect on the body, which creates more dehydration within the body. Research suggests these drinks have increased the diabetes problem through the unnatural levels of acidity and sugar. Visits to the doctor's surgery or time off work could be reduced just by properly hydrating the body everyday and not drinking processed substances. Unfortunately, people aren't being educated enough on the benefits of drinking water, which is where the integration of other organisations working alongside the NHS can be of benefit in terms of the reduction in GP appointments and a stronger workforce.

As you've probably noticed, the complimentary and alternative medicine (CAM) industry is growing every year with 1 in 10 of the population now trying it, mostly going private. A recent poll also suggests the majority of people want CAM to be available to all on the NHS. The government have responded to pressure and are now funding initiatives to help the CAM industry become even more professional by improving guidelines and regulations within it. NHS Trusts and clinics are starting to see the benefits both financially and practically from integrated healthcare.

So, apart from tap water, filtered water and bottled water, is there any other water to drink? Through thorough research, water ionization was found to be the way forward in providing not only clean water but more importantly scientifically proven healthy water. The process of water ionization or electrolysis is achieved using water ionizers.

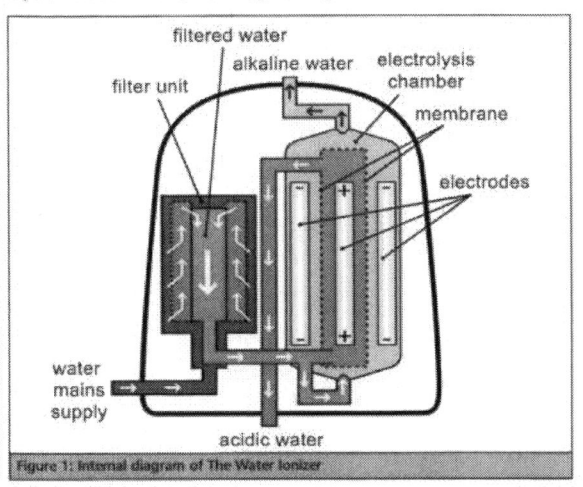

Figure 1: Internal diagram of The Water Ionizer

Useful resources

This list is by no means conclusive and many more references may be found by buying one or two of these books, or browsing online. The journey has begun!

Books;
- The pH Miracle. Dr R. Young [Time Warner pub.]
- Cellular Awakening. Barbara Wren
- The Healing journey. Matthew Manning
- Chronic Fatigue, ME, and Fibromyalgia. The Natural Recovery Plan. Alison Adams
- Fibromyalgia Naturally. Patti Chandler
- The Acid-Alkaline Diet. Christopher Vasey. [Healing Arts Press]
- Candida Albicans. Shirley Trickett
- Cooking without. Barbara Cousins [Thorsons]
- The Alkaline Diet Recipe Book. Ross Bridgeford
- The Alzheimer's Prevention Plan Patrick Holford

Questions may be raised further with Angela Bea
www.healthy-life-ways.co.uk

Notes

Notes

Notes

Printed in Great Britain
by Amazon.co.uk, Ltd.,
Marston Gate.